American Studio Glass

American Studio Glass
1960–1990

An Interpretive Study
by Martha Drexler Lynn

HUDSON HILLS PRESS

NEW YORK AND MANCHESTER

This book is dedicated to those who expand craft scholarship worldwide.

First Edition
© 2004 Martha Drexler Lynn

Published in the United States by Hudson Hills Press LLC, 74-2 Union Street, Manchester, Vermont 05254. Distributed in the United States, its territories and possessions, and Canada by National Book Network, Inc. Distributed in the United Kingdom, Eire, and Europe by Windsor Books International.

Co-Directors: Randall Perkins and Leslie van Breen
Founding Publisher: Paul Anbinder

Editor: Frances Bowles
Designer: David Skolkin
Indexer: Susan DeRenne Coerr
Printed and bound by Tien Wah, Singapore

Library of Congress Cataloguing-in-Publication Data
Lynn, Martha Drexler.
  American studio glass, 1960–1990 / by Martha Drexler Lynn.— 1st ed.
      p. cm.
Includes bibliographical references and index.
  ISBN 1-55595-239-9 (alk. paper)
  1. Art glass—United States—History—20th century. I. Title.
  NK5112.L97 2004
  748'.0973'09045—dc22

                                          2003027582

Frontispiece: *Lillies of the Valley PWV 034* (from the Paperweight Vase series), 1976. Mark Peiser (United States, b. 1938). Blown and cased glass; 8 ½ inches high, 5 inches in diameter. Indianapolis Museum of Art, gift of Marilyn and Eugene Glick (IMA 2000.64)

Contents

1 INTRODUCTION

Common or Exalted?

5 CHAPTER 1

From Art Glass to the Studio Movement—
Shifting Terminology

21 CHAPTER 2

From Factory Glass to Craft Glass—
Shaping a Movement

35 CHAPTER 3

Proto-Studio Glass Pioneers—
Leading the Way

49 CHAPTER 4

Critical Mass—
Aspiring to High Art

69 CHAPTER 5

Marketing, Exhibitions, and Collecting—
Spreading the Word

93 CHAPTER 6

Dealers, Galleries, and Auctions—
Creating the Market

107 CHAPTER 7

A Measure of Success—
Escalating Prices

123 CHAPTER 8

Private and Public Patronage—
Displaying a Passion for Glass

141 CHAPTER 9

Studio Glass in the Museums—
Validating the Collections

155 EPILOGUE

Glass Becomes Art

159 Acknowledgments
160 Glossary
163 Selected Reading
164 Index
170 Photography credits

Common or Exalted?

Throughout history, people have suspected that glass is magic. How else can a material be explained that imitates other materials but cannot itself be imitated? That is five times stronger than steel, yet can be broken by the human voice? That is invoked by heating sand and ash and then bewitched into an infinite variety of forms and textures in an astonishing array of colors? That is hot liquid and frozen solid, transparent and opaque, common and exalted?

—Tina Oldknow, *Clearly Inspired*

Untitled, 1968. Dominick Labino (United States, 1920–1987). Blown and manipulated glass; 6 x 5 x 6 ½ inches. Indianapolis Museum of Art, gift of Marilyn and Eugene Glick (IMA 2000.399)

Y ES, BUT IS IT ART? Traditionally, high art was restricted to painting on canvas and wood and to sculpture in stone; work made of so-called craft media was excluded. In the twentieth century the art that was deemed worthy was determined by an urban elite. The list became more fluid, however, in the years following World War II and in the past few decades the high-art world has been increasingly flexible about admitting new media—when it sees fit. Photography and even clay have found acceptance; other craft-based media with their utilitarian associations and antecedents as hobbies still hover uneasily at the border, despite the evident ambitions and efforts of practitioners, dealers, collectors, and public institutions. [*]

Art scholars often insist that glass is a new medium. With roots in ancient Mesopotamia, glass is, however, new only to the world of high art, which is unfamiliar with its history and often has a limited knowledge of the decorative arts as a whole. The high-art world long ago elected to focus its attention on a short list of media considered appropriate for art making, a list that has been presented as absolute but is, in fact, constructed. [1]

Three developments that occurred between 1960 and 1990 affected studio glass and its relationship with the world of fine art. First, the production of American studio glass reached a critical mass, whereas before 1960, activity had been comparatively minor. Second, art ceased to be rigidly defined in terms of the material used. Third, utilitarian forms began to be assimilated into the high-art world, so that the function of a vessel or chair, for instance, was not necessarily restricted to

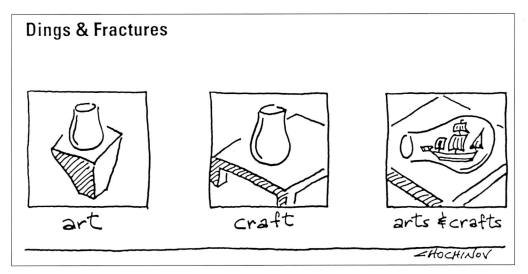

Dings & Fractures

art   craft   arts & crafts

CHOCHINOV

A cartoon by Allan Chochinov that appeared in *Glass Quarterly* in 1996 under the title "Dings and Fractures." This rendering vividly captures the central debate about glass: Has it moved from being a craft medium to being art—or does it vacillate between the two and land on the coffee table?

its use as a container or a seat. Consequently, object-centered forms could assume a content greater than its formal language implied.

Despite this increased openness, the traditionally conceived high-art world continues to occupy the central position in the mental art universes of many. For those who seek the status to be found within this rarefied environment, as well as the financial recompense that accompanies admission to it, that world must truly appear to be a paradise. The desire for entry into this magic kingdom is only part of a complex story when it comes to glass, for while well-known glass artists, such as Dale Chihuly (see page 10), Howard Ben Tré, and others, operate in both the glass community and the high-art world, some members of the glass community (and of communities that have developed around other craft-related media) wish to remain separate. Some artists who work in the high-art world dabble in glass, using the medium occasionally (see page 154), but pointedly maintain their status within the community of the fine arts.

Little has been written to date about American studio glass from a scholarly perspective. When reviewing an art medium, one expects that certain categories of literature will exist—periodicals, histories, catalogues raisonnés, exhibition catalogues, technical treatises, and critical analyses. For studio glass there exist one journal, a few histories and magazines, many technical works, a good number of exhibition catalogues, and no catalogues raisonnés. Critical analysis is also thin. Writers have been reluctant to make judgments about

the close-knit glass-making community wherein aesthetic criticism was often interpreted as personal attack. Not surprisingly for such a young movement, a debate arose about whether there is a need for a new set of criteria and a critical methodology specific to the material, or whether existing critical standards could be applied. This debate continues.

Perhaps the most coveted form of literature for the scholar is the periodical, but there are no periodicals that span the period under examination and focus exclusively on contemporary glass. The few magazines devoted solely to studio glass that do exist begin in the 1970s with a series of short-lived publications that quietly faded. Early articles simply noted developments in American glassmaking, usually in factual, often unattributed, one- or two-page stories. This style of reporting was typical of the period and reveals the hobbyist roots of the field. The significance of these articles, however, lay in their chronicling of the glass fabrication occurring outside factory settings and raised the visibility of studio glass as a medium. The American studio glass movement does boast one journal, the *Glass Art Society Journal*, which is published by the Glass Art Society (GAS) and written by practitioners, curators, and teachers for themselves. Another source of documentation is the newsletter, a category represented in the studio glass community by *Glass Focus*, the newsletter of the Art Alliance for Contemporary Glass, an organization of collectors.

The books about studio glass are written, as one might expect, from varying viewpoints—those of the

Pierced Celestial Ambit, 1985. Michael Glancy (United States, b. 1950). Blown glass, blue industrial plate glass, copper; 5 x 13 x 12 inches. Courtesy of the artist.

Corn Dolly, United Kingdom, ca. 1980. Wheat straw, 24½ x 7½ inches. Neutrogena Collection, Museum of International Folk Art, Santa Fe, New Mexico. Modern example of a traditional craft updated by a large-scale interpretation.

artist, the dealer, the collector, the curator, and the historian. And, because American glassmakers often define themselves by the forming methodology (that is, hot glass, cast glass, and so on) that they use, technical treatises constitute an important genre for the community. Nonetheless, in spite of the proliferation, David Huchthausen, writing in 1984 for the *Americans in Glass* exhibition catalogue, lamented the absence of a body of critical analysis of the American studio glass movement. "The success of a piece," he observed, can rely "on the material alone," thus rendering glass as a medium "suspect on a conceptual level."[2] This missing critical perspective continues to haunt American studio glass and to perpetuate its exclusion from the realm of fine art media, an exclusion that is keenly felt by many glass artists and their supporters. The other side of this equation—the stance of much of the fine, or high-art, world toward glass—is reflected in Robert Silberman's

opinion: Studio glass artists should not be assimilated into the fine arts world lest they lose their unique traditions.[3] These two observations—one from a practicing glass artist, the other from a high-art critic sympathetic to craft—illustrate the contradictory forces that have shaped the American studio glass movement since World War II.

The studio glass movement offers an opportunity to examine the power structure of the high-art world and to analyze the boundaries—real and imaginary—that exist between it and the rest of art production. The late twentieth century was a time when this hegemony was challenged, making the recounting of the history and acceptance of the studio glass pertinent to art history as a whole and perhaps determining "whether the studio movement is an answer or merely a cul-de-sac."[4]

NOTES

1. In antiquity there was no distinction between art and craft. The Greek term *techne* and the Latin *ars* were used to refer to both. The distinction emerged as each art medium jockeyed for status in later eras. The list of acceptable Western art-making media has long been fluid. Aristotle placed architecture, as the "queen of the arts," ahead of painting and sculpture. The medieval and Renaissance periods viewed the arts differently—divided into guild activities and defined by specialized knowledge, rights, and attendant prestige. Consequently, for Renaissance patrons Benvenuto Cellini's silver saltcellar was as much art as were the ceilings and walls painted by Michelangelo.

During the baroque period, with its preoccupation with classifying all phenomena, various art disciplines vied for equal status with architecture and sculpture. The most successful of these was painting; see Thomas Crow, *Painters and Public Life in Eighteenth-Century Paris* (New Haven: Yale University Press, 1985). The repositioning of painting as a significant art is captured in *Las Meninas* by Diego Velasquez (1656), in which the artist depicts himself as a gentleman, operating within the royal circle: the painter as artist and aristocratic intimate; see Michel Foucault, *The Order of Things: An Archaeology of the Human Sciences* (New York: Random House, 1970).

While each discipline worked to have itself considered the most significant, levels operated within each. So a listing of activities covered by the mercer's corporation for 1723 includes "paintings, bronzes, furniture, clocks etc for furnishing" as one subdivision; see Carolyn Sargentson, *Merchants and Luxury Markets: The Marchands Merciers of Eighteenth-Century Paris* (London: Victoria and Albert Museum and the J. Paul Getty Museum, 1996), 12.

Clearly, paintings employed as decorations for furniture fronts were seen as of lesser import than those created as stand-alone works of art.

But in the eighteenth and nineteenth centuries, the separation of the arts into high and lesser was predicated in part on the means of production and purpose. Kant wrote in 1790 that "Art also differs from Handicraft; the first is called 'free,' and the other may be called 'mercenary'" (*The Critique of Judgment*, trans. J. H. Bernard [New York: Hafner Press, 1959], 146). This implied that craft was commissioned and hence circumscribed by the buyer's needs and that art emanated solely from the artist's own invention. As the study of actual painting and sculpture practice has deepened, it has become clear that commissions by great painters were requested by patrons for use in specific locales, to communicate piety or status, to record a particular event, or just to titillate. The imposition of the hand and the exchange of money for art as a spoiler of artistic legitimacy would linger in public perception until the late twentieth century. Those with vested interests proclaim this canonical hierarchy infallible. Meanwhile, artists reach for any medium that can facilitate their expression.

2. David Huchthausen, Introduction, in *Americans in Glass*, exh. cat. Leigh Yawkey Woodson Art Museum, Wausau, Wisconsin, 1984, 7.

3. Robert Silberman, "Americans in Glass: A Requiem," *Art in America* 73, no. 3 (March 1985): 47–53.

4. R. Craig Miller, "Betwixt and Between: Contemporary Glass in American Art Museums," *Glass Art Society Journal* (1991): 27.

Chapter 1

*From Art Glass
to the Studio Movement—
Shifting Terminology*

THE ROAD FROM the *art glass* to *studio glass* is paved with an array of ever-changing terms. An examination of this shifting language and its contested terminology will clarify the complex tensions that simultaneously repel and attract glassmaking toward the separate realms of craft and high art.[1] In the nineteenth century the term *art glass* was used to describe *objets d'art* made of glass.[2] Objects falling under this rubric were made in factories by designers and manufacturers; they were fashioned in large quantities using high-quality art material. Although they made reference to utility, they were primarily intended for display in middle- and upper-class homes; having art glass elevated the status and confirmed the taste of its owners. In the United States, Louis Comfort Tiffany manufactured some of America's most prestigious art glass in his various production entities during the last years of the nineteenth century and into the beginning of the twentieth. By consciously pairing the word *art* with the word *glass*, he and other makers increased the cachet of their products, implying the aesthetics of high art, enlivened by virtuoso technical achievement. In scholarly literature, museum publications, and books for a general audience, the term *art glass* has since become firmly attached to this specific type of glass, made at this time.

Mid–twentieth-century studio glassmakers would express their disdain for this historical material and intentionally avoid referring to their own work as art glass, even though the adoption of this term would have seemed logical as it did link their ambition to make art and their chosen medium efficiently and vividly. In the 1960s, glass artists echoed this earlier nomenclature by speaking of themselves as makers of glass art, shifting the emphasis to *art* with the word *glass* functioning as a modifier and thus relegating the medium to a secondary, or qualifying, position relative to the elevated activity of art making. This new coinage helped ambitious studio glassmakers to distance themselves further from factory-related work and closer to the high arts.

Two other nineteenth-century terms continue to be relevant to the discussion of studio glass today. They are *applied art* and *decorative arts*. These terms refer to items made of clay, fiber, glass, metal, and wood that have utilitarian forms (or make reference to utility) with appended decorative passages.[3] The term *applied arts* denotes utilitarian objects that have aesthetic elements added to the basic form as a way of softening or obscuring crude functionality. In contemporary usage, the adjective *applied* can suggest decoration ill-suited to the form it adorns. By the middle of the nineteenth century, the term fell into disfavor as the field split in two, with machine-made items becoming known as *production* (*design*) and individually crafted works as *crafts* and later as *studio crafts*.[4]

The term *decorative arts* implies skill in expression and execution, paired with a high level of aesthetic sensitivity, a combination that holds the potential to produce masterpieces. The masterpiece sensibility is aptly

Electric Lamp with Dragonfly Shade and Twisted Stem Waterlily Standard, c. 1910. Tiffany Studios. Glass, copper foil, bronze; 27 inches high. Chrysler Museum of Art, Norfolk, Virginia; gift of Walter P. Chrysler, Jr.

illustrated by Louis Comfort Tiffany's *Dragonfly Lamp* (ca. 1910; above),with its utilitarian lampshade decorated with a motif that dictates the general form and adds visual interest and drama. The utility of the lamp is not affected by this design, but its decorative power is enhanced, as is its usefulness as a marker of high status. Skilled execution, scarcity, and a named maker guarantee it a place in the desired masterpiece category. A more nuanced meaning of decorative arts would therefore include its function as decoration for the domestic interior and as a status symbol.[5] Thus, the best Tiffany lamps embody a constellation of meanings. The expression "decorative arts" as used today continues to suggest connoisseurship, rarity, and masterpieces.[6] It is ironic that Western art historical discourse has determined that anything referred to as "decorative," being useful, or having intrinsic beauty (all applicable to a fine Tiffany lamp) is of lesser worth and incapable of expressing content, a requisite component of high art. This bias would have far-reaching ramifications for studio glass.

The original manifestation of craft in the United States is now termed *traditional (vernacular) craft* or *folk art*.[7] It may be distinguished from *applied arts* or *decorative arts* by its rural associations and its naive sensibility (see *Corn Dolly*, page 3). Traditional crafts are fabricated by usually anonymous master-trained, rural makers who learn their trade through an apprenticeship system that passes empirical knowledge about forming and materials from one craftsman to the next in a generational stream.[8] Producing almost identical objects through repetitious methods of fabrication, these craftsmen neither seek nor prize artistic or technical innovation and often make items that are anachronistic in form as well as meaning.[9]

George Kubler, seeking to determine what separated the indigenous arts of Africa (traditional craft) from the realm of high art, observed that "a great difference separates traditional craft education from the work of artistic invention. The former requires only repetitious actions, but the latter depends upon departures from all routine."[10] This fundamental trait also distinguishes traditional craft from the production of studio craftsmen, who, like fine artists, strive for personal expression and communication of content, achieved with the aid of technical innovation and skill.

Another characteristic of vernacular crafts relates to their marketing. Most makers sell their works to those in close proximity and, as a rule, do not seek recognition or market support from urban centers.[11] In this way they represent the conservative end of the craft spectrum, the studio craftsman being at the opposite end.[12] As with all classifications, there are practitioners who do not conform in all aspects; for example, there are traditional craftsmen who are located adjacent to urban centers but continue to market their works through individual associations.[13] The studio glass community began in this way but later consciously adopted urban high-art strategies for building an audience and marketing its wares.

Another characteristic that links traditional craft to studio work in the twentieth century is that traditional craftsmen make objects that are not essential to the marketplace or to contemporary culture. Markets exist for factory production and for studio work because, although a factory-made glass goblet may function adequately, a handblown one pleases the eye, hand, and soul while providing a culturally meaningful statement. Additionally, the ownership of studio work signifies an appreciation for craft and testifies to a sophisticated aesthetic sensibility. This cultural distinction, initially derived from traditional crafts, remains embedded within the sensibility of American studio glass and affects its valuation and place within the larger art community.[14]

CONTEMPORARY + CRAFT = AMERICAN STUDIO GLASS

The word *craft* used as both a noun and an adjective has diminished the standing of the studio movement vis-à-vis the high-art world since the movement's inception. In the discourse about craft—whether within the craft world or without—the term refers to handmade, utility-linked objects made of clay, fiber, glass, metal, or wood, either alone or in combination. Originally, it denoted the conservative end of the craft movement, but in current usage it implies the contemporary, and because of this, it has supplanted the term *decorative arts* within the museum world, although not within academe.[15] In the university, specifically in cultural studies and anthropology, *craft* refers to items made by native peoples in rural settings. The implication is that crafts are not art and are subject only to the rules that govern material culture.[16] Craft in art historical discourse still retains the association of kitsch that became attached to it after the appearance of Clement Greenberg's essay "Avant-Garde and Kitsch" in 1939.[17] At its most rudimentary level, *craft* means a skill and has the connotation of power or strength derived from its Saxon linguistic roots. In this context the term implies a high level of competence in the manipulation of the chosen art material.[18] Today *craft* is teamed with *contemporary* to indicate works that manifest high skill *and* artistic intent—and this is the classification into which contemporary studio glass most properly fits.

Kenneth R. Trapp, curator-in-charge at the Smithsonian Institution's Renwick Gallery in Washington, D.C., states that craft (read here *studio glass*) is "always concerned with *materials*, craft makes reference to *traditions*, craft involves a 'constant play with *function*,' [and] craft makes constant reference to the *human body* [Trapp's italics]."[19] As all of these attributes position craft outside the realm of high art and serve as the basis for the tensions between the two worlds, the ramifications of each are worth examining.

The first attribute, materiality, refers to the potential inherent in the medium—a potential that affects the finished product. Materiality is critical to craft-based art, and the selection of one craft material (or, for that matter, one fine-art medium) over another is a primary artistic decision.[20] For example, the glass artist Dan Dailey was first a ceramist but shifted to glass because he sought its slick surface. His work, however, still demonstrates an interest in opaque material, a quality not usually associated with glass. This can be seen in his piece *Café* (1979; page 8), where he uses Vitrolite, an opaque glass building material. Dailey eventually became "hooked on glass; [and there was] no going back" even when it did not prove the most logical choice for the visual effect he desired. But the medium itself proved seductive and glass became fundamental to his artistic expression.[21]

Transparency is a significant aspect of the materiality of glass. Larry Bell was drawn to glass in the late 1960s when he sought to explore transparency in his *Terminal Series of Boxes* (see page 8). Fabricated, with the help of glass technicians, out of plate glass and articulated with chrome binding, these works use the refractive nature of glass to explore transparency and strategies of display. In other words, the materiality is an important component of the content of the work.[22]

Another aspect of materiality is expressed in the passion glassmakers have for the process of making glass art. If glass is a way of knowing (as painting has been described), then the effect of the making of glass is critical and reveals a way of seeing that is unique to the medium.[23] This interest in the process was at the heart of David Huchthausen's refusal to abandon glass when the painter Richard Dahle urged him to adopt a more "appropriate" artistic medium. Huchthausen

Café, 1979. Dan Dailey (United States, b. 1947). Cut, polished, sandblasted, acid-polished, and assembled Vitrolite and plate glass, fabricated brass and steel fittings; 29½ x 21½ inches. The Corning Museum of Glass, purchased with the aid of funds from the National Endowment for the Arts (80.4.63)

The Vitrolite obscures the expected transparency of glass.

Untitled, 1986. Larry Bell (United States, b. 1939). Glass and rhodium-plated brass; 14⅛ x 14⅛ inches; on Plexiglas base, 36 x 14 x 14 inches. Fine Arts Museums of San Francisco, partial gift of Dorothy and George Saxe (A358096)

The interesting reflective qualities of glass and Plexiglass are clearly illustrated here.

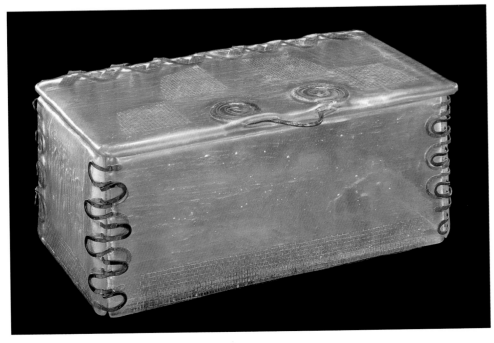

Sowed Box, 1948–1949. Michael Higgins (United States, 1908–1999). Fused glass with screen inclusions, copper band joints, hinge, and handle; 3¼ x 7½ x 4⅞ inches. The Corning Museum of Glass (89.4.9)

Detail of *Three-Part Vessel*, 1973. Harvey Littleton.
Marked [To Bernard Harvey K. Littleton UCLA 1973].

Three-Part Vessel, 1973. Harvey Littleton
(United States, b. 1922). Blown and altered
glass; 5½ x 7¼ x 3¼ inches. Private collection.

continued to work in glass because its forming potential and visual effects intrigued him.[24] The process, the inherent transparency, and the slick surfaces associated with glass became the subject of his work, just as they had for Bell, an artist of the high-art world Huchthausen has pointed to the materiality of glass as its essential liability vis-à-vis the high-art world, because the advent of conceptual art and other nonobject-centered art practices has made the physical reality of the artwork, which is of primary importance to the craft-based arts, subordinate to concept.

The second inherent characteristic of craft is its reliance on tradition. Tradition here means practices relating to formal vocabulary and forming technologies. Glass objects have existed since the fourteenth century B.C.E. In part an effect of the nature of working (forming) glass—from a liquid to a solid—a predictable and uniform formal vocabulary developed. For example blowpipe forming, prized by the early American studio glassmakers, produced bubbles and blobs that were then readily attenuated to make vessels (or vessel-shaped objects), such as, for example, Harvey Littleton's blown and altered *Three Part Vessel* (1973; see above). Forming these objects did not require sophisticated skills, for bubbles are the natural outcome of the introduction of hot air into a lump of molten glass. Generously termed "art" by their makers, these modest early works were really the continuation of the traditional (natural) forms of blown glass and rely on the inherent visual appeal of the medium for their merit.

Many aspects of traditional glass-forming methodology have been lost and subsequently rediscovered.[25] Each time a so-called lost technology has been recovered, it has been updated and put to innovative use. For example, Dale Chihuly rediscovered threaded decoration and used it in his *Sea Forms* series of the 1980s (see page 10). The technique had long been known on Murano, one of five islands located near Venice and renowned for the skill of the glassmakers there, whose knowledge was a closely guarded secret. A form and technique closely related to Chihuly's can be seen in sixteenth-century century Venetian *tazza*. Chihuly's two-part *Sea Forms* is formally related to the bowl of

Sea Forms, 1981. Dale Chihuly (United States, b. 1941). Two parts, blown in an optic mold, with threaded decoration; 9 ¼ x 14 ½ x 10 ⅝ inches. The Corning Museum of Glass (81.4.43)

the Venetian goblet, but it has been presented in a larger scale and is without a stem. All glassmakers are aware of both the technological and formal history of their medium and use this knowledge as an inspiration and a point of departure.[26] Within the glass community this continuity of knowledge confers cultural significance; within the high-art world it is often seen as a liability.

Intangible qualities and associations influence the valuation of glass. Comprising the relatively inexpensive elements of silica and an alkali, glass could be made to imitate the sparkle and shine of jewels such as diamonds, rubies, and other precious stones and used in their place on high-status decorative objects. The natural, and only recently understood, refractive and transparent qualities of glass also made it a metaphor of God's own brilliance.[27] These associations contribute to the appeal that studio glass has for artists, dealers, and public and private collectors. And made it prey to devaluation as an imitative material.

The third attribute of craft objects that must be considered is function. This can be overt, as in a vessel made for drinking, or it can be symbolic, as in display items made of silver and intended to communicate their owner's wealth.[28] Utility can be seen in the traditional crafts, but an attenuated, implied functionality is more usual in contemporary work. Jane Bruce, for instance, makes works that appear utilitarian until the viewer realizes they are too large or too fragile for actual use (see *Black "Window" Bowl*, page 156). As contemporary craft loosened its ties to traditional craft, it increasingly united two types of function: utility and status or display. This latter aspect remains a key factor in the desire of individuals to collect studio glass and has influenced the patterns of patronage and commodification.

The fourth distinctive attribute of crafts is the relationship to the body. Also linked to utility, this aspect has proved to be a barrier to the acceptance of craft-based work in the high-art world. The connection to the body reveals itself in scale (objects are usually made to be held or placed on a tabletop), the selection of textures, and the real or implied functionality. Scale, which in some craft media is dictated by the inherent structural limitations of the material, permits the viewer to relate to craft items without feeling domi-

nated by them. The traditional tabletop size of most crafts contrasts with the vogue for large-scale paintings that marked the second half of the twentieth century. Interestingly, as the idea caught on that large-scale works were art, studio glass artists with art ambitions also increased the scale of their works.[29] In the 1970s Chihuly collaborated with Jamie Carpenter, among others, to make large-scale installation works. When it became evident that collectors could not easily put an installation in their living rooms, many artists reincorporated tabletop-sized works in their repertoire.

Tactility is another body-related aspect of glass. First appreciated through the eyes, texture is subsequently registered by the hand, adding a sensuality beyond the visual with which to seduce an audience. This hand-to-glass connection, unlike the sensual connection of other craft media, contains an element of danger. Glass breaks easily and broken glass cuts. Glass can also shatter spontaneously (because of errors in metal formulation and annealing processes). Thus a personal and, at times, intimate and charged relationship is established between a glass object and the viewer.[30]

All of those characteristics combine to create a seemingly insurmountable boundary of associations separating craft from art. This essential tension between contemporary craft and the high-art world was further deepened as craft—including studio glass after 1960—sought to challenge the boundaries. Studio glass artists choose, however, to see the aforementioned qualities not as limitations (as the high-art world has positioned them) but as virtues, and from this stance they have developed a dual ambition: to create functionally related objects *and* to express artistic content.[31] This second goal impelled studio glass to challenge established artistic categories. Joseph Alsop notes: "If there really is an unbridgeable gulf between 'high art' and 'mere craftsmanship' then hand axes are not works of art." The notion of an unbridgeable gulf continues to be accepted as reality within the high-art world. With the word "craft" clearly evoking utility and, by implication, the hand or body, an apotheosis to a higher realm is blocked. For "art to be true," Alsop continues, "it must be, and can only be an 'end in itself' produced with no other primarily in mind."

The usefulness, attenuated or not, of craft objects diverts them from the straight path to high art. But high art has its own utility. Painting and sculpture have functions as expressions of piety, wealth, or status, to name only a few. When the utility of the high arts is decoded, the distance between craft and art is diminished.[32]

THE FACTORY OR THE STUDIO

When the word *studio* is combined with *glass*, it is generally understood that the antonym is *factory*. The distinction made between the studio and its perceived opposite, the factory, permits glass artists to distinguish their work from the industrial and from traditional craft, often a home-based activity. Studio and factory are indeed different in terms of how production occurs, who controls it, and how many items are produced. A glass factory produces thousands of objects for utilitarian or aesthetic purposes through a process of repetitive acts that are facilitated by machines. The extent of the role of the machine depends on whether it is guided by a maker's hand or simply overseen by a technician observing routine functioning. In factories, the method of production is from the top down, with designers—who may or may not have an intimate technical knowledge of glass-forming methodologies—directing glassmakers by means of drawings or verbal instructions to execute the designers' concepts. This method separates conception from production and the creative process from fabrication. The use of industrial machines further distances creativity from fabrication, essentially eliminating any

individual expression by the technician or machine operator. The repetitive nature of the mechanical process removes spontaneity, and the large number of identical items produced further dilutes unique expression. Commercial factory production may yield thousands of identical glass tumblers in a week with the glassmaker working merely as a functionary. A factory can be small, as they are in Europe, or large, as they are in the United States, so the governing distinction rests on the number of identical items produced and the method of production, the key element being the reliance on the machine over the individual expressions of the maker.

While a factory worker performs a repetitive task many times in a day, the studio artist engages in a range of activities repeated solely at his or her discretion. Within the realm of studio glass, the process from the initial conception through the production is governed by a single person who often also oversees the marketing of the work. Within these general parameters, there are of course variations in involvement and intent. Some studio craftsman desire to make competent handmade objects and others want to make art; all, however, are united in their search for autonomous self-expression.

Studio glass practitioners consider themselves artists in the sense understood by the high-art world on the bases of the locus in which they make their art and their complete control over all aspects of the creative process. The sociologist Howard Becker posits "a perfect correlation between doing the core activity and being an artist. If you do it, you must be an artist.

Vessel, 1964. Harvey K. Littleton (United States, b. 1922). Blown glass; approximately 7–8 inches high. Courtesy of the artist.

opposite
Three Bottles, 1962. Harvey K. Littleton (United States, b. 1922). Blown glass, #475 glass marbles; tallest approximately 8–9 inches high. Collection of the artist.

Conversely, if you are an artist, what you do must be art."[33] Unfortunately for those who make studio glass, which is viewed as tainted by its roots in craft, this correlation is not universally accepted. The fact that they may work in an artist's setting has not automatically secured their acceptance as artists. Interestingly, the high-art world locates the essential artistic activity within the end product; the studio community positions it within the process. Consequently, much writing about studio craft focuses on the conflict with the factory and breaking free from it.[34] By making items that are not demanded by the market and in an artistlike manner, studio glassmakers engage in a "conscious, gratuitous act" that they claim makes them artists.[35]

The problems inherent in considering the location of production a condition of art making are exemplified by the production methods of Howard Ben Tré. To produce his works, the artist rents a commercial glass-casting foundry where he directs the workers and his assistants to execute his concepts with the aid of machines. This method of creating his large-scale, totemic and anthropomorphic works clearly positions Ben Tré closer to factory production than to the methods associated with studio fabrication.[36] But because his intent is to make unique, art-ambitious works, he is considered to be operating within the studio-and-art definition. Indeed, his sculptures are esteemed by the high-art world, where he is referred to as an "artist who works in glass." Within the glass community he is a fellow studio glassmaker.[37]

In reviewing the terminology associated with the American studio glass movement, it becomes apparent that the origin of the phrase "studio glass" is itself murky. In the period immediately following 1962, studio glass referred only to free-blown works. During those early years, "the ethos of the North American Studio Glass movement assumes that one is talking about hot work, specifically freehand, off pipe, in which one works with molten glass oneself, shaping it, forming it or letting gravity do its thing."[38] This remained the case until the late 1970s and effectively placed the trailblazing proto-studio artists of the 1930s and 1940s, who had used cold- or warm-glass techniques, outside the movement.[39] The authors of this exclusionary definition were Harvey Littleton and his followers (see page 49).[40]

However, studio glass has no single proper manifestation. Instead, it encompasses the methodologies used by many individual makers. This has not precluded some from claiming that blown glass is the sole correct expression of the movement. Blown glass has without a doubt been important to the expansion of the movement, Littleton's declaration that free-blown glass is true "studio glass," effectively privileging it over other methods of glass forming (casting, mold blowing, cold working, assembling, and so on), was exclusionary. It was a conscious component of a strategy to lend credibility to the movement by separating it from the taint of the craft world and of the earlier proto-studio glass artists who were part of that world. Littleton's stance was determined by his interest in glass as an art medium and his feeling that it had potential for the creation of art. As to the origin of the term *studio glass*, Littleton as the putative founder of the glass movement said that "studio and glass were used in the earliest proposals [for grants] as two separate nouns, not as an adjective modifying a noun" and that he was not "sure of the first use of the phrase 'studio glass.'"[41] The joining of the two words may thus have resulted from a shorthand that was quickly adopted without much thought. In this volume the term *studio glass* will include the work made by any practitioner working outside the factory and using any technique, hot, warm, or cold.

Some other terms that illustrate aspects of the craft sensibility that still appears in the studio movement and influences its relationship to the high-art world merit discussion. The term *hand arts*, for example, first came into currency in the late 1940s and indicated the importance that makers placed on the direct hand-to-object connection both in making and in use.[42] The reverence for the hand is one of the hallmarks of the craft movement and diminishes its status in the eyes of the high-art world.

In the 1950s and 1960s the hybrid term *designer/ craftsman* also came into use. Favored by the leading craft magazine of the day, *Craft Horizons*, the phrase sought to include the factory designer and the studio craftsman, thereby resolving the tension between factory and studio. It also assumed that there was the potential for art making within the factory. During the

1950s this possibility was considered more attainable as Americans became increasingly aware of European factory practice, where artists worked in direct association with factory craftsmen. A similar practice had existed earlier in the United States when art glass was produced during the late nineteenth century and early twentieth century. European factories were smaller than their American counterparts, and a closer working relationship between designer/craftsmen and gaffers was possible. This small-factory model may still be seen in Scandinavia, Germany, Czechoslovakia, and Italy. Littleton observed it in 1957 while visiting Italian glasshouses, and it was this experience that led him to set up a studio at his home designed for the making of glass by a single practitioner.[43]

At about the same time, the term *artist craftsman* was applied to studio makers, and this phrase continues in use today with some modifications. Again, this terminology appeared in *Craft Horizons* magazine and referred to someone who worked in craft media (clay, glass, fiber, metal, or wood) with the intention of creating art-ambitious objects. This term—describing a maker positioned between the high-art artist and the craftsman (read "traditional craftsman")—signaled the developing ambitions of craftsmen who had begun to see themselves as artists and thus as worthy of that recognition. In the early 1980s another phrase found favor: *studio glass artist*, which eventually became *glass artist*. Here, the medium functions as an adjective modifying the activity and the term is used to describe artists who happen to work with glass, such as the Czech artist Dana Zámečníková, for whom glass was simply one of many materials available. She chose it, not because she was glass artist, but because it offered her the best possible way for expressing her ideas.[44]

By the late 1980s, those who had once called themselves "glass artists" dropped this appellation in favor of "sculptors," thereby attempting to disassociate themselves entirely from the taint of glass with its complicating craft associations. This appellation was quickly picked up by enterprising dealers and artists alike. Then Dale Chihuly took yet another direction, limiting his exhibition titles to his name and the word *glass*, with perhaps one other word used in conjunction: *Dale Chihuly: Glass Cylinders* (1976–1977; see page 61), *Dale Chihuly Glass* (1981–1982), and *Chihuly: Master Glass* (1990).[45] All of these naming strategies are clearly rhetorical bids for inclusion in the more lucrative and rarefied high-art community.

Forming technologies have long been used as a system of classification within the glass world, and with this comes a reliance on skill as the demarcation of success, rather than the emphasis on content that exists in the high-art world. Glass-forming technologies can be broken into three general types: cold-worked glass, warm glass, and hot glass. Cold-worked glass encompasses cutting, polishing, engraving, painting (before firing), fabricating, and assembly.[46] Warm-glass techniques include slumping, fusing, *pâte de verre*, *filet de verre*, and drawing with canes of glass. Lampworking, another warm-glass technique, was most often used in factories to make paperweights; after the studio movement was underway, it was also used in small studios.[47] Hot-glass techniques include mold blowing, free blowing, and casting. During the past decades warm- and cold-glass techniques have found increasing favor with artists. Dan Klein, the former director of Christie's auction house and a studio glass collector, has noted that hot glass, which had "enjoyed what seems in retrospect a disproportionate degree of popularity during the 1960s, lost ground to other techniques, until it was felt during the 1980s that it had been almost completely phased out."[48] This shift in the hierarchy of forming methodologies reveals significant aspects of the progression of glass toward art status.

The last word used in connection to studio glass that should be examined is the word *movement*. It is problematic when applied to studio glass. As understood in a theoretical, art historical sense, *movement* implies a group sharing a unified set of goals—sometimes expressed in a written manifesto. There is, however, no uniformity of vision or theoretical discourse among studio glass artists that relates to artistic goals, use of technologies, or even how many craftsmen can work in a studio. Perhaps the only unifying element is a raw enthusiasm for the material itself. Although this does not constitute a true movement as understood within art historical discourse, it does provide the basis for the creation of a community. Nonetheless, studio glass is referred to as a movement by its practitioners and supporters, as well as in craft literature. The fact that it does not conform to a definition established by the high-art world is of no concern to those involved.

Indeed, a disdain for high-art rules has been a source of pride.

NOTES

1. For the purposes of this discussion, the term *high-art world* will be used instead of *mainstream* or *larger art world*. *Mainstream* indicates that anything included under this rubric is widely considered to be such. This is not the case, as *high art* (as defined by urban galleries and museums) is not necessarily supported by greater numbers than those who favor craft-based works. This distinction is critical to a fair discussion of both the reality of the urban gallery world and its disproportionate influence over the taste of the country. It is also a source of the continuing separation of the arts into high and other—whether described as *low* or *outsider* or *folk*. For the same reasons, *larger art world* is an unsatisfactory term.

2. Art glass is a "general term applied to glassware made for ornamental rather than utilitarian purposes, with primary regard to the quality of the *metal* and the artistic nature of the form and decoration. It was used usually in connection with modern glassware from c. 1850." Howard Newman, *An Illustrated Dictionary of Glass* (London: Thames and Hudson, 1977), 27. For a detailed discussion, see Wendy Kaplan, *"The Art that is Life": The Arts and Crafts Movement in America, 1875–1920* (Boston: Museum of Fine Arts, 1987), especially the sections about Louis Comfort Tiffany.

3. Susanne K. Frantz, formerly the curator of twentieth-century glass at the Corning Museum of Glass, prefers the term *decorative arts* over *craft*. She also distinguishes between art that is functional and art that is decorative. A work that is just decorative cannot qualify as art; see "What Ever Happened to the Decorative Arts," *Glass Art Society Journal* (1987): 29.

4. The nominative use of the word *design* will not be discussed here at length. By the time period under examination, design had become a separate concern and discipline, exclusively focused on factory mass production. The word is significant within the studio world as a verb, which indicates, as it does in many other fields, the activity of formal composition.

5. For the effect of domestic context on decorative arts, and subsequently on the production of the studio movement, see chapter 8. The issue of domestic space and women reveals itself in the "placeness" of craft (see Douglas Crimp's terminology). This association works against glass as it contrasts with the modernist notion of "placelessness," an assumed attribute of successful modern painting and sculpture. Ever since the production of both domestic and business wares outside the home was made possible by the advent of the machine, craft has been located in the home, produced as a leisure activity separate from work. The location of craft in the domestic realm means that it is dismissed as a serious art medium. Glass, however, at least during the first part of the period under discussion, could be produced only in a factory and was thus decidedly located outside of the domestic sphere. When glass is linked to craft, the historical connotation of a female domestic activity affects its valuation. See Douglas Crimp, *On the Museum's Ruins* (Cambridge, Mass.: MIT Press, 1993); and Christopher Reed, ed., *Not at Home: The Suppression of Domesticity in Modern Art and Architecture* (London: Thames and Hudson, 1996). Another shift occurred that reversed the value of homemade and handmade. In the nineteenth century, "handmade" meant "amateur," or shoddy and of lesser value. The studio movement discussed here inverted this paradigm: "handmade" currently implies something unique, rare, and of greater value. See Arthur J. Pulos, *American Design Ethic: A History of Industrial Design to 1940* (Cambridge, Mass.: MIT Press, 1986); Susanne K. Frantz, "This is Not a Minor Art: Contemporary Glass and Traditions of Art History," *Glass Art Society Journal* (1985–1986): 7–11; and Robert Silberman, "Domesticity and Beyond: Irve Dell, Christie Hawkins, and the Place of Craft," *American Craft* 57, no. 4 (August/September 1997): 48.

6. This is in marked contrast to the nineteenth-century term *minor arts*, which assumed that anything other than painting, sculpture, or architecture was minor. Susanne K. Frantz and the ceramics scholar Garth Clark agree that the classification of works made in craft media as art is determined by the intention of the artist. If the artist is not successful, the result will not be art, just as bad painting is not admitted to the temple of art. See Frantz, "This Is Not a Minor Art," 7; Garth Clark, conversations, 1985 and on.

7. The terms *traditional crafts* and *folk art* are sometimes distinguished. Traditional crafts imply a knowledge of previous technologies; folk art carries with it the notion of an untutored and naive sensibility. Both may be anonymous. Traditional craft makers are trained but in a way that teaches them to make an established range of forms from time-honored materials in the same manner over decades of time. Michael Owen Jones makes similar distinctions in *Exploring Folk Art: Twenty Years of Thought on Craft, Work, and Aesthetics* (Ann Arbor, Mich.: U.M.I. Research Press, 1987); see specifically the chapter "Violations of Standards of Excellence and Preference in Utilitarian Art," 13–39.

8. Unlike the maker of fine arts, who usually signs the artwork, the rural artisan usually works anonymously, a difference that reflects issues about the importance of the individual and of authorship. Studio glass makers from the beginning signed and often dated their work, thereby linking their practice to that of high art.

9. Joel Samuel Yudken, "The Viability of Craft in Advanced Industrial Society: Case Study of the Contemporary Crafts Movement in the United States" (PhD diss., Stanford University, 1987), 1:136–78.

10. George Kubler, *The Shape of Time: Remarks on the History of Things* (New Haven, Conn.: Yale University Press, 1962), 15.

11. With institutional support for collecting and study emanating from the Smithsonian Center for Folklife, traditional craft and folk art have recently taken on some of the gloss of the high-art world. Like studio craft, they are now faced with tension between their original roots and the ambitions evident within the field. See Adele Earnest, *Folk Art in America: A Personal View* (Exton, Penn.: Schiffer Publishing, 1984); and Jones, *Exploring Folk Art*. The way in which folk art began to move toward contemporary craft or studio craft is outlined by Steven M. Gelber in "A Job you Can't Lose: Work and Hobbies in the Great Depression," *Journal of Social History* 24, no. 4 (winter 1991): 741–66.

12. Howard Becker states that there are two types of craftsmen: the craftsman and the artist-craftsman; "the two types not only carry on the craft in distinctive ways, but also constitute distinct groups of people." See Becker, *Art Worlds* (Berkeley: University of California Press, 1982), 276. This is a distinction that studio glass has sought to eliminate.

13. Yudken, "The Viability of Craft," 2:452–67.

14. Both Bernard Kester, the noted textile expert and former professor of art at the University of California, Los Angeles, and Edith Wylie, the founder and director of the Craft and Folk Art Museum, Los Angeles, represent this point of view. Kester never desired to have his work considered as high art. When Wylie founded her museum, her goal was to reinvolve herself with objects and figuration, counteracting the trend toward abstraction that prevailed at that time. Kester, conversations, 1990–1994; Wylie, conversations, 1996–1997.

15. There are two new institutions, both in North Carolina, devoted to the issues of crafts and studio work: the Mint Museum of Craft + Design has opened a new facility in Charlotte, and the Center for Craft Creativity and Design is located in Asheville. With Penland School of the Crafts and Black Mountain College in the vicinity—both are traditional craft centers and are located just outside Asheville—the term *decorative arts*, with its urban and academic connections, was never a possibility in this context.

16. For a schematic view of the way in which the connotation of *craft* moves from a material culture to an art association, see A. J. Greimas and François Rastier, "Semiotic Square," as modified by James Clifford, "On Collecting and Culture," in Russell Ferguson et al., eds., *Out There: Marginalization and Contemporary Culture* (New York: MIT Press, 1990), 147.

17. Clement Greenberg, "Avant-Garde and Kitsch," in *Art and Culture: Critical Essays* (Boston: Beacon Press, 1965), 3–21.

18. For a discussion of the root meaning of *craft*, see "What Criteria for the Crafts," *Craft Horizons* 20, no. 2 (March–April 1960): 38.

19. Bob Sinclair, "Kenneth R. Trapp: I Start with the Work of Art Itself," *Renwick Quarterly* (summer 1997). Susanne K. Frantz modifies these same notions; see "What Ever Happened to the Decorative Arts?"29. A similar definition is presented by Howard Becker (*Art Worlds*, especially 272–99), who adds "beauty" to the characteristics of craft (276). This is an issue in glass, but it is not strictly true of all contemporary craft. Indeed, to position themselves closer to high art in their sensibility, craft artists have come to embrace the ugly as content.

20. The notion of materiality is often misunderstood by scholars of painting and sculpture. A case in point is found in John Varriano's "Caravaggio and the Decorative Arts in the Two *Suppers at Emmaus*," *Art Bulletin* 68, no. 2 (June 1986): 218–24. As Varriano analyzes the two paintings, he focuses on the maiolica tableware, specifically the *boccaletto*. He comments that the decoration of the vessel (a jug or tankard) is at odds with that of those known from the period (222). But what he does not allow for or understand is that Caravaggio may have taken license with the decoration because he was not working in a concave, volumetric form but rather rendering in two dimensions. Decorative motifs that are successful in one-dimensional iterations are often not successful in three-dimensional applications. This is evident to anyone who has tried to paint on a curved surface and create a pleasing pattern across the entire form. This was the topic of long debates in nineteenth-century British design literature about appropriate decorative applications.

21. Dan Dailey, letter to author, September 13, 1995.

22. See Robert C. Morgan, "Michael Taylor's Metaphors of Light and Energy," *New Work* 33 (spring 1988): 14–16; and Melinda Wortz, "Larry Bell," *Glass Art Society Journal* (1986): 58–61. Glass has unique visual properties. Plexiglas, a seemingly similar material, refracts light differently and when used in large sheets deforms the desired optics. Artists such as Larry Bell did not execute their works in Plexiglas. Other artists from the high-art world have also used glass, among them, Mario Merz, Lynda Benglis, and Robert Rauschenberg.

23. See John Berger, *Ways of Seeing* (London: British Broadcasting Corporation and Penguin Books, 1972).

24. See Martha Drexler Lynn, *Masters of Contemporary Glass: Selections from the Glick Collection*, exh. cat. Indiana Museum of Art, Indianapolis (Indianapolis: Indiana University Press, 1997), 70–73.

25. *Pâte de verre* and off-hand blowing are two technologies that were lost and when revived in the twentieth century became especially important forming methods for American studio glass, the latter defining studio glass during its first fifteen years.

26. In their books both Dominick Labino and Harvey Littleton included extensive sections about the history of glassmaking because, they felt, knowledge about the history would impart additional legitimacy to their work. See

Dominick Labino, *Visual Art in Glass* (Dubuque, Iowa: William C. Brown, 1968); and Harvey K. Littleton, *Glassblowing: A Search for Form* (New York: Van Nostrand, Reinhold, 1971).

27. See Lynn, *Masters of Contemporary Glass*, 15.

28. The display function of silver is evident in Timothy B. Schroder's exhibition catalogue *The Gilbert Collection of Gold and Silver* (Los Angeles County Museum of Art, 1988), in which the provenance of objects in silver that are described as "monumental" reveals their royal and aristocratic connections. The dramatic scale and design of these works proclaim their utility as signifiers of wealth and power. Also see Elizabeth De Castres, *A Guide to Collecting Silver* (London: Bloomsbury Books, 1980). Both these authors focus on technique, provenance, formal decorative elements, and forming methodologies, which are often presented without any clarification of their physical or social ramifications. As is typical of texts about even masterpieces in the decorative arts, there is no discussion of larger cultural issues (of class, power, the uses of and strategies for display, and so on) pertaining to silver.

29. The artist and ceramist Ron Nagle is known for his sculptural pieces that may be considered cups. These functional and body-referent works are executed in sizes ranging from 2½ × 2 feet (*My Compliments*, 1988, Los Angeles County Museum of Art) to 1 × 1½ inches (*Untitled Cup*, ca. 1989, Los Angeles County Museum of Art). The first was considered sculpture and displayed in the sculpture galleries of the Andersen Building at the museum. The other would have won a place only in the wall case in the decorative arts galleries.

30. Thomas McEvilley, "Essay: The Sound of Glass Breaking," *Glass* 73 (winter 1998): 34–39. Karla Trinkley purposely uses this aspect of glass as part of the content of her work. *Pâte de verre*, her usual technique, leaves rough and sharp edges at the seams of the mold. Trinkley retains this imperfection in order to make her works simultaneously enticing and dangerous.

31. Much of the ethos attached to the craft sensibility in the United States during the 1940s and 1950s was modeled on the Mingei-kai (short form of *minshu-teki Kogei*, meaning "common people's craft"), a movement that was begun by Sōetsu Yanagi (1889–1961). Yanagi dedicated his life to the rediscovering and dispersing of the real truth of beauty, which he fixed within handcrafted everyday utilitarian objects. As he wrote in "The Kizaemon Tea-Bowl" (1931), an essay published in *The Unknown Craftsman: A Japanese Insight onto Beauty* (Tokyo: Kodansha International, 1984, 90–196), this movement prized the craftsman as maker of objects that have "effortless peace" and "peaceful beauty." The addition of a spiritual dimension led American craftsmen, whether traditional in orientation or artistic in ambition, to believe they were part of a higher calling. See Kyoko Utsumi Mimura, "Soetsu Yanagi and the Legacy of the Unknown Craftsman," *The Journal of Decorative and Propaganda Arts 1875–1945*, 20 (1994): 208–23. See also Rose Slivka, "The Art/Craft Connection: A Personal, Critical and Historical Odyssey," in Marcia

and Tom Manhart, ed., *The Eloquent Object: The Evolution of American Art and Craft Media since 1945*, exh. cat. Philbrook Museum of Art, Tulsa, Oklahoma (Seattle: University of Washington Press, 1987), 67–103.

32. Joseph Alsop, *The Rare Art Traditions: The History of Art Collecting and Its Linked Phenomena Wherever These Have Appeared* (New York: Harper and Row, 1982), 34.

33. Becker, *Art Worlds*, 18, 272–99.

34. See Leslie Graves, "Transgressive Traditions and Art Definitions," *The Journal of Aesthetics and Art Criticism* 56, no. 1 (winter 1998): 39–48. Here Graves notes two separate conditions for the making of art. The functional theory of art definition requires that an object must conform to at least a general standard of what makes something art; the procedural theory maintains that art is made when it is designated as art according to certain privileged procedures, regardless of what function it serves.

35. Slivka, "The Art/Craft Connection," 86.

36. Dan Dailey and Dale Chihuly have also used commercial facilities to create their works.

37. Howard Ben Tré graduated from the Rhode Island School of Design, which would have qualified him as a studio craftsman, and he also worked at the Blenko Glass Factory. But he quickly found representation in Charles Cowles's New York gallery in the mid-1980s. He then received a one-man exhibition at the Phillips Gallery in Washington, D.C. From that time on he has been associated with the high-art world and only tangentially with the glass community. See Lynn, *Masters of Contemporary Glass*, 38–41. See also the gallery exhibition catalogues: *Columns*, Hadler-Rodriguez Galleries, New York City, 1982; *Howard Ben Tré*, Charles Cowles Gallery, New York, 1985; and *Howard Ben Tré: Vessels of Light*, Charles Cowles Gallery, New York, 1991.

38. Louise Berndt, letter to the editor, *Glass* 63 (summer 1996): 6.

39. Because warm glass can be worked at a lower temperature than is necessary for melting glass for blowing, the heat levels required were easily attained outside the factory, often through use of ceramics technology. Warm glass refers to slumping or the fusing of pieces to form the desired shape. In this volume I am describing as studio glassmakers all of those artists who work, in any glass technique, outside the factory setting.

40. With the emergence of the so-called new art history, the application of the primacy of any single "big man" connected to any movement has been brought into question. Studio glass owes its existence to a number of elements coming together at a time and place.

41. William Warmus, "Harvey Littleton: Glass Master," *Glass* 72 (fall 1998): 34. Others were using warm-glass or cold-glass techniques, but after 1962 only hot glass was considered studio glass. By the 1980s this situation changed and other glass-forming techniques (cold, warm, assembled, and so on) made in a studio setting were also called studio glass. In this way studio glass became defined by the

structure of the working environment and not by the forming methodologies used.

42. The term *designer/craftsman* was used to described handmade work of the period, but this combination of design and craft did not last long; see *Craft Horizons* 13, no. 6 (November–December 1953): 12–18.

43. Susanne K. Frantz, *Contemporary Glass: A World Survey from the Corning Museum of Glass* (New York: Harry N. Abrams, 1989), 46.

44. Needless to say, the term *glass artists* does not refer to artists made of glass. Kristian Suda, "Zámečníková: A Singular Encounter," *Glass* 45 (fall 1991): 30–37.

45. *Dale Chihuly: Glass Cylinders*, Wadsworth Athenaeum, Hartford, Connecticut (1976–1977); *Dale Chihuly Glass*, Tacoma Museum of Art, Tacoma, Washington (1976–1977); and *Chihuly: Master Glass*, Museo Nacional de Bellas Artes, Santiago, Chile (1990).

46. Stained glass, one cold-working methodology, falls outside of the scope of this text. A different history and artistic challenges link stained glass to architecture and to painting. Its planar quality contrasts with the volumetric and sculptural nature of most studio glass. "It's only relatively late that medieval stained glass gained the status of fine art as distinct from decoration, and it has done so as pictorial art, not glass-making" (Clement Greenberg "Glass as High Art," *Glass Art Society Journal* [1984–1985]: 15). Studio glass as discussed here is three dimensional and object or figure related. Stained glass did not suffer the decline that handmade glass did during the late nineteenth century and the early twentieth century. So despite the ease of working flat cold glass in a studio setting, the focus of stained glass is not that of what has come to be called studio glass.

47. John Burton and Charles Kaziun were two mid-twentieth-century American flameworkers who had their own studios. Knowledge of flameworking techniques was jealously guarded by factory practitioners, so Burton and Kaziun sought independent training. Burton taught himself how to make his eccentrically decorated vessels and considered himself an artist. Kaziun built his own furnace during the late 1950s and encased his lampworked forms inside glass ingots. See Yoshiko Uchida, "John Burton: Fluid Breath of Glass," *Craft Horizons* 20, no. 6 (November/December 1960): 23–27.

48. Dan Klein, *Glass: A Contemporary Art* (New York: Rizzoli, 1989), 28.

Diatretum Vase, 1953. Frederick Carder
(1863–1963, born United Kingdom, active in the
United States after 1903). Cast in a cire-perdue
mold; 6 ³⁄₈ x 7 ¹⁄₄ inches. The Corning Museum of
Glass, gift of the artist (53.4.26)

Chapter 2

*From Factory Glass
to Craft Glass—
Shaping a Movement*

Aᴍᴇʀɪᴄᴀɴ ᴛʀᴀᴅɪᴛɪᴏɴᴀʟ or vernacular crafts were at the outset modeled on European practices and forms that were commercially and functionally driven.

For the most part the colonial craftsman did not consider himself to be a designer, but rather the instrument by which the desires of his patrons could be satisfied. To show his familiarity with the most recent styles, he imported examples that could be displayed to attract business and could also be copied. And he sought out and purchased special tools and patterns, or made his own from such samples as he could lay his hands on. That enabled him to work in the latest continental or English styles. However, the artisan often found it necessary to modify a design—not only to suit the client's whims, but sometimes because of inadequate tools or limited talents.[1]

This legacy led to an American traditional crafts practice in which items were fabricated using time-honored methods and innovation was valued only when dictated by the client or required for successful production. This approach gave vernacular crafts a conservative ethos that persists even to the present.

In the late nineteenth and early twentieth centuries, the reform-based Arts and Crafts movement contributed, albeit indirectly, to the philosophical development of American studio craft. Based on the writings and theories of the English art critic John Ruskin

(1819–1900) and the designer and theorist William Morris (1834–1896), the tenets of British Arts and Crafts were transformed when they passed into pragmatic American hands. Ruskin wrote at length about his distaste for the machine; Morris (and the Americans) accepted it as a tool of production with the understanding that it should not be used for excessive flights of decorative fancy.[2] American Arts and Crafts were more commercially based, and their producers did not reject mechanized production out of hand. In fact, most American Arts and Crafts items were fabricated in what would now be viewed as factorylike settings (when compared with high-art practice), and this was especially true of glass. [3]

The unique relationship of glass to the factory must be explained here. This long association is perhaps the most important factor informing the studio glass sensibility and differentiating it from the other contemporary crafts. Ironically, it also represents an instance of the survival of craft—craft in the simplest sense of knowledge of workmanship—for it was only within the commercial setting that knowledge of glass technology endured. All seventeenth- and eighteenth-century glass had been of necessity handmade; by the nineteenth century glass production flourished predominately within the factory. With the advent of machines, the hand was distanced from production, and in a strange turn of events, craftsmanship in the sense of original aesthetic expression was devalued. The term *handmade*, once positive in connotation, became pejorative. Arthur J. Pulos notes that, as the result of advertising by manufacturers in the United States during the nineteenth century, *handmade* became synonymous with *substandard* and *shoddy*. Machines, in contrast, were praised for uniform production and for meeting the goals of mass production.[4] These factors, combined with the expense of running a glasshouse, drove glass into the factory.[5] Factory beliefs about how and how not to form glass and concerns about how many workers were needed for glassmaking also delayed the emergence of glass as a craft activity.[6]

Glass yields reluctantly to the amateur hand. Clay can be formed (thrown, hand-built, coiled, slab-rolled, and so on) in an informal setting—hence its popularity in summer camp and art school—glass cannot. Reasons for this abound. Raw glass (cullet) that is free of impurities is difficult to obtain; furthermore, carefully guarded so-called secret formulas affect its stability and visual properties. Higher temperatures are needed to melt glass into a malleable material than are required to fire ceramics, and these are difficult to achieve on a small scale outside a glasshouse. Attempts by early studio glass artists to modify ceramics technology were successful only for working glass cold or warm—to slump (partially melt or soften) glass over molds or to fuse it into desired shapes. These techniques offered little formal variety.

High fuel costs and the necessity of round-the-clock operation also combined to make the expense of operating a glass furnace, which is necessary for blowing or casting hot glass, prohibitive. Only cold working (cutting, painting, gluing, and so on) is really possible in a small studio. Blowing was, however, the elusive technique and it became the goal of the early studio glassmakers. Ironically, the more accessible warm- and cold-glass techniques would not return to favor with studio glass artists until the technologically challenging hot-glass skill of blowing had been conquered.

In the late nineteenth century the work of Louis Comfort Tiffany and the Tiffany Studio epitomized American Arts and Crafts glass.[7] Working in a guild-based tradition of team-crafted production, Tiffany thrived because it was a commercial enterprise.[8] By the 1920s, however, fashion had changed, and designs from other manufacturers found favor with the public.

In an effort to remain profitable, Tiffany moved away from producing expensive artwork and increasingly catered to urban, middlebrow tastes with less expensive items. Even with this shift, the firm failed to reach a large enough market, and it was sold in 1928. Others who relied less on hand-finished works (the bedrock of the Arts and Crafts ideal) and successfully marketed mass-produced glass came to the fore. The most important of these for studio glass was the Steuben Glass Works, a subsidiary of the Corning Glass Works.

It is often assumed that the Arts and Crafts movement was directly responsible for the subsequent development of American studio crafts and, by extension, studio glass. This is not the complete story. Although American Arts and Crafts communities were established in both rural and semi-urban areas, the movement was informed by an urban sensibility. Reacting to the imposition of the machine between the worker (and consumer) and the product manufactured—an intrusion that separated life and livelihood—the Arts and Crafts movement sought a return to hand-based craftsmanship and "truth to materials," among other things.[9] It is this focus on the machine, however, that reveals the movement's urban base, for in the country the hand still prevailed as the primary mode of production. Indeed, the Arts and Crafts movement and its philosophy must have seemed an urbanite's bucolic fantasy to traditional rural makers, who had never been separated from hand production and were, as a rule, true to their materials. Consequently, the movement had a limited and indirect effect on the later studio movement. It was only after the wane of Arts and Crafts enthusiasm in the 1920s and 1930s that crafts—perceived as a wholesome contrast to big-business manufacturing and its Depression era failures—became part of the next reform impulse and were freighted with redemptive social virtue.[10]

During the 1930s regionalism and an interest in figurative, as opposed to abstract, rendering of form characterized the prevailing high-art style. As well, rural crafts were valued as expressions of the virtues of the American heartland. Figurative artists, such as Thomas Hart Benton, Grant Wood, Paul Cadmus, John Steuart Curry, and Millard Sheets, among others, depicted craftsmen at work or representational land-

Sun, Sea and Rocks of Sonoma, ca. 1970. Millard Sheets (1907–1990). Watercolor on paper; 40 x 28 inches. Sheets represented the regionalist impulse that favored representational art over the avant-garde abstraction championed by Clement Greenberg in New York.

scapes in order to celebrate the common man and the virtues attached to his activity.[11]

During the Depression a life in the crafts was believed to express the democratic values that could restore faith in the American system. Craft became a component of national culture and renewal. Handcrafted works would improve social conditions in rural areas and in urban centers, and were viewed as an untapped source of healthy creative energy.[12] Crafts were also thought to improve the quality of life for those who were "seeking a creative outlet, convalescents needing occupational therapy, or a retired person seeking an interest in later life."[13] These associations had an ironic outcome, however, for the connection of craft with the less fortunate, the elderly, convalescents or the countrified, attached itself to the later studio

crafts—including glass—thereby ensuring their second-class status in relation to painting and sculpture. Indeed, "craft is what other people make—women, people of color, savages, hippies, farmers, crazy people, the poor . . . 'normal' people make art," observed John Perreault, a critic who would later become the director of UrbanGlass in Brooklyn. These associations helped perpetuate the divide between art and craft.[14] Eventually, the desire of studio glassmakers to be considered artists, which increased after the 1970s, succeeded in removing this taint.

The Depression also left a legacy of relating craft to individualism. Before 1929, the public had increasingly placed its faith in government and big business for economic security.[15] Eileen Boris notes that concerns about a professional class in which autonomy and creativity are placed second to labor reflected anxiety over the possible loss of control in an America where people were becoming employees of corporations and witnesses to class conflict.[16] When the Depression hit, self-sufficiency and an honest day's labor seemed an

Vase, 1923. François-Emile Décorchemont (France, 1880–1971). *Pâte de verre*; 3 ½ x 4 ½ inches. Los Angeles County Museum of Art, gift of the 1987 Collectors Committee (M.87.137)

This finely finished work contrasts with the rough exterior maintained by Karla Trinkley in her more contemporary interpretation of *pâte de verre*; see page 145.

Plate, 1940s. Glen Lukens (United States, 1887–1967). Slumped glass with oxides; 7 ½ inches in diameter. Los Angeles County Museum of Art, gift of Daniel Ostroff (M.90.1)

Lukens successfully slumped glass over his ceramic mold forms.

appropriate antidote to the losses and hardships suffered by the working man after the market crashed. These events engendered a desire to return to core values, and self-reliance became a siren's song.

In this way, craft activity came to embody an egalitarian vision and stood in marked contrast to the callous corporation. Even the government, with its New Deal alliances between farmers and craftsmen, came to value this rediscovered self-sufficiency. This connection helped to solidify the image of the craftsman as a social type imbued with positive virtues. In the early years of the studio-glass movement, self-sufficiency and a position outside the establishment once again proved powerful lures for would-be practitioners.

A less-tangible component of the philosophical architecture of glass resides in its reputed spirituality. Ultimately the values of self-reliance and righteousness were presumed to suffuse the handmade object itself. "Themes of individualism, independence and freedom are connected with those of spirituality and humanism in the life and work of the craftsman."[17] This spiritual quality was also noted by Rose Slivka, the editor of *Craft Horizons* (who carefully replaced the word *craft* with the more elevated term *art*), when she wrote that "in 1945, at the close of World War II, there was only a small group of artists in New York City. We had no idea art would become not only a respectable profession but a crowded one. To us it was not a profession, it was a priesthood—a spiritual calling."[18]

Spirituality was attributed to all crafts, but was particularly associated with glass. This in part accounts for the devotion to studio glass professed by both its producers and collectors. It can be said, in fact, that it is this quality that assured the success of glass as an art medium. Artists and collectors are often drawn to the medium because of this perceived spiritual essence— glass moves almost magically from liquid to solid, from fire red to clear crystal. This and its vaunted transparency and translucency are discussed by artists, dealers, and collectors in terms that suggest a glimpse of the divine.

HISTORICAL FOUNDATIONS

In addition to the foregoing philosophical roots, a number of circumstantial factors shaped the development of studio glass. One was the growth in hobbies that occurred in the 1930s and 1940s. The connection with hobbies and faith in crafts as useful for solving social issues or providing work relief deepened during the 1930s, when hobbies were promoted as therapeutic for both society and the individual for they

> taught discipline, instilled focused behavior, and redeem[ed] idleness . . . [t]he word "hobby" became a strategic term used less to be descriptive than to carry weight of authoritative approval when applied to individual activities. In other words the term "hobby" as used in the Thirties was more an ideological construct crafted to distinguish between "good" and "bad" pastimes, than the natural category of leisure activity.[19]

The enthusiasm for hobbies (then synonymous with craft) led to the founding of *Craft Horizons* magazine in 1941, the only magazine devoted to reporting on craftsmen and their activities. In the 1950s as leisure time increased, crafts, practiced as hobbies, continued to be seen as a social good. The linking of virtue and working with the hands and the emphasis on seriousness of purpose and consummate skill in the making of items became guiding precepts of the studio-glass movement. At this time, however, the number of those who dabbled in glass as a hobby were few; but they were significant to the movement—working alone, fashioning items out of glass in their spare time, and relying on technical knowledge gleaned from commercial glass factories or transferred from ceramics.[20]

Two governmental actions helped to propel crafts to greater acceptance in the 1930s and 1940s, the Works Projects Administration and the GI Bill. In 1935 the Works Progress Administration Federal Arts Project (after 1939, the Works Projects Administration [WPA]) created employment for approximately five thousand artists and craftsmen. By placing craftsmen on a par with painters and sculptors, the WPA implied that being a craftsmen was a worthy profession; and with their being perceived as a single class of worker, the seeds were sown for the GI Bill.[21]

The GI Bill (Public Law 346; the Readjustment Act), signed into law by President Franklin D. Roosevelt on June 22, 1944, was intended to provide productive activity for veterans returning from World War II, but it was actually adopted to avoid the unrest and riots that had followed the return of World War I veterans. Among its provisions, the bill offered to pay tuition for college-level classes in the arts and sciences.[22] No one, however, foresaw the stampede that would take place as returning vets flocked to colleges and graduate schools. Even more surprising was the number of veterans who chose the arts as a viable professional and personal choice.[23] This led to increased demand for art courses, which in turn, necessitated the creation of permanent faculty positions to accommodate the influx of new students. As a result, the arts and crafts—led by clay and glass—became institutionalized, and for the next three decades many craftsmen survived on university salaries, which augmented income from the sale of their artwork. Another consequence of the war contributed to the emergence of studio glass. As returning veterans formed new families, they required housing and furnishings. Household wares were therefore produced in great quantity to compensate for lingering wartime shortages and meet this increased demand. This fostered a trend toward mass-produced, anonymous objects, which threatened to make every home look alike.[24] Handcrafted items, in contrast, were anomalous, refreshing, and capable of expressing individuality. Rose Slivka noted that "the object makers are commenting on their middle-class culture of mass-produced, standardized good taste as a domesticated, housebroken, sanitized sensibility."[25] Crafts were seen as an antidote to suburban Levittowns and as a means of returning individuality to the new American tract house.[26] The result was an expanded market for studio crafts and a shift in its center from the rural, often lower-class, milieu of vernacular crafts to the middle-class, suburban high-craft community.

Craft items, represented as part of a European avant-garde aesthetic, were touted through the modernist *Good Design* exhibitions held during the 1950s at the trendsetting Museum of Modern Art in New York. Crafts seemed to offer relief from the chilly avant-garde modernity of steel and glass, harking back soothingly to time-honored materials. To those with more discriminating taste, they also offered the touch of individuality. Clay works by Peter Voulkos and Beatrice Wood (see page 41) were found next to furniture designed by Charles and Ray Eames for Herman Miller, Inc.

The last spur to the increased popularity of crafts was the fact that handcrafted items, while not inexpensive, seemed to offer value for money, unlike mass-produced modernist design items that, although advertised as inexpensive, were not.[27] The interest in the handmade was appealing enough for factories to develop their own line of craft pieces, as Blenko Glass Factory, Inc., of West Virginia did in the 1940s. Later Joel Phillip Myers would work at Blenko and use factory made elements to construct his famous *Dr. Zarkhov's Tower* in 1971 (see page 135).

GLASS AFTER WORLD WAR II

The American studio glass community was the smallest studio community to develop after World War II. Clay, textiles, furniture, and even metals (in the form of enamels, decorative wall pieces, and room dividers) boasted more practitioners and supporters. Even today the studio glass community consists of only a few thousand top-level artists, teachers, students, collectors (representing public and private interests), dealers, and suppliers.[28] The impact of this small number is seen in a variety of ways. Most importantly, it accounts for the relatively few studio glass items produced.[29] The written record lags, too. Books about glass, including ancient glass, number fewer than a third of those devoted to clay. These factors have lent a hothouse quality to the glass community: artists who teach and their students compete on a very personal basis with one another.[30] The small numbers have also led to a canonical history that privileged a few key players and, initially, permitted glassblowing to be valued over other methods of working glass.

By the end of the nineteenth century glassmaking was largely restricted to factories. American factories were larger and less flexible than their older European counterparts. They typically focused on the efficient production of utilitarian objects such as beakers, bottles, and tubes. Supported by the marketplace, these facilities trained their own workers and built the specialized equipment they needed. The smaller-scale glass furnaces and annealing ovens that had been used in the creation of unique glass objects during earlier periods (by Tiffany Studios or Handel Glass Company, for example) were replaced by larger glasshouses in the nineteenth and early twentieth centuries. By the time Tiffany Studios and other, similar establishments closed and began to fade from memory, only commercial production remained.[31]

Determining what is properly called a glass factory is difficult. As a general rule, a factory is a facility that brings together a number of workers who repetitively carry out discrete tasks that result in the creation of a predetermined form. Implicit in this definition is the fact that each factory worker is skilled in a limited number of tasks and that artistic guidance is separate and provided by a designer who oversees the total production but who may or may not be able to actually work glass. Factory work can therefore be seen as an assembly-line activity with the workers taking little creative risk. To increase production, supplementary teams of workers are added; successful large glass factories employed hundreds of skilled glassworkers.[32]

The time-honored approach of separating glassmaking into tasks made the existence of teams of six to eight the custom. Glassblowing, a primary method used by industry for forming glass, is a time-critical activity. The various tasks relating to forming objects are broken down into actions that are carried out quickly by each specialist. It was considered impossible to melt glass in small batches and even more outlandish for an individual alone to attempt to form objects from start to finish. Based on the realities of fabrication, the custom of having groups create glass became embedded within the American factory system. This article of faith, with its potential for featherbedding, precluded attempts to establish small glassmaking facilities.

One interesting custom, which grew out of the factory setting, can, however, be considered an early manifestation of the studio glass impulse. Owing to the size of factory enterprises, fuel costs for sustaining the high temperatures needed to melt glass for forming were considerable, as was the time necessary to melt large quantities of glass cullet. Consequently, it proved most economical to leave the furnaces on all the time. This practice provided an opportunity for glassmakers to create off-hand glass objects, called "whimsies" or "friggers," for their own amusement outside work time. While not conceived as or termed *art* by their makers, these works ranged from impressive displays of technical virtuosity to artistic expressions. They were glass objects formed without concern for utilitarian applications, and in their own way, they moved glass one step further away from its functional, factory roots and toward a studio sensibility.

In the main, however, factory attitudes fostered contempt for those who tried to be amateur glassworkers. In *The Making of Fine Glass* (1947), Sidney Waugh, a designer for the Steuben Glass Works in Corning, New York, wrote: "It must be emphasized that glassblowing, as described on these pages, is not within the scope of the amateur or even the most talented artist or craftsman working alone."[33] Yet previously, in his *Art of Glass Making*, written in 1937 (below), he pronounces no such admonition. Perhaps ten years later

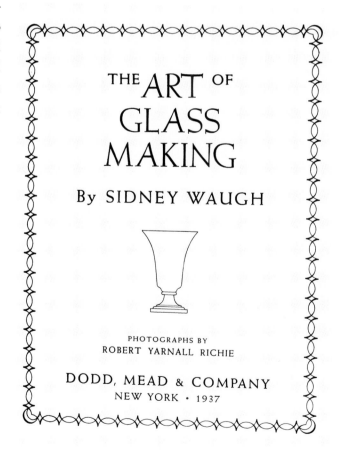

Cover of *The Art of Glass Making* by Sidney Waugh, 1937.

company men like Waugh were already feeling the hot breath of the independent glassmakers to come.

This glass-factory sensibility contributed to a split in the American glass-forming community that would haunt it well into the 1970s: the specialized knowledge needed for working glass resided within the industrial community, but the interest in using glass as an expressive art medium lay in the crafts and art communities. Although linked by a passion for the medium, these two communities had little or no contact with each other. Consequently, the first twenty years of the studio glass movement were spent rediscovering, inventing, and transferring glass forming technologies to the service of art.

By the 1930s glassmaking had begun to appear outside the factory. Established in 1903, Steuben Glass Works, an upscale subsidiary of the Corning Glass Works, emerged as a dominant force in national and international glass. Frederick Carder (1863–1963) arrived at Corning from the British glassmaking firm of Stevens and Williams, Brierley Hill, near Stourbridge, and brought with him a knowledge and respect for the medium. A great innovator of colored-glass formulas and glass compositions, Carder was also a sculptor, a skilled form designer, and ultimately responsible for most of the colored Steuben glass manufactured from 1904 until 1933.

It was Carder's later career, however, that influenced the studio glass movement. In 1932 he was relieved of many of his responsibilities at Steuben,[34] and from the 1930s to the 1950s, he worked at a small kiln in his studio to develop various glass-molding techniques for his original sculptures, rendered in *pâte de verre* and cire perdue (lost-wax) techniques. Most ambitious were his loose interpretations of ancient Roman carved *diatreta* vessels, or cage cups, such as his *Diatretum Vase* (1953) executed in cire perdue (see page 20).[35] These independent experiments, coupled with his stature within the glass world, made his explorations, which prefigure a studio glass practice, widely known.

Meanwhile, European trailblazers also influenced American studio glass. European factories were organized differently from their American counterparts and reflected the historical guild system from which they grew.[36] Positioned between the definition of *factory* in

the American sense and of *studio* in the contemporary sense, European glassmaking had not lost its respect for the traditional, artistic, and artisan-based activities of the glassmaker. This extended to all forming and decorative technologies, the hot-glass skills of free blowing and mold blowing being valued equally with warm-glass slumping or cold-glass etching or engraving skills. Unlike American factories, those in Europe made both production pieces (those produced in large quantity) and art pieces (few in number) as a matter of course. The prices paid reflected the amount of individual work provided by the gaffer and the contribution of the master designer. This "touch of the designer's hand" justified (and still does) the marketing of these works as high-end glass art. In studio work, the artist's hand confers value.

French glass factories also influenced the American studio movement. The establishments of the French art-glass manufacturers and designers Emile Gallé (1846–1904) and René Lalique (1860–1945) were typical of the European glass factory. Professional designers made sketches for works to be executed by a glassmaking team. As the team worked, the designer might come through the work area and alter or augment the gaffer's work, generally in a managerial capacity.[37] The distinction between the artistic aspect and the fabrication of works would ultimately be eliminated in American studio glass practice. It should be remembered, however, that although French art glass was manufactured in quantity, the plants were smaller and the workers fewer than in American factories of the same period; the French factories could be compared with some contemporary studio makers working now.

Even more directly influential on the American studio glass movement were the pioneer French glassmakers who carried out explorations on their own, using factory facilities in off hours or working in their own studios. Henry Cros (1840–1907), Gabriel Argy-Rousseau (1885–1953), and François-Emile Décorchemont (1880–1971; see page 24) had rediscovered the warm-glass technique of *pâte de verre,* an ancient Egyptian technique that had long been lost. Suitable for fashioning small pictorial or sculptural objects, the technique involved placing crushed glass, colored with oxides, in a mold and applying heat to fuse the mixture into a solid form. Experimentation resulted in formulating a new mold-release technology that returned *pâte de verre* to the glassmakers' palette. American proto-studio glassmakers[38] also worked in *pâte de verre*, which as a warm-glass technique required only an annealing oven (often modified from a clay kiln), rather than the large glassblowing furnaces required for hot work. It thus offered technology for proto-studio artists to explore in their studios.

Hot-blown glass, so important to the studio glass movement in the 1960s, intrigued the pioneering early twentieth-century French glassmakers, and their experience directly affected the American movement. Maurice Marinot (1882–1960), who was trained as a painter and affiliated with the Fauves, participated in the Salon d'Automne in 1905. In 1911, however, he transferred his interest to making vessels from molten glass. Previously Marinot had commissioned functional tableware blown in the factories to his specifications, which he then decorated with enamel paints. In 1912, he apprenticed himself to the M. M. Viard factory in Bar-sur-Seine, which was owned by friends. He worked there after hours to form small vessels with stoppers and veiling (air bubbles trapped between layers of molten glass) resembling his later *Vessel* (c. 1934). Describing his works as sculptures, not vessels, Marinot labored alone or sometimes with one assistant

Vessel, c. 1934. Maurice Marinot (France, 1882–1960). Blown and acid etched glass; 6¹¹/₁₆ x 6¾ inches. The Corning Museum of Glass, gift of Mlle Florence Marinot (65.3.48)

Footed Bowl, c. 1930–1940. Jean Sala (1895–1976, born in Spain, worked in France). Blown glass, with hot applications; 3 1/8 inches high, 4 1/8 inches in diameter. The Corning Museum of Glass (75.3.15)

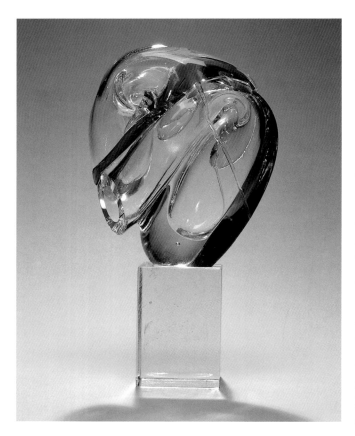

Blue Lined Loops #14, 1975. Harvey Littleton (United States, b. 1922). Blown glass; 10 1/2 x 5 3/4 x 3 inches. Racine Art Museum, gift of Gerald G. Stiebel and Penelope Hunter-Stiebel in honor of Douglas Heller (1998.23)

to create acid-etched, moderne patterns in the exterior of his thick-walled forms. In 1937 the Viard factory closed, and Marinot discontinued his work in glass.[39]

Marinot influenced American studio glass in several ways. By working as an independent artist in a factory, he bridged the divide between artistic vision and the ability to execute it. He was an established artist who chose glass as his medium, a choice that would be made later by several glass artists who ushered in the crossover phenomenon that developed between high art and studio glass in the 1980s. He imputed a spiritual character to the activity of forming glass and he believed that art made of glass had to come directly from the hands of the artist. This belief would come to lie at the core of the American studio glass movement and would ultimately inspire its adherents to call themselves "glass artists."

Another important intersection between European glass and the emerging American studio glass movement occurred when the Spaniard Jean Sala (1895–1976) and the American Harvey Littleton crossed paths in 1958. From the 1920s through the early 1950s, Sala pioneered glassblowing in a studio setting. The sons of Bienvenido Sala, a Catalan gaffer, Jean and his brother Joachim learned their father's craft in Spain. The family then moved near Paris, where Jean maintained a private hot-glass facility in Montparnasse and worked in the family antique shop on the rue Bonaparte. In his small, self-made furnace, which he fanned with a hand bellows, Sala made *pâte de verre,* melted glass batch and cullet, blew glass, and produced small vessels and glass animals in a bubbly, porous metal called *malfin.* Adulterated with impurities, his work in time took on the appearance of devitrified glass (a condition associated with ancient glass).

Sala's studio, probably the first designed and built for glassblowing by an individual, remained in operation until his failing eyesight forced him to close it around 1952. Fortunately for the American studio glass movement, Littleton visited Sala in 1958. Sala had photographed his studio before dismantling it and was able to show Littleton his small furnace, built with an annealing oven on top. This confirmed Littleton's belief that glass could be blown on a small scale outside the factory.

NOTES

1. Arthur J. Pulos, *American Design Ethic: A History of Industrial Design* (Cambridge, Mass.: MIT Press, 1983), 19.

2. See Wendy Kaplan, "The Lamp of Precedent: An Introduction to the Arts and Crafts Movement," in Kaplan, *"The Art that Is Life": The Arts and Crafts Movement in America, 1875–1920* (Boston: Museum of Fine Arts, 1987), 54; in the same volume, see Eileen Boris, "'Dreams of Brotherhood and Beauty': The Social Ideas of the Arts and Crafts Movement," 208–22. For a discussion of the differences between the American and British manifestations of Arts and Crafts, see Isabelle Anscombe and Charlotte Gere, *Arts and Crafts in Britain and America* (New York: Rizzoli, 1978). Regarding Morris's position, see Peter Shansky, *Redesigning the World: William Morris, the 1880's, and the Arts and Crafts* (Princeton, N.J.: Princeton University Press, 1985); esp. 21–47 for a detailed discussion of Morris's later thoughts about the machine; and Tanya Harrod, *The Crafts in Britain in the Twentieth-Century* (New Haven, Conn.: Yale University Press, 1999), 15–24.

3. The Arts and Crafts firms of L. & J. G. Stickley, Gustav Stickley's Craftsman Workshop, and Newcomb Pottery, among others, sold their work through catalogues, from which the buyer could select the style and finish desired —a manufacturing and marketing approach unlike the studio system in which unique items are produced See Judson Clark, ed., *The Arts and Crafts Movement in America, 1876–1916* exh. cat. (Princeton, N.J.: Princeton University Press, 1972); Kaplan, *"The Art that Is Life"*; and Kaplan, ed., *The Encyclopedia of Arts and Crafts: The International Arts Movement, 1850–1920* (New York: E. P. Dutton, 1989).

4. The art critic Howard Risatti traces the decline of craft status to John Ruskin's skirmish with James McNeill Whistler in 1877. Ruskin was outraged by what he perceived as Whistler's lack of technical ability. Whistler won the "art for art's sake" argument (and the ensuing trial) thereby separating the making of art from craftsmanship. See Howard Risatti, "Craft after Modernism: Tracing the Declining Prestige of Craft," *New Art Examiner* 17, no. 7 (March 1990): 32–35; see also Pulos, *American Design Ethic*, 64–89, 228–50.

5. This association persevered to the extent that in the 1950s, Rose Slivka, then editor of *Craft Horizons*, referred to a lingering of "the machine aesthetic [indicative] of a time in which 'made by hand' carried with it the stigma of the inferior human touch, clumsy and full of mistakes." It has only been since the studio movement emerged that the term *handcrafted* was returned to a state of (selective) respect. The fact that today we praise the handmade and associate it with uniqueness and taste is a direct result of the effectiveness of the studio crafts movement in shaping social and aesthetic sensibility; it is also a reflection of our growing discomfort with technology and mass culture. This shift began with the expansion of the post–World War II craft movement. See Rose Slivka, "The Art/Craft Connection: Personal, Critical and Historical Odyssey," in Marcia and Tom Manhart, eds., *The Eloquent Object: The Evolution of American Art in Craft Media since 1945*, exh. cat. Philbrook Museum of Art, Tulsa, Okla., 1987 (Seattle: University of Washington Press, 1987), 68.

6. Studio clay and textiles emerged in the 1930s and 1940s respectively, wood turning in the 1950s, glass in the 1960s, and furniture in the 1980s. For a detailed look at the relative time frames and the coalescing of the various craft movements, see Davira Taragin, ed., *Contemporary Crafts and the Saxe Collection* exh. cat. Toledo Museum of Art, Toledo, Ohio (New York: Hudson Hills Press in association with the Toledo Museum of Art, 1993), 21–90, 149–78, and esp. Martha Drexler Lynn, "Clay Leads the Studio Crafts into the Art World," 90–131, in the same volume.

7. Tiffany's formal vocabulary and use of color have also been associated with an antihistoricizing, Art Nouveau sensibility. Dirk Van Erp (1908–1977), active in Oakland and San Francisco, is really a better example of the Arts and Crafts ethos. Van Erp was a metalsmith who strove to create functional items that valued the beauty of the materials used. For a seminal work on Art Nouveau, see Paul Greenhalgh, *Art Nouveau 1890–1914* (London: Victoria and Albert Museum and the National Gallery of Art, 2000).

8. It was later derisively characterized by the studio glassmaker Harvey Littleton as managed by "the great merchandising family of New York City." Harvey K. Littleton, *Glassblowing: A Search for Form* (New York: Van Nostrand, Reinhold, 1971), [23].

9. Interestingly, American Arts and Crafts furnishings were not prized until the 1970s after a group of enterprising dealers in New York began to write about and collect the material. Chief among these was Todd Volpe, whose gallery was located in Soho. This revived interest was furthered by the exhibition, *The Arts and Crafts Movement in America, 1876–1916*, and catalogue of the same name edited by Judson Clark, which placed the movement within an intellectual framework.

10. Later studio glass, however, would be linked to the American Arts and Crafts movement in terms of its passion to reunite art and life, to create an "art that is life." Urban middle-class Arts and Crafts aficionados had been obsessed with these issues, and the same desire would inform the lifestyle choices of many in the studio glass movement. In the 1960s and 1970s American studio glassmakers sought to create handmade glass art within a studio, and in so doing embraced the counterculture, assuming an anti-establishment stance. The phrase "the art that is life" was the subtitle of William Price's Arts and Crafts periodical, *The Artsman*. See Kaplan, "The Lamp of British Precedent: An Introduction to the Arts and Crafts Movement," in *"Art that Is Life."* 52–60. This goal was similar to that of the Japanese *mingei* movement of about the same period. Indeed, many of the formal and aesthetic influences seen in the crafts from the late 1800s through the 1950s were orientalizing and took their philosophical underpinnings from Asian sources.

11. Following the Depression, however, abstracted images

gained currency in the high-art world and figuration was considered passé. Abstraction was the avant-garde and became the rage in urban centers. Figurative artists and craftsmen fell from favor. Crafts were viewed as too literal for the avant-garde, abstraction-oriented, "art for art's sake" world. The shift toward abstraction was sanctified in the writings of Clement Greenberg. See his *Art and Culture: Critical Essays* (Boston: Beacon Press, 1961); and Erika Doss, *Benton, Pollock, and the Politics of Modernism from Regionalism to Abstract Expressionism* (Chicago: University of Chicago, 1991), 31 passim. For a discussion of the role of New York in this transformation of styles, see Serge Guilbaut, *How New York Stole the Idea of Modern Art: Abstract Expressionism, Freedom, and the Cold War,* trans. Arthur Goldhammer (Chicago: University of Chicago Press, 1983); Jean Baudrillard, "Hot Painting: The Inevitable Fate of the Image" in *Reconstructing Modernism: Art in New York, Paris, Montreal 1945–1964* (Cambridge, Mass: MIT Press, 1990), 17–29; and Diana Crane, *The Transformation of the Avant-Garde: The New York Art World, 1940–1985* (Chicago: University of Chicago Press, 1987), 19–83.

12. Allen Eaton, *Handicrafts in New England* (New York: Harper, 1949).

13. Aileen O. Webb and David Campbell, "The American Craftsmen's Council: A Look at the Future," *Craft Horizons* 16, no. 2 (March/ April 1956): 10.

14. John Perrault, "The Situation in the USA 16th Biennial, Lausanne," as quoted in *Neues Glas* 3 (1995): 9.

15. See Mary Douglas, "Philosophical Aspects of the Studio Crafts Movement, 1945–1965" (unpublished essay commissioned by the American Craft Museum, 1996), for a discussion of Aileen O. Webb's enthusiasm for figurative and regionalist art and her role in the founding of various crafts organizations, including America House in 1941 and eventually the American Craft Museum, New York City. Intriguing parallels with the development of abstraction and its highest expression, abstract expressionism exist within the craft world as clay moved from favoring functional vessels to objects that only reference function. See Martha Drexler Lynn, *Clay Today: Contemporary Ceramists and Their Work* (Los Angeles: Los Angeles County Museum of Art and Chronicle Books, 1990), 13–15, 154–57; see also Doss, *Benton, Pollock, and the Politics of Modernism.*

16. Eileen Boris, "'Dreams of Brotherhood and Beauty,' 214 passim.

17. Douglas, "Philosophical Aspects of the Studio Crafts Movement," 1.

18. Slivka, "The Art/Craft Connection," 67.

19. Steven M. Gelber, "A Job You Can't Lose and Hobbies in the Great Depression," *Journal of Social History* 24, no. 4 (winter 1991): 741.

20. Harvey Green, "Culture and Crisis: Americans and the Craft Revival," in Janet Kardon, ed., *Revivals! Diverse Traditions: The History of Twentieth-Century American Craft, 1920–1945* (New York: American Craft Museum and Harry N. Abrams, 1994), 31–40.

21. Slivka, "The Art/Craft Connection," 72.

22. Edwin Kiester Jr., " Uncle Sam wants you . . . to go to college," *Smithsonian* 25, no. 8 (November 1994): 128–41.

23. One of the most famous veterans to take advantage of this opportunity was Peter Voulkos, who returned to Montana State University, Bozeman, to study ceramics and ultimately led the way to "the new ceramic presence." Slivka, "The New Ceramic Presence," *Craft Horizons* 21. no. 4 (July/August 1961): 30–37.

24. Just as houses became uniform, the furnishings offered for them, even when touted as avant-garde or so-called good design (Scandinavian Modern and the designs of Charles Eames) offered only a limited range of forms. See Avi Friedman, "The Evolution of Design Characteristics During the Post–Second World War Housing Boom," *Journal of Design History* 8, no. 2 (1995): 131–46; Douglas, "Philosophical Aspects of the Studio Craft Movement."

25. Slivka "The Object: Function, Craft and Art," *Craft Horizons* 25, no. 5 (September/October, 1965): 11.

26. For a particularly clear discussion of the growth of suburbia during the war years and immediately afterward, see the exhibition catalogue edited by Donald Albrecht for the exhibition he curated, *World War II and the American Dream: How Wartime Building Changed a Nation* (Washington and Cambridge, Mass: National Building Museum and MIT Press, 1995). See especially Robert Friedel, "Scarcity and Promise: Materials and American Domestic Culture during World War II," 42–89.

27. Specifically, the designs of Ray and Charles Eames were advertised as cost effective, while in fact, they were priced on the high end, and many could not afford them. Author's conversations with collectors of 1950s furniture about why, in the late 1950s, they bought the work of Paul McCabe and other lesser designers instead of Herman Miller's Eames furniture, 1992–1994.

28. This number is based on the assumption that only the top level of participants—those who, either as artists or collectors (or institutions), have a chance of being noted and remembered. The craft movement in general, because of its hobby roots, has spawned many who dabble. The artists included in this study are those with significant track records of exhibitions and works in important collections. The collectors are defined as those who have spent (a crude measure) over two hundred thousand dollars or purchased approximately ten or more significant works. The institutions under consideration have high-quality examples and works donated as gifts and bequests.

29. For example, when the American Craftsmen's Educational Council put on *Young Americans 1953,* its fourth annual exhibition of work by craftsmen under thirty years of age, there were no glass submissions.

30. "Young Americans 1953," *Craft Horizons* 13, no. 5 (September/October 1953): 38–39. Historical glass scholarship was led by German historians.

31. Handel Glass Company, founded in 1885, was located

in Meridian, Connecticut. The company made bronze and glass lamps in a style similar to those made by Tiffany and was known for its patented process in which the design was sandblasted, filled with glue, and reheated; this caused it to contract and fall away, together with some surface glass, resulting in a frosted surface. The company closed in 1936.

32. During the 1940s and 1950s in the United States there were several very small glass facilities in the southern and midwestern regions. Most of their glass was obtained by melting bottles and used to produce trinkets for the tourist trade. There were also many small factories that made paperweights and employed gaffers from shops in Ohio and West Virginia. This type of establishment blurs the crisp distinction between what is factory and what is studio. One practitioner was Charles Kaziun who came from a craftsman, not a factory, tradition. He was an outsider who sought training in lampworking so that he might incorporate it into paperweights. In the late 1950s he built his own furnace and was encasing the lampwork in the glass himself. In this way he can also be considered part of the proto-studio glass (see note 38, below) community.

33. Sidney Waugh, *The Making of Fine Glass* (New York: Dodd, Mead, 1947), 19; Waugh, *The Art of Glass Making* (New York: Dodd, Mead, 1937). Also, "This is Steuben Glass," *Craft Horizons* 15, no. 5 (September/October 1955): 35–36.

34. Because he was considered old-fashioned and not responsive to the modernist trend toward colorless glass, Carder was replaced by Arthur Amory Houghton Jr. as director of Corning Glass Works. Houghton shifted Steuben Glass Works away from colored art glass to modernist clear glass.

35. The antique forms are believed to have been carved from a thick glass blank, leaving a surrounding, raised envelope of openwork and narrow connecting struts. There has long been a controversy about how these pieces were made.

36. French factories are discussed here because Littleton first came into contact with what can be called studio glass in the workshop of Jean Sala, who was working in France. The factories of Scandinavia were organized somewhat differently and less clearly on a studio model, so had less direct influence on the American studio glass movement.

37. Hands-on participation by Gallé or Lalique with glass was not usual, but it is possible that Lalique may have made cire perdue castings himself. See Susanne K. Frantz, *Contemporary Glass: A World Survey from the Corning Museum of Glass* (New York: Harry N. Abrams, 1989), 14. These factories separated their production into categories designated by the amount of handwork and the level of original creativity. The most prized works were made with some direct contact by the named designers. Corning Glass Works continues this practice today with its designer Steuben line, relying on the reputations of designers such as Eric Hilton, George Thompson, and David Dowler. See the Steuben 1990 catalogue (Corning: Steuben, 1990).

38. The term *proto-studio* glassmaker is introduced here to differentiate the early makers from those who followed.

39. Many others followed in Marinot's footsteps: among them, André Thuret (1898–1965) and Henri Navarre (1885–1971). Navarre combined the working of molten glass pioneered by Marinot with *pâte de verre*.

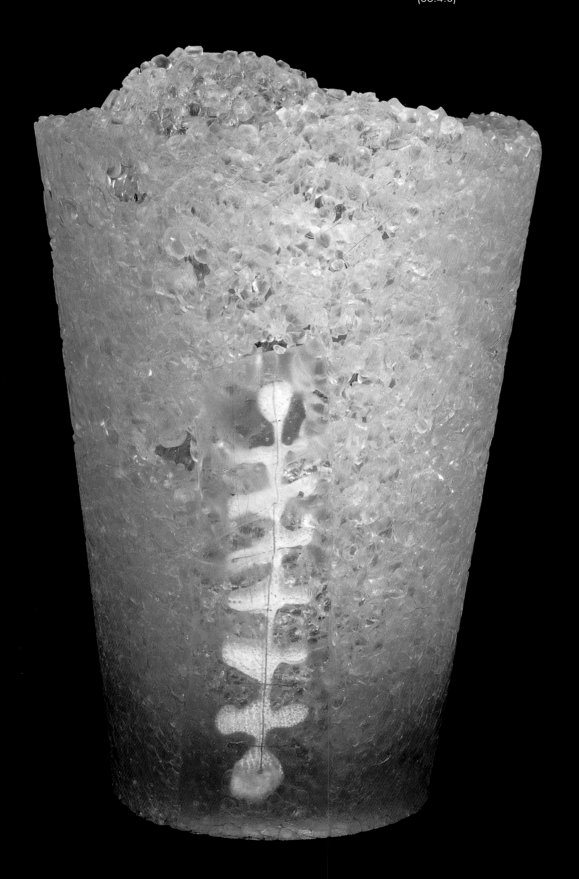

Chapter 3

Proto-Studio Glass Pioneers—
Leading the Way

ONE OF THE COMMONPLACES of the studio movement is that it began in Toledo, Ohio, on March 23, 1962, when Harvey Littleton held a glass workshop on the grounds of the Toledo Museum of Art. This event was important, but the belief in a single progenitor of studio glass is an oversimplification that privileges one moment and one person over a number of others. As the historian Susanne K. Frantz has written: "What is often forgotten is the fact that there were plenty of other artists working with glass in various states long before Harvey. Sometimes overlooked, too, is the fact that most of these precursors were not Americans, and for them, the idea of an artist working with glass was not the revelation it had been in the United States."[1] This point of history pits the followers of Littleton against those who are aware that there were others working with glass in a studio context at least two decades before and that they, too, were instrumental in the founding of the American studio glass movement.

The passion of the Littleton group had a considerable impact on the development of studio glass and the intensity of their belief can be glimpsed in the title of an article by Paul Hollister: "And on the Sixth Day He Rested. . . ." Published in *Neues Glas* in 1989, this essay (like many others) dramatically casts Littleton as the sole leader of the American studio glass movement. Similarly, Karen S. Chambers, a New York writer for *American Craft* and *Art in America*, stated in 1999 that "the Studio Glass Movement *can* be said to have a definite birthdate: 23 March 1962, the beginning of a ten-day workshop organized by Littleton at the Toledo

Museum of Art (italics original)."[2] Although her assertion is partially true, the reality is more complex. There is no question that Harvey Littleton was important to the development of the American studio glass movement, but there are numerous factors behind the emergence of studio glass after World War II, and there were other Americans working independently. making glass in studios. In Europe Marinot and Sala had made artistic glass in a studio setting long before the Toledo workshops in the 1960s.

In the United States a handful of independent glassmakers worked in varying degrees of isolation from one another and outside the factory. Their education, their attitude toward glass as a potential art medium, and their methods prefigured sensibilities seen later in the movement. They qualify as peers of the Europeans because they earned their livelihood from sales of their glass and were not simply hobbyists. Working in the period between the decline of Tiffany, Handel, and the glass *objet d'art*, and the rise of a formalized studio glass movement in the early 1960s, these artist-craftsmen used warm- and hot-glass techniques at a time when little was known about how to fabricate glass in a small studio.

The precise number of these independent glassmakers is difficult to determine, but four pioneers deserve attention because of their influence on the development of the studio glass movement.[3] Independently, these pioneers set up studios to experiment, using the warm-glass techniques of fusing, slumping, and enameling to make small functional items. Three of them—Maurice

Plate; 1960s. Michael and Frances Stewart Higgins (United States, 1908–1999 and b. 1912). Kiln-formed glass; approx. 15 inches diameter.

Country Gardens, Arabesque Apple, Buttercup, and Sunburst, 1960s. Michael and Frances Stewart Higgins (United States, 1908–1999 and b. 1912). Kiln-formed glass; approx. 15 inches to 5 inches diameter.

Their designs recall enamel platters of earlier eras.

opposite:
Africa, 1948. Maurice Heaton (United States, 1900–1990). Kiln-formed glass, powdered glass and enamel decoration; 2 9/16 inches high, 14 5/8 inches in diameter. The Corning Museum of Glass (51.4.533)

Heaton and Michael and Frances Higgins—owed their success to European training and one—Edris Eckhardt—to the transfer of technology from studio ceramics to glass.

Maurice Heaton exemplifies the multigenerational and artisan-based European tradition. The son of an Arts and Crafts cloisonné enameler and the grandson of a stained-glass maker, who specialized in Gothic Revival-style windows, Heaton was born in London and moved to New York in 1914. He attended the progressive Ethnic Culture School and then spent a year at Stevens Institute of Technology. Armed with a cultural and technical education, Heaton had decided by 1923 that his future lay in glass, and he worked with his father on large, stained-glass commissions. In 1928 the textile designer Ruth Reeves asked Heaton to create glass shades for polished steel floor lamps, a commission that led to similar work throughout his career. Executed in an Art Deco style, these and the lighting scones and ceiling fixtures that were to follow, demonstrated his knowledge of enameling. Soon, he was designing for the manufacturer Lightolier, and his work appeared in industrial design shows at the Metropolitan Museum of Art. Conversant with the formal language of art moderne and cubism, Heaton employed the traditional *verre églomisé* and gold-enamel techniques used in ancient times.

Heaton also made plates decorated with brightly colored enamels. Typical of these are three works in the collection of the Corning Museum of Glass: *Africa* (1948; opposite), *Free* (1951), and *Fish Bowl* (1955). Each uses the warm-glass techniques of kiln forming (slumping) and the application of powdered glass enameled decoration. As described at the time, Heaton

cuts and grinds the glass to shape and then attaches the glass to a plate glass turntable. He makes his design directly on the shaped glass by tapping powdered enamels through graded sieves and over curved and angled templates to create overlapping shadows. The completed design is fixed with an adhesive spray, placed in a sheet iron mold into which it is slumped in the kiln while the enameled design is fired on. Heaton himself makes the molds and all his tools.[4]

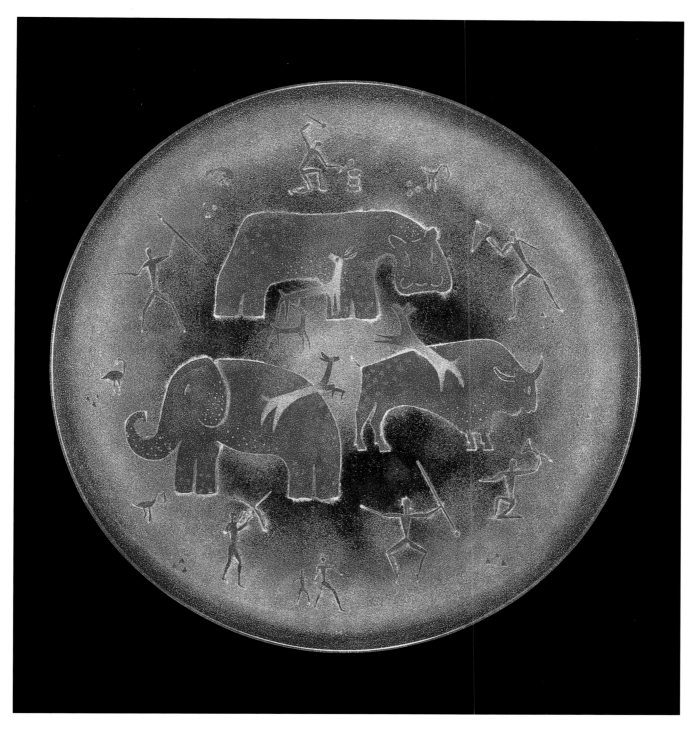

In May 1932 Heaton created *The Flight of Amelia Earhart across the Atlantic*, a large window for Radio City Music Hall in New York. Using a combination of techniques, he applied vitreous glazes to glass with an airbrush and then kiln-fired them. Several of Heaton's commissions, including large, paneled windows for Stern Brothers and L. P. Hollander & Company in New York City, glazed elevator doors for apartments on Park Avenue, and several salesroom windows, were illustrated in an article in *Architecture* (1931). These are the only images that survive; in 1974 Heaton's studio burned to the ground and many of the installations had been dismantled by that time. Heaton also fabricated objects in his studio during the 1940s and 1950s using the warm-glass techniques of fusing and slumping. For equipment, he scavenged and modified items associated with ceramic production. Both the means and the location of his production place his activity within the definition of studio glassmaker.

Two other trailblazers were the husband-and-wife

Uriel, 1968. Edris Eckhardt (United States, 1910–1998). Glass, cast in a cire-perdue mold; 9 7/8 x 7 7/8 inches. The Corning Museum of Glass, gift of the artist (68.4.28)

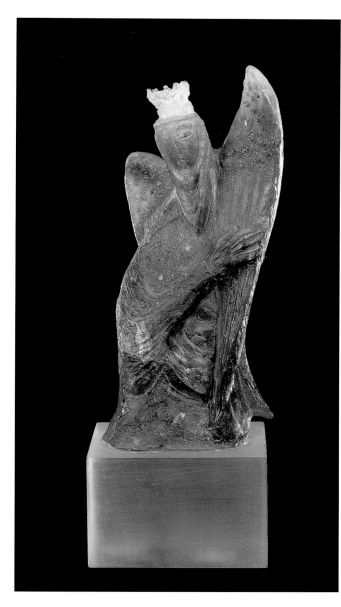

Archangel, 1956. Edris Eckhardt (United States, 1910–1998).
Glass, cast in a cire-perdue mold; 8 5/8 x 3 15/16 inches. The
Corning Museum of Glass (61.4.64)

Aside from their numerous commercial tableware lines made for Dearborn Glass from 1959 to 1965, the Higginses produced a range of unique objects in their studio. Michael constructed ingeniously hinged boxes with connecting joints of copper wire screen and folded metal bands fused into glass (see page 8). Equally sensitive and innovative were the vessels made by Frances during the late 1950s with granules of fused colorless glass that mimicked fractured ice. By leaving the top edge of the simple, tapered vessels irregular and the upper half of the vases intermittently punctured, she heightened the visual effect of ice melting (see page 34). Interested in creating an optical dialogue between the surface and the three-dimensional ground, Frances also added gold enamel to the vases. The work looks dated now, overdecorated and too clearly utilitarian in comparison with current studio glass, but clearly the artists strove to return an individual aesthetic touch to glassware.

The Higginses also adapted a silk-screen technique resulting in designs that required as many as twelve laminations to yield the rich colors they desired. One of their trademark styles involved mother-of-pearl lustered glass. To achieve this effect, chips of glass were dipped into water, then sprinkled with colorant for the design, and lustered on top. Their largest commission was the window for the front of the First National Bank of Appleton, Wisconsin, which was twenty-eight feet high and eighty feet wide. In the early 1980s the bank was remodeled and the window was lost.

During the 1950s the Higginses made a line of utilitarian ware for Marshall Field, Bloomingdales, and Georg Jensen. Many of the pieces retailed for five dollars each. Highlighting the differences between the factory and the studio, Michael Higgins remarked in 1985: "If we had had the money that Tiffany had, what we could have accomplished! But of course Tiffany didn't blow glass: he was a designer and designer is a very different act."[5] The Higginses are prime examples of the "designer-craftsman," a designation that was the hallmark of the proto-studio glassmaker and linked production to unique expression.

The fourth of these early glassmakers was Edris Eckhardt (1905–1998). Trained as a sculptor at the Cleveland School of Art in the late 1920s, she was

team of Michael and Frances Higgins, who are known for their brightly colored, geometric-patterned glass enamel tableware made using warm-glass technology. Michael (1908–1999), who was trained as a graphic designer and painter, attended the Visual Design Department at the Chicago Institute of Design in 1948. Frances (b. 1912) received her master of fine arts degree from the Chicago Institute and was an assistant professor at the University of Georgia. Attracted to working in all scales, from jewelry to church windows, by 1962 the Higginses were fusing glass into large sheets to make screens, panels, and sculptures.

employed as a Works Projects Administration supervisor in the ceramic arts program until 1941. As with many of the later studio glassmakers, Eckhardt chose to work in the craft-based medium of clay and then transferred those technologies to forming glass. During the 1950s she experimented with making her own glass from batch in her basement studio, and for her innovative work received one Tiffany and two Guggenheim fellowships.[6] Among her innovations were sculptures combining glass with other materials, notably bronze, and a tool for drawing with hot glass. By 1953 Eckhardt had rediscovered the technique of laminating gold or silver between two or more layers of glass. The sheets of the metal were engraved with a stylus, then slumped between two sheets of glass and rolled with a rolling pin on a marble marver (a type of table on which hot glass is worked). She, too, went on to rediscover the *verre églomisé* technique and the procedure for casting of glass in lost-wax molds. She used the latter technique to form plaques (see page 39) and freestanding, figurative, sculptures, such as *Archangel* (1956). This work was included in the important survey exhibition *Glass 1959*, mounted by the Corning Museum of Glass, and is now in the permanent collection.

"I'm only happy," said Eckhardt in 1985, "when I am working with three-dimensional forms. I work in glass from an artist's viewpoint, not a craftsman—as I am a sculptor."[7] This perception, by which she separates herself from craft and aligns her work with art—and glass not at all—places her within the studio camp ahead of her time. This focus on art prefigured the attitude of studio glass artists in the late 1970s.

CRAFTSMEN UNITE: ASILOMAR 1957

Professional conferences were, and are, a galvanizing force in the growth of the American studio glass movement. It was at these gatherings that the work of proto-studio glassmakers, which was little known to other craftsmen and sometimes not even to other glassmakers, was first shared. Of special importance was the First Annual Conference of the American Craftsmen's Council, which was held at the Asilomar Conference Center, Pacific Grove, California, June 12–14, 1957. Four hundred and fifty craftsmen and women from thirty states and many from abroad met to talk and

Exhibition installation, Asilomar Conference, 1957.

attend the five discussion panels, which were organized by medium and included more than forty speakers.

The scope of the conference—with representatives from Mexico, Japan, Denmark, Sweden, and Afghanistan—was important to the studio movement in general for it showed the worldwide popularity of crafts. For glass, however, it was critical, because other countries were ahead of the United States in seeing its potential as an art medium.[8] Articles appearing as early as 1955 in *Craft Horizons* had shown work by European glass designers and served to highlight the differences between the European factory model and the evolving American studio model. Many of the works shown in the conference exhibition were made at glass factories (such as Orrefors Glasbruk A-B in Sweden and the Royal Dutch Glass Works at Leerdam in the Netherlands), where designers, not independent glassmakers, worked.[9] Nonetheless, the work had a galvanizing effect on the studio glass movement, revealing the potential of glass and inspiring a sense of camaraderie. As Rose Slivka recalled, craftsmen "traveled from all parts of the country to meet each other," and for many the conference was their first encounter with fellow craftsmen working in similar media.[10]

The topics explored at the conference included the socioeconomic outlook for craft media, the importance of technique and professional practices, advice on marketing, and the valuing of craft as a cultural good. It

top left: *Ceramic Vessel*, 1950s. Harvey K. Littleton (United States, b. 1922). Ceramic; approximately 8–9 inches high.

top right: *Large Footed Luster Bowl*, 1987. Beatrice Wood (United States, 1893–1998). Earthenware, glaze, and luster; 14¾ inches high. Collection of Marian Skeist.

bottom left: *Container with Cover*, c. 1953. Peter Voulkos (United States, 1924–2000). Stoneware and glaze; 22 inches high. Collection of Frank Lloyd, Los Angeles.

bottom right: *Brown Crater Bowl*, 1960. Gertrud and Otto Natzler (Austria, active in the United States, 1908–1971 and b. 1908). Earthenware, glaze; 3¾ inches high, 7¼ inches in diameter. Los Angeles County Museum of Art, gift of Howard and Gwen Laurie Smits (M.87.1.108)

was generally felt that sincerity and a belief in the goal of "making craftsmanship universally recognized as a vital element of our nation's life" would pave the way for "contemporary craft [to acquire] a separate identity."[11] This desire for a separate identity, distinct from traditional craft or factory-based design, indicates the uncertain status of craft (and of glass) at this time and also indicates that glassmakers had not yet evidenced the ambition to be high-art artists. Interestingly, the conference participants referred to themselves as "craftsmen" or "designers," not as artists (or glass artists.)

At the conference, glass was subsumed under the category of enamels. Michael Higgins and Edris Eckhardt appeared on various panels. They spoke about their work and shared their enthusiasm for glass as an appropriate medium for art.[12] Higgins, referring to himself as "work[ing] for industry," and not wanting to "accept patronage," discussed his choice of glass as a medium for expression; Eckhardt reviewed the realities of marketing and offered practical advice about using brochures as sales tools.[13] This blending of artistic yearning and businesslike advice—an early manifestation—is typical of craftsmen's discourse and was still evident over thirty years later when David Gruenig wrote in 1989 that "one gets tired of living on a shoestring, and it does become apparent that if you want to be a glassmaker, you are in business, and you must pay rather large bills."[14] With the later emergence of galleries, dealers, and collectors devoted to glass, such discussions shifted to the profitability of making art out of glass—whether that was possible and, if so, how to accomplish it.

Another important conference with ramifications for the studio glass movement was held four years later at the University of Washington, Seattle. At the Fourth National Conference of the American Craftsmen's Council in 1961, Harvey Littleton participated in a panel chaired by Kenneth Wilson, then curator at the Corning Museum of Glass, to discuss the future of glass as an art medium. Paul Perrot, later director of the Corning Museum of Glass, stated in his opening remarks to the panel that

> for years we have been hearing that glass would become one of the basic materials available to contemporary craftsmen. Indications can now be

seen on many sides that this prediction has come true. That such a development has occurred is due to the tireless efforts of a few craftsmen who, not to be discouraged by the prediction of specialists, have boldly explored and experimented with the material and its properties. Obviously, the surface has only been dented and the true potential of this fascinating material will only burst forth with the entry of many more craftsmen into the field.[15]

The panel represented the same cross-section of interests seen at Asilomar, but four years later, the development in the conceptualization of glass as an art medium was apparent. In discussing his latest experiments, Littleton explained that his initial tests (and most likely his visit to Jean Sala in 1957) convinced him that it was possible for the craftsman to undertake glassblowing entirely alone. He displayed pieces that he had melted, ground, and polished in his studio and presented several blown bubbles. His fellow panelists, glimpsing the potential, encouraged Littleton to pursue glassblowing as a viable medium for artists. Even the factory community revised its position, and Dr. Frederic Schuler, a scientist for Corning Glass Works, spoke on the properties of glass and its suitability for use by craftsmen.

THE CORNING MUSEUM OF GLASS AND THE GLASS 1959 EXHIBITION

On May 19, 1951, the Corning Museum of Glass was opened. It was established as a nonprofit, tax-exempt, educational institution dedicated to the art, history, research, and exhibition of glass, and supported by the patronage of the industrial glassmaker Corning Glass Works. In its first few years, several exhibitions devoted to historical glass were organized, but by far the most significant in terms of the studio glass movement was the international survey *Glass 1959: A Special Exhibition of International Contemporary Glass*.

The impetus for this exhibition came from the impressive architectural glass displayed in the Czechoslovakian pavilion at the Brussels World's Fair of 1958. It awakened the determination of the directors of

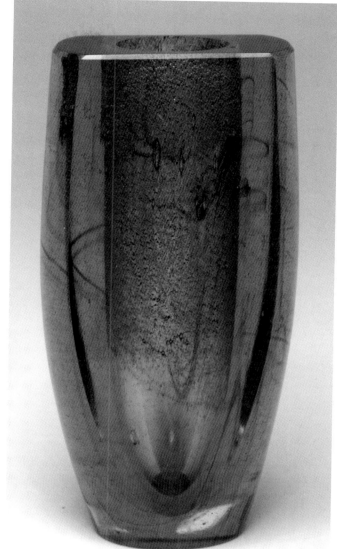

Vessel, 1966. Dominick Labino (United States, 1920–1887). Dimensions unknown.

right: *Vase*, 1963. Harvey K. Littleton (United States, b. 1922). Blown glass, from #475 glass marbles, rolled in cobalt carbinate between gathers; 5¾ x 2½ x 1 inches.

In the early and middle 1960s vessels were the dominant form for studio glass.

the Corning Museum of Glass to assess developments in contemporary glass worldwide. This international survey exhibition was a collaboration with Corning of four participating institutions: the Art Institute of Chicago, the Metropolitan Museum of Art, the Toledo Museum of Art, and the Virginia Museum of Fine Arts, Richmond. Writing in the preface of the accompanying catalogue, Thomas S. Buechner, the director of the Corning Museum of Glass, cozily positioned the need for this exhibition within the context of the Cold War and clearly reflected a manufacturing sensibility: "glass capacitors and resistors [that] contribute to miniaturization in electronics and glass dosimeters [that] record radiation," coupled with the "sixty car loads of table glass" recently ordered by the Strategic Air Command,

place glass as a primary material of the future, he said. He also ambitiously linked the exhibition to the Triennale in Milan and the Brussels World's Fair.[16]

Choosing an original approach toward curating the exhibition, the museum, guided by Buechner, did not seek a panel of jurors who were experts in glass technology or history. Instead, they selected recognized authorities on design and connoisseurship. Leslie Cheek, the director of the Virginia Museum of Fine Arts, Edgar Kaufmann Jr., an architectural historian and critic, Russell Lynes, an editor at *Harper's Magazine*, the studio furniture maker George Nakashima, and Gio Ponti, the editor of the Italian design publication *Domus*, selected 292 objects from 1,814 submissions made by 173 manufacturers located in 23

Vase, 1967. Samuel J. Herman (United States, b. 1936). Glass; 4 x 5¾ x 2¾ inches. The Metropolitan Museum of Art, anonymous gift, in memory of Edith Gaines, 1995 (1995.582)

countries. Of the works shown by European manufacturers, fewer than fifty were designed and crafted by individual artists, and most of those were executed in cold-glass decorating techniques, by kiln-forming, or by flameworking. The most expressive work came from Czechoslovakia and Italy, confirming the seminal position of these countries and their long history of glassmaking. These pieces, notable for their use of brilliant color and their fresh approach to the traditional skills of enameling, engraving, blowing, and casting, stood in contrast to the spare, modern aesthetic of northern Europe and Scandinavia.[17]

The jurors' statements, accompanied by photographs of each juror's three favorite pieces, focused on issues of functionality and formal beauty. The natural seduction of the material was evident in their descriptions: "beautiful containers," "brilliantly caught," "glistening high-lights," and "delicacy of the components."[18] The American proto-studio glassmakers were represented by Heaton, the Higginses (for the Dearborn Glass Company, Dearborn, Michigan), and Eckhardt; and were joined by Priscilla Manning Porter, Earl McCutchen, and the paperweight maker John Burton.

Frantz notes that among the factory-made works exhibited by the foreign countries were a few intriguing examples of free-blown glass and one figural vase, the expressiveness of which recalled Marinot's work and reflected a sensitivity to contemporaneous painting and sculpture. It was submitted by Lucrecia Moyano de Muñiz of Buenos Aires, the artistic director of Cristalerias Rigolleau, S.A., and was identified as designed and "fashioned" by Mrs. Muñiz. Although this piece represented something very different from the other works produced outside the United States and prefigured the studio glass to come, it aroused little interest at the time. Only Gio Ponti expressed the wish to "steal the barbaric vase by Mrs. Muñiz!"[19]

Witch's Ball, 1967. Richard Marquis (United States, b. 1945). Blown glass; 12 inches high, 7 inches in diameter. Racine Art Museum, gift of Karen Johnson Boyd (1992.4)

A common thread that linked all of the proto-studio glass artisans was the need to learn their techniques from industry sources, from ceramics, or through trial and error. While some information was available from trade schools and from Alfred University in Alfred, New York, the skills taught there were considered technical and not applicable to artistic endeavors. This division was underscored in the article for *Craft Horizons* written in 1955 by Earl McCutchen, an instructor at the University of Georgia, who noted the limited number of sources for glass and the primitive state of prevailing technique. He then naively suggested that glass be obtained from the junkyard or salvaged from mirror shops, and remelted.[21] Had readers followed his recommendations, they could have been working with a type of *malfin*, which would not produce stable glass

Marvin Lipofsky, Roger Lang (?), and Sam Herman at Madison, Wisconsin, July 1964.

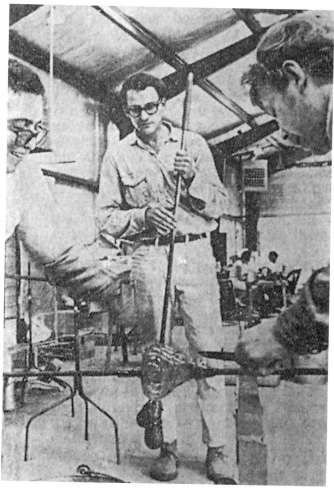

As a result of *Glass 1959*, Paul Perrot, then director of the Corning Museum, assessed the state of contemporary glass by observing that in 1960 there was a rising number of artist-craftsmen who were making kiln-formed glass in the United States, while in Europe, apart from cutters, engravers, and enamelers, there were few independent artists using the material. In his article "New Directions in Glassmaking" that was written for a special issue of *Craft Horizons* magazine, Perrot, in an attempt to unearth previously unknown experiments, asked to hear from craftsmen working in the medium. Neither Perrot nor anyone in the United States at the time was aware of the work of Erwin Eisch of Frauenau, Germany (who became a seminal link between America and Europe as a result of his friendship with Littleton), and the independent work of Mrs. Muñiz was regarded as an eccentric offshoot.[20]

due to the high level of particulate impurities. This type of technical problem highlighted two other issues for the nascent studio glass movement.

First, limited technical choices resulted in works that were essentially vessels (see page 43). Second, technique became the means of determining who the true studio glass artists were. The reality of the first problem led the ceramist and sculptor Robert Arneson to declare in 1967 that "if I see another drippy glass bubble, I'm going to blow my mind."[22] Only after technical limitations ceased to restrict the forms produced could glass move ahead and begin to address issues of content. Indeed, it was by rejecting utility and the references to utility implied in the vessel form that the glassmakers emerged as artists.

NOTES

1. Susanne K. Frantz, a former curator of contemporary glass at the Corning Museum of Glass, and Patricia Failing of Seattle, also agree with this assessment of Littleton. See Susanne K. Frantz, "Not So New in '62," *The Glass Art Society Journal* (1988): 15, and "Studio Glass 1945– 1965/ Revised Essay" (1996), written for the American Craft Museum; unpublished.

2. Karen S. Chambers, *Clearly Inspired: Contemporary Glass and Its Origins* (San Francisco: Pomegranate and Tampa Museum of Art , 1999), 31; Paul Hollister, "And on the Sixth Day He Rested. . . ." *Neues Glas* (1989): 34–39; and William Warmus "Nature Transformed: The Legacy of Studio Glass," *New Work* 28 (winter 1987): 18-21.

3. There were also pioneers who worked part-time in glass using simple ceramic kilns (made and designed with the aid of such manuals as Bernard Leach's *A Potter's Book*, 1941). While working as the ceramics instructor at the University of Southern California in Los Angeles, Glen Lukens (1887–1967) slumped glass into the molds he used for his clay pieces. This example of technique shifting was typical at mid-century. Interested in color and the expression of the basic materials in the final work, Lukens both colored his batch glass and dribbled oxides casually over the clay forms used in slumping the glass. Such explorations in small studios fit the definition of studio glass as it is now understood. David Gruenig, another independent glassmaker, began blowing glass in 1949 at the age of ten, using his father's gasoline pump-up torch and found shards of glass. He went on to publish a newsletter for glass blowers, *The Independent Glassblower*, from his studio in Vermont. Others working outside the factory system were itinerate, probably originally factory trained, and turned to melting glass bottles to make tourist trinkets. A still smaller group tried to form glass objects in their homes. The four glassmakers cited above were well-known members of the studio crafts community, hence their importance to the development of studio glass.

4. See Eleanor Bittermann, "Heaton's Wizardry With Glass," *Craft Horizons* 14, no. 3 (May/June 1954): 10–14. Enameling was a favorite technique of these early glassmakers. Enameling on metal was also popular for at-home studio artists in the same period. Heaton continued to produce pieces based on his original 1940s and 1950s designs well into the 1980s, making dating problematic; Paul Hollister, "Studio Glass Before 1962: Maurice Heaton, Frances and Michael Higgins and Edris Eckhardt," *Neues Glas* 4 (1985): 234–35.

5. Ibid., 235.

6. In 1968 Eckhardt was honored with a one-person show at the Corning Museum of Glass.

7. Hollister, "Studio Glass Before 1962," 236; and Oppi Untracht, "The Glass of Edris Eckhardt," *Craft Horizons* 22, no. 6 (November/December 1962): 36.

8. At the time of this conference the distinction between traditional crafts and what was becoming known as contemporary crafts was not as clear as it would become in the following decades.

9. Ingeborg Lundin represented Orrefors Glasbruk A-B, Arthur Percy represented Georg Jensen, and A. D. Copier and Floris Meydam represented the Royal Dutch Glass Works.

10. See the original report in " Designer's Choice: Contemporary Glass," *Craft Horizons* 15, no. 2 (March/April 1955): 22–24; and Rose Slivka, "The Art/Craft Connection: Personal, Critical and Historical Odyssey," in Marcia and Tom Manhart, eds., *The Eloquent Object: The Evolution of American Art in Craft Media since 1945*, exh. cat. Philbrook Museum of Art, Tulsa, Okla. (Seattle: University of Washington Press, 1987), 70.

11. An article and photos of the conference were published in "Craftsmen's Conference at Asilomar," *Craft Horizons* 17, no. 4 (July/August 1957): 17–32. They show what by a decade later would be deemed a sober crowd. All the women were in high heels and stockings, and the men in ties. Only the occasional beard and pipe indicated a bohemian sensibility. See also J. L., "Recalling Asilomar," *Craft Horizons* 57, no. 3 (June/July 1997): 66–68.

12. Susanne K. Frantz, *Contemporary Glass: A World Survey from the Corning Museum of Glass* (New York: Abrams, 1989), 32–39.

13. American Craft Council, *Asilomar: First Annual Conference of American Craftsmen* (June 1957): 144.

14. David Gruenig, "The Independent Glassblower; or, The Glass Bug vs. Survival," *The Glass Art Society Journal* (1989): 46; Susanne K. Frantz, "Should Making Art Be a Career?" *The Glass Society Journal* (1991): 33–38.

15. American Craftsmen's Council, *Research in the Crafts: Papers Delivered at the Fourth National Conference of the American Craftsmen's Council* (New York, 1961) 29.

16. Thomas S. Buechner, Preface, in *Glass 1959: A Special Exhibition of International Contemporary Glass*, exh. cat. Corning Museum of Glass, Corning, New York, 1959, [2]. One wonders about the relationship that might have existed between Corning and the military-industrial complex and possible links to funding from that sector.

17. The works in the exhibition were grouped by nationality, the United States being represented by Blenko Glass Company, West Virginia; Harriton Carved Glass, New York City; Glass Guild, Inc., New York; Fostoria Glass Company, West Virginia; Erickson Glass Works, Ohio; Owen-Illinois Glass Company, Libbey Glass Division, Ohio; Rainbow Art Glass Company, West Virginia; United States Glass Company, Ohio; and Viking Glass Company, West Virginia.

The monumental cast, blown, and leaded glass sculpture by Jaroslava Brychtová, Stanislav Libenský, Jan Kotik, and Rene Roubicek displayed in the Czechoslovakian Pavilion of the World's Fair in Brussels had been well documented in Europe, but went unmentioned in American publications. Nevertheless, their work was a revelation. *Glass 1959* was followed in 1961 by the Museum of Contemporary Crafts' exhibition *Artist-Craftsmen of Western Europe*, which included the work of glass crafters—Hanns Model (West Germany), Roberto Nierderer (Switzerland), and Alfredo Barbini (Italy)—alongside that of designers. In 1964 the museum mounted similar displays for Czech and Italian glass. The proximity of the 1967 Montreal Expo afforded thousands of visitors from the United States an opportunity to see the spectacular monumental glass sculpture in the Czechoslovakian Pavilion. Again, the new display was almost completely ignored in the pages of *Craft Horizons*. However, Libenský and Brychtová's cast double-panel *Blue Concretion* was brought temporarily to New York in 1968 as part of the exhibition *Architectural Glass* by the Museum of Contemporary Crafts.

18. *Glass 1959*, 10, 12, 14.

19. See Frantz, *Contemporary Glass,"* 43.

20. Paul Perrot, "New Directions in Glassmaking," *Craft Horizons* 20, no. 6 (November/December 1960): 23–25. The museum glass community was also not aware of the obscure cottage industry of small family plants scattered throughout the southern United States, in which glass bottles were remelted for simple items for the tourist trade.

21. Earl McCutchen, "Glass Molding: Experimenting on a Budget," *Craft Horizons* 15, no. 3 (May/June 1955): 38–39. For some forms of preworked glass there was the risk of its not forming or annealing properly or not melting well in the small, cooler studio furnaces.

22. Robert Arneson in a review of the glass exhibition *Six Glassblowers,* held at Centennial House Barn Gallery, Deer Isle, Maine, July 21–August 16, 1967, as printed in *Craft Horizons* 27, no. 5 (September/October 1967): 39–40.

Torso, 1942. Harvey K. Littleton (United States, b. 1922). Slip-cast Vycor Multiform (97 percent silica glass), fused; 11¼ x 5 inches. The Corning Museum of Glass, gift of Dr. and Mrs. Fred A. Bickford (78.4.38)

Fabricated by Littleton when he had a summer job as a moldmaker for the Corning Glass Works.

Chapter 4

Critical Mass—
Aspiring to High Art

THE ACCOMPLISHMENTS of the proto-studio glass artists of the 1950s and early 1960s prepared glass to shed its factory and hobbyist roots and to adopt high-art ambitions.[1] In studio glass, the years 1962 to 1975 were characterized by energy, knowledge, and fortuitous timing.

Glass art since 1962 has added a whole new dimension to American culture. Before this, most Americans working in glass were either designers for industry or industrial technicians. They had few artistic pretensions and their main aim was to make good consumer products. But whereas the industrial designer has a customer and his needs to consider when working on a product, the artist needs to impose no such restraints on himself.[2]

From the efforts of a small band of craftsmen would flow enthusiasm for glass as an art medium, a reconnection to factory-based skills, the use of these skills in studios, and the development of glass-centered university curricula, which in turn would attract practitioners (artists and teachers) and supporters (dealers and collectors), who would insure the success of glass as an art medium.[3] Three conditions were necessary for this to occur: a focused artistic ambition, access to adequate technical knowledge, and validation from cultural institutions. All were present in 1962, requiring only Harvey Littleton, Dominick Labino, and Otto Wittmann of the Toledo Museum of Art to fuse them together. The contributions of these men deserve recognition.

The accepted recounting of the origins of the American studio glass movement casts Harvey Littleton as its sole progenitor. He was, however, only one of several individuals who sought to use glass for art making, and he was heir to the educational and technological successes of his proto-studio predecessors. Littleton's timing was fortunate. Shifts in art practice after World War II opened the door for materials not previously considered appropriate for art making. Evolving social concerns also coincided neatly with Littleton's vision and ambitions. He had a significant effect on the evolution of studio glass during its first decades, but he was not the only "big man of glass." The persistence of this

Harvey K. Littleton, 1980s.

Harvey K. Littleton blowing glass in 1964.

Dominick Labino, 1966.

myth has, nonetheless, shaped the studio glass movement in key ways.

AMBITION AND TECHNIQUE COALESCE

Littleton's passion for hot glass led him to restrict the definition of studio glass to that blown in a studio. This excluded work produced with other technologies, such as warm or cold glass, and created tensions during the first two decades between practitioners using different forming techniques. It was not until the late 1970s—after others rediscovered the potential of warm- and cold-glass techniques and after Littleton had moved on to making intaglio prints with glass sheets—that this issue faded. Littleton's other passion (the potential of glass as an artistic medium) also left its mark on the movement, providing the impetus for art-based, glassblowing classes in universities. These eventually led to university-level training in all glass-forming methodologies. He pushed studio glassmakers to move beyond technique and toward presenting content through their work.

Littleton was born into glass. His father Jesse Littleton, a physicist, was hired by Dr. E. C. Sullivan at Corning Glass Works to develop new consumer products for the growing middle-class domestic market. Dr. Littleton was particularly interested in the nature of glass insulation and its application to cooking devices.[4] As the son of a physicist and inventor, Harvey had a certain status within the glass community at Corning, but it was his visits to the plant on Saturdays, when his "father would give [him] to some stockman to take around the factory, or sit in front of a Bunsen burner to melt some tubing, or otherwise keep [him] entertained" that made glass integral to his life.[5]

Despite his father's influence, Littleton's interests were artistic, rather than scientific. From an early age he attended extension classes at nearby Elmira College, where he learned the rudiments of figure drawing and modeling under Enfred Anderson.[6] In 1939, however, he bowed to family expectations and enrolled at the University of Michigan, Ann Arbor, to study physics. After a two-year stint, he transferred to Cranbrook Academy of Art in Bloomfield Hills, Michigan, where he served as an assistant to the sculptor Carl Milles. Milles did not encourage his artistic ambitions, and Littleton returned to the University of Michigan to study industrial design in the fall of 1941.

After the outbreak of World War II, Littleton spent three years in the army, working with the 849th Signal Intelligence Corps on codes and ciphers for the British and traveling through Italy and France as a teletype maintenance man. His passion for art resurfaced, and he concluded his tour with a few months at the Brighton School of Art in England. This exposure to European culture, combined with his early scientific and artistic experiences, would serve him well later.

Returning from Europe, Littleton took advantage of the GI Bill to complete his degree in industrial design at the University of Michigan. His view of the postwar climate is revealing: "There were ten million of us who came back, and suddenly free of our parents . . . [we] could go to the university and we didn't have to compromise with [our] parents."[7] For Littleton this meant taking a number of jobs relating to industrial glassmaking; at Corning he inspected blown-glass cookware and made molds for the fused-glass product, Vycor Multiform. While there he made his first glass sculpture, a female torso originally made in clay, which he then copied in Vycor Multiform (see *Torso*, page 48). In 1946 he displayed this piece at the *Michigan Artists Exhibition* in Detroit, but he did not show his glass again until 1962.

In 1947 Littleton married and moved to Ann Arbor. A casual request to build several potter's wheels steered him toward the business of ceramics supply, and he took over the private Goat's Nest Ceramic Studio, renaming it the Potter's Guild of Ann Arbor. This small clay studio grounded him in practicalities, requiring him to sell pots, teach technique, and build wheels for throwing. It also provoked his interest in starting "what was called a studio group, or a group of potters who had been there long enough so they didn't need to take a class, but they wanted a place to work."[8] This made him a professional, focused on producing work instead of studying, and provided him with a paradigm for future independent glass studios.

The years 1949 to 1951 were devoted to working with clay (see page 41). In 1949 Littleton again attended Cranbrook Academy of Art to complete his master of fine arts degree in ceramics with the Bauhaus-educated Finnish ceramist Majlis (Maija) Grotell.[9] Under her guidance Littleton formulated a

central tenet of his artistic philosophy, one that he would soon apply to studio glass: neither the type of material used nor its implied or referenced utility circumscribed its potential as art. This meant that even functionally referent forms made of craft media could aspire to being art.

Searching for recognition for his ceramic work, in 1950 Littleton entered the *Syracuse National Exhibition*, which featured utilitarian ceramics, and the next year he won a prize at the *Michigan Designer Craftsman Exhibition*. His prize-winning piece was acquired by the Detroit Art Institute and provided a tantalizing taste of museum validation.[10] An acquaintance of Littleton's, whose father was a judge in Toledo, helped him to secure a position teaching ceramics at the Toledo Museum of Art, School of Design from 1949 to 1951. This proved fortuitous for his return to glass. The position gave him access to the fine ancient and nineteenth-century glass in the museum's collection, and he met the director of the Toledo Museum of Art, Dr. Otto Wittmann. Responsible for the economic well being of his institution, Wittmann was always looking for ways appeal to a broader public. Indeed, Wittmann struck Littleton as especially concerned with increasing attendance at his museum, giving the impression that he might even "divert the sidewalk to put more people through the front door, because that was his stock in trade."[11] This desire to expand the museum's audience may have been what made Wittmann so receptive later to Littleton's proposal to hold a glassblowing workshop at the museum.

In 1951 Littleton secured a faculty position at the University of Wisconsin, Madison. For the next few years he continued to focus his interest on clay, although he still wanted to move into glass. After attending the First Annual Conference of the American Craftsmen's Council at Asilomar in 1957, he decided to do extended research on glassmaking in Europe, where he knew that the tradition of small factories might inform his own studio ambitions. He planned to visit European factories and technical schools to see at firsthand how the historically based apprenticeship training functioned. He also hoped to see small-scale furnaces and fine glass craftsmanship.

Before leaving for Europe, Littleton met with Paul

Perrot, the director of the Corning Museum of Glass, who shared his concern about the increasing mechanization of glass factories and the potential loss of the craft of glassblowing. At that time, Perrot was using the engineering resources at the Corning Glass Works to explore plans for a small melting furnace that could work for studio applications. Recognizing that they had similar interests, Perrot asked Littleton to prepare a report on the Italian glass factories of Murano for inclusion in the catalogue for an upcoming exhibition, *Glass 1959*—a request that was the first gesture of encouragement from an important institution.

Further support was forthcoming when Littleton asked Arthur A. Houghton Jr. the president of Corning Glass Works, if he knew of any individuals working with molten glass in Europe. Houghton mentioned Jean Sala, Thomas S. Buechner, the founding director of the Corning Museum of Glass, had seen Sala blowing glass in his Parisian studio in 1951. This connection led Littleton to a historic meeting with Sala (see page 30) in Paris. On leaving Paris, Littleton visited small glass factories in Naples and on the island of Murano, where he spent two and a half months observing factory organization and glassblowing techniques. These experiences convinced him that it was possible to set up a one-person studio. He remembered that "it was the impact of again watching the fascinating technology of the small glass shops in Murano that made me resolve to discover for myself if glassblowing was within the scope of the artists."[12]

When he returned to Wisconsin in the summer of 1958, Littleton attempted to melt glass in a ceramic kiln.[13] Using his modified clay-forming equipment, he improvised a small furnace and a tiny thirteen- by fifteen-inch firebrick kiln, which he heated with a propane blowtorch. For a crucible Littleton used one of his thick, wheel-thrown stoneware bowls. Restricted by the limited literature available on glass technology, Littleton remembers that he "looked at [Samuel R.] Scholes's *Handbook of the Glass Industry* and picked the simplest formulas for lead glass. Using my own clay pots, I couldn't expect the perfection of Steuben, but results were satisfying."[14] To economize on fuel, he built a small annealing oven, patterned after Jean Sala's design, on top of the furnace, and then carried out primitive blowing experiments. A year later he wrote to Michael Higgins that his goal was to show that the individual craftsman working alone could, without being born in the industry and without going through an arduous apprenticeship, melt decent glass and handle the technical aspects of blowing and annealing it. "On the basis of the five melts (two soda-limes and three lead compositions) and of course, the 'bubbles' that I was able to blow, I believed that is possible."[15]

Eager to share the news of his progress, Littleton presented his experiments to the Third Annual Conference of the American Craftsmen's Council at Lake George, New York, in 1959, and exhibited glass he had formed hot and altered in a cold state. A panel moderated by Littleton discussed eleven methods of glassworking, and Paul Perrot, a fellow panelist, seconded Littleton's belief that glass offered endless potential for creativity. The panel concluded that there were currently no more than half a dozen American artists working with glass outside the factory. By 1960, buoyed by collegial enthusiasm and clear in his goals, Littleton asked to be relieved of his teaching duties for two months in order to study all stages of the glass-melting process.

To proselytize for studio glass, Littleton participated in a panel chaired by Kenneth Wilson, then curator at the Corning Museum of Glass, at the 1961 Fourth National Conference of the American Craftsmen's Council held at the University of Washington, Seattle.[16] He discussed the future of glass as an art medium, and Perrot, who also attended, again reinforced Littleton's position by stating in his opening remarks to the panel that

> for years we have been hearing that glass would become one of the basic materials available to contemporary craftsmen. Indications can now be seen on many sides that this prediction has come true. That such a development has occurred is due to the tireless efforts of a few craftsmen who, not to be discouraged by the prediction of specialists, have boldly explored and experimented with the material and its properties. Obviously, the surface has only been dented and the true potential of this fascinating material will only burst forth with the entry of many more craftsmen into the field.[17]

Stirring language and mutual encouragement seemed to assure that what was characterized as Littleton's dream could be realized. Once again reviewing his latest experiments, Littleton explained that his initial tests convinced him that it was possible for the craftsman to blow glass entirely alone. He displayed pieces that he had melted, ground, and polished while working alone in his studio. Fellow panelists, glimpsing the potential, encouraged Littleton to pursue glassblowing as a viable medium.

In what would become a typical pattern, Littleton neatly positioned himself as an artist uninterested in technical issues and opposed to the uniformity of industrial manufacturing. Declaring glass technique as "no more difficult than pottery," he wrote in 1964 that "an aura of impossibility has prevented artists from realizing [the] expressive potential [of glass], particularly in the field of offhand glassblowing. This technique most needs the artist's uninhibited approach to counter the uniformity of almost all industrial production."[18] The skill was, however, at this time, still in the domain of the factory.

Littleton had met the second key figure in the studio glass movement, Dominick Labino. Then vice president and director of research at Johns-Manville Fiber Glass Corporation, Labino was taking evening hobby craft classes at the museum and he and Littleton came to know each other well; they frequently played poker when Littleton stayed overnight in Toledo after teach-

Cover of *Craft Horizons*, July/August 1966, with picture of *Vessel* by Dominick Labino, c. 1966.

The prominent featuring of studio-made objects encouraged others to form glass in residential studios.

ing ceramics on Wednesdays. With his knowledge of glass chemistry and devotion to glass, Labino embodied the movement as it sprang from the factory and from the hobbyist's passion. Trained as an electrical engineer at the Carnegie Institute, Labino had a lifelong love of tools, inventing, and problem solving, which he coupled with a passion for artistic endeavors: as a child he had carved wood and later designed jewelry and painted. A true inventor, Labino felt that "machines were more beautiful than art because they are *doing* something, and they are doing it for a *purpose* [italics original]."[19] At this juncture in the development of American studio glass, it was Labino's tools and inventions that the studio movement needed.[20]

Just as Frederick Carder had done at Steuben, Labino carried out glassblowing experiments while working at Johns-Manville. During the 1930s Labino had run the milk bottle plant belonging to Owens-Illinois Glass Company. There he had a small laboratory in which to concoct new glass formulas. In 1940 Ben Alderson, Labino's predecessor at the plant, showed him how to blow glass. Although Labino enjoyed the experience, he did not pursue it as an art but rather as an occasional hobby. He noted later that, while he was working at Johns-Manville, he had a home furnace where at night he would blow glass more or less as a hobby. But the hobby had noteworthy successes: in 1958 Labino fabricated a paperweight as a retirement gift for a friend, and by 1960 he had melted a batch of glass and fashioned a primitive blowpipe on which to blow bottles in his studio.[21]

Labino's interest in studio glass grew out of his frustration with industry. As he recalled, "I had just had it in industry. I would say to myself, 'How many years will I have to stay here until I can decide to do something that I don't have to get approved by fourteen to twenty people?'"[22] Labino's home studio gave him the chance to fuse his interest in the potential of glass for art and his understanding of glass chemistry

THE TOLEDO WORKSHOPS

For the future of glass, the third necessary element was institutional interest. Otto Wittmann, perhaps sensing the appeal of glass to the general public, provided this with his interest in the notion of studio glass. Wittmann invited Littleton to consider using the resources of the museum and the city of Toledo—known for its Libbey Glass factory—as a site for an experimental workshop in glassblowing. A garage that had been part of the recently razed director's residence on the museum grounds was offered as a venue.[23] The dates were set for March 23 to April 1, 1962. Norman Schulman, an art education supervisor and ceramics instructor at the museum's School of Design, and Charles Gunther were assigned to help organize the weeklong program. In addition to glassblowing, information about kiln construction, glass composition, glass melting, casting, lampworking, and finishing techniques was also offered. An overview of historical glass was given by the museum staff, and a tour of the Libbey Glass plant was arranged. The afternoons would be devoted to glassblowing.

Seven students signed up and a handful of others joined unofficially as the workshop progressed. The students ranged from beginning ceramists to faculty members of the university art department.[24] Edith Franklin, one of the few women participants, remembers that "at first the course was only for college instructors, but later [Norm Schulman] came to me and said I could take it if I paid fifty dollars. I ran to get the money."[25] Further institutional validation was conferred when all the registered students received three college credits from the University of Toledo.

To help with technical aspects, Littleton enlisted Labino, who provided glass marbles for melting into a malleable batch and technical advice about which bricks to use for the construction of the furnace.[26] Labino also donated the steel and burner and Littleton brought the furnace bricks from Wisconsin. Companionable in their curiosity about technique and their passion for glass, Littleton and Labino focused on how to prepare molten glass that could be blown. The first batch of glass did not melt into a workable consistency, and the stoneware container (one of Littleton's vessels) used as the crucible broke apart in the high heat. Labino suggested that they remove the failed batch and melt directly into the tank. He also urged them not to waste time on perfecting glass formulas, but instead to use his #475 glass marbles, which were used by Johns Manville to make fiberglass. The marbles melted at a lower temperature and the result had a pliable consistency suitable for blowing. Annealing was accomplished by placing the exploratory bubbles in a vermiculite-filled can. After overcoming such technical hurdles in a rudimentary way, the students were able to experiment with molten glass for the first time.

But Littleton dreamed of blowing glass and for that professional glassblowing knowledge was still needed. It was provided by Harvey Leafgreen, a retired blower from the Libbey Division of Owens-Illinois in Toledo. Intrigued by the activities at the museum, he decided to visit, and as Edith Franklin remembered, "the first day Harvey Leafgreen came, no one knew what he was there for. He took off his coat, got a blowpipe and some of the melted glass marbles from the furnace, and blew a bubble by putting his thumb over the blowpipe hole. I remember it was like magic that there was this bubble on the other end."[27] Leafgreen was later joined by Jim Nelson, another retired factory glassblower, who was then a guard at the museum. In this way factory knowledge combined with artistic energy and received the museum's cultural imprimatur.

The first workshop was followed by another three months later, running from June 18 through 30. Through the efforts of Wittmann and Littleton, the second workshop was funded by grants from the Scandinavian silversmithing company Georg Jensen, Inc., and the University of Wisconsin Research Committee. This led to a more ambitious workshop schedule that included lectures on the history of glass and a lecture on furnace and annealing oven technology by Larry Gagan from Johns-Mansville Fiber Glass. There were more demonstrations of glassblowing by Leafgreen and Nelson, and Nils Carlson of Detroit demonstrated lampworking.[28] Again, each student had the goal of completing a simple blown object from start to finish, thereby demonstrating work in a studio rather than a factory.

But even in those heady days of experimentation, an attitude that was to mark one of the fault lines within the movement surfaced. Not all who were there were interested in blowing glass. As Clayton Bailey, a ceramist who attended both workshops, remembers, "I was always very sensitive about being seen as one of Harvey Littleton's followers. So I didn't blow glass at the workshop. Instead I was the only one working with the torch, making strings of glass beads."[29] By choosing not to work with blown glass, Bailey was effectively placed outside the studio "definition." Interestingly, he made his mark through his work as an artist and teacher in clay.

After the first workshop, the newly energized Littleton became an evangelist with a missionary bent, promoting glassblowing as the true studio glass activity. In an article appearing in *Life* magazine, Littleton was described as a "glassblower who deliberately crafts bubbles and flaws" and was quoted as saying that "my pieces are experimental and intended to show the breadth of glass as a medium."[30] As the only glass-maker mentioned in the article, which included eleven other craftsmen, Peter Voulkos among them, Littleton found his image as the leader of the studio glass movement further enhanced.

To spread the news of the success of glassblowing by artists, the *Glass Workshop Report* (1962) on the second Toledo Workshop was published in mimeographed form. This document recorded the workshop's accomplishments, disseminated technical information, and formalized the vision. In addition to including comments from the students, a technical section about glass formulas, and a list of equipment sources, the report (written with input from Littleton) stated that the purpose of the workshop had been "to introduce the basic material (glass), the molten metal, to the artists and craftsmen—to design and test equipment which they might construct for themselves—to investigate techniques for the artist working alone—to look with this knowledge at the glass of the past and present—to look at education possibilities within the secondary, college and university systems."[31]

In this way the workshop participants, led by Littleton, defined themselves (that is, studio glass artists) as those who worked with hot glass and who had a commitment to expanding education about glass forming into the university. For the next fifteen years, this statement served as the informal manifesto of the American studio glass movement. With the success of the workshops and a manifesto in place, studio glass had managed to distance itself from both the factory and the

Moon Bottle, 1973. John Lewis (United States, b. 1942). Blown glass; 5 ¼ x 4 inches. Racine Art Museum, gift of Karen Johnson Boyd (1992.9)

Glass Form, 1966. Marvin Lipofsky (United States, b. 1938). Blown Glass; 8½ x 7 inches.

Super Star-Studded Charlotte 500 Winner, 1970. Fritz Dreisbach (United States, b. 1941). Glass; 6 x 10 inches. Mint Museums, Charlotte, North Carolina; museum purchase from the 8th Annual Piedmont Craft Exhibition (1971.5)

hobbyist, had reconstituted itself, with the museum's blessing, and had achieved a new identity. Now it embarked on the process of institutionalization by establishing itself within university art departments.

GLASSMAKING IN THE UNIVERSITIES

The period from 1962 to about 1975 was a time of new energy and high excitement. In those days I went to Toledo a lot thanks to Dominick Labino's support. Around the country people were doing lots of workshops, blowing glass, doing big things . . . there were few glass exhibitions, few collectors of glass—not very much to glass then as I look back and remember.

—Fritz Dreisbach

As Driesbach observed,[32] the Toledo Workshops marked a watershed. Before the workshops, glassmaking—then termed *glass technology*—if it was included at all in academic settings was part of the manual arts curriculum or taught as a hobby. After the workshops, it moved into university and college programs and, significantly, into fine arts departments. This development was critical for glass; it meant that after 1964 glass artists were increasingly college educated in fine arts degree programs that required the same coursework demanded of painting or sculpture majors.[33]

And other venues for the study of glass were opening up. Courses in studio glass were being offered in the already established seasonal and regional craft centers across the country. Often held for a few weeks in the summer, the workshops were informal and provided intensive learning opportunities with master makers. Most attendees were students who were beyond or not yet connected to university degree programs. Mark Peiser remembers the casual screening he received in 1967 on applying for the first hot-glass artist residency at the Penland School of Crafts. When he asked if he could become a resident, although he had little training in glass, the director William Brown "nonchalantly said 'sure'" and Peiser joined the team.[34] Typical of such programs were those offered at the Haystack Mountain School of Crafts, Deer Isle, Maine, and Southern Illinois University at Carbondale. Within this milieu, where requirements were few and

compatibility important, a tightly woven glass community developed.

The interest in having glass included in the art-based curricula had begun several years earlier. In 1956 the glass artist Robert Willson had received a national study grant to undertake research at the Corning Museum of Glass on the historical and technical background of glass used in art, architecture, and crafts worldwide. In order to understand the European approach to glass education and its long history, Willson visited Murano in Italy and while there collaborated with Alfredo Barbini and other craftsmen in fabricating glass sculpture. Willson's work helped to establish a climate favorable for the inclusion of glass in college curricula.

Workshops were also held by artist-teachers who traveled nationally and internationally making glass. Haystack and Penland became regular stops on the workshop circuit. Inspired by Willson's and Littleton's experiences in Europe, visits to Italian and German glasshouses would also become part of glass culture. Richard Marquis received a Fulbright-Hays Fellowship to study traditional techniques at the Salviati and Venini companies in Italy. Marvin Lipofsky became a "glass ombudsman" to Europe for his work at small factories in Holland and Italy.[35] These international contacts facilitated exchanges of the exuberant and casual American style and the highly skilled but more formal European glass practice. The expanding net-

Marvin Lipofsky working at Berkeley, 1965.

Pair of Vessels, 1965. Marvin Lipofsky (United States, b. 1938). Green blown glass; 5 inches high and 3 inches high.

below: *California Loop Series*, 1969. Marvin Lipofsky (United States, b. 1938). Glass, paint, electroplating; 10 ½ x 22 x 7 inches.

work of traveling glassmakers created an infrastructure of artists, teachers, and eventually collectors who became the international studio glass community.

Another program began in the 1950s at New York State University at Alfred. Known for its technological expertise and long association with industry, the Alfred campus offered a laboratory course in glass technology that included an opportunity to blow glass. Each Saint Patrick's Day, a small outdoor furnace was lit, and blowers from the nearby Steuben factory in Corning would demonstrate their craft. Andre Billeci, a ceramist and drawing instructor at Alfred, arranged to keep the furnace going throughout the summer of 1962, and with assistance from two retired Corning Glass Works gaffers, he started blowing glass. In the early 1960s there were no hot-glass training courses available in the United States, except those that taught the related activity of scientific lampworking. By the fall of 1963 Billeci established an independent study course in glassblowing, and by 1966 it had become an undergraduate course in the Alfred art department.[36] As it would turn out, this development coincided with Littleton's activities at the University of Wisconsin. Perhaps Alfred's long affiliation with clay overshadowed glass, or perhaps because of its connections with the ceramics industry, these accomplishments did not receive as much attention as Littleton's work did.

Following on the successes of the Toledo workshops, Littleton instituted an independent study course in glassblowing through the ceramics department at the University of Wisconsin in the fall of 1962. It was a groundbreaking course, offered in the informal setting of Littleton's pottery studio on his farm outside Madison. In the spring of 1963 Littleton tried to secure funding from Corning Glass Works to establish an independent art glassworking center and to continue the Madison-based pilot glassworking program, but he was turned down. In the fall of 1963, however, the Department of Art and Art Education at the university accepted Littleton's proposal to inaugurate Art 176 Glassworking as a graduate art class to begin that September. The university approved the plan with the proviso that funds from outside the university be found to purchase the equipment needed. Once again Labino came to Littleton's aid and arranged for Johns-Mansville Fiber Glass to donate a thousand dollars and twenty-four hundred pounds of #475 glass marbles to the nascent program. As before, Littleton designed the curriculum around glassblowing, excluding other forming methodologies.

Soon other glassmaking opportunities developed. In 1966 and 1967 Labino presented three workshops on glassblowing at his studio under the auspices of the Toledo Museum of Art, School of Design. The museum also sponsored classes and built a studio specifically for glassblowing. Responding to the increased interest in glass, the museum opened a new gallery in 1969 to house its collection of ancient glass and nineteenth-century glass. A joint art program was established between the University of Toledo and the museum's School of Design, with Fritz Dreisbach (see page 56) as the glass instructor.[37] Dreisbach remembers that there were many workshops, a lot of glassblowing, but few exhibitions or collectors. One year later the Philadelphia College of Art included glass in its ceramics department curriculum, and the future glass artists William Bernstein, Dan Dailey, and Wayne Filan built their first glass furnace.[38]

All of these programs required teachers, and the newly minted glass artists gladly took the jobs. Aware that object-based art was vulnerable to the caprices of art fashion, they wanted glass to achieve a permanent place within the university hierarchy. For the artists-turned-instructors, teaching offered access to bigger and more sophisticated kilns and other equipment than they could afford on their own. It also provided the security of a regular paycheck to balance the less-reliable income derived from sales of their work. Thus even those with slender credentials and minimal training were tempted to accept the newly established posts.[39]

As Littleton had taught most of the studio glassblowers during the first few years following the Toledo workshops, his students became the majority of permanent faculty members and it was they who perpetuated the mythology of the singularity of Littleton's contribution and privileged glassblowing. Tom McGlauchlin (see page 60), for example, who had attended the Toledo workshops and then settled at the University of Iowa, Iowa City, typifies the prevailing minimal training

NS38, 1982. Tom McGlauchlin (United States, b. 1934). Blown glass; 8 ¾ x 5 x 4 inches. Racine Art Museum, gift of Donald and Carol Wiiken (1994.4)

below: *Teddy Bear on Bird Throne*, 1972. William Bernstein (United States, b. 1945). Glass; 9 ½ x 6 ½ inches. Mint Museums, Charlotte, North Carolina; museum purchase from the 9th Annual Piedmont Craft Exhibition (1972.37)

and passion for blowing. He remembers that he "came away [from Toledo] bursting with enthusiasm for this new material—couldn't wait to get started on my own. I remember that when I got a job teaching glass in Iowa in 1964, I had about six hours of glassblowing experience."[40]

As a result of the small and closely knit group, generational links between teachers and students were established and can easily be traced: Marvin Lipofsky, while working at the University of California, Berkeley, taught Richard Marquis, who eventually settled at the University of California, Los Angeles; Norman Schulman founded the program at the Rhode Island School of Design (RISD) in the fall of 1965 and was soon assisted there by Littleton's graduate student Dale Chihuly; Dan Dailey studied with Chihuly and went on to found the glass program at Massachusetts College of Art in Boston; Therman Statom attended Pilchuck Glass Center and RISD with Chihuly and headed the glass program at the University of California, Los Angeles, for two years until it closed in 1985. The close-knit studio glass community espoused the belief that if your glass education could not be traced back to study with Littleton or one of his students, you were an outsider. By the late 1980s, with the emergence of glassmakers and teachers working in other methodologies—and not trained by the first generation of Littleton's followers—this hegemony had receded.

In 1973 glass programs had penetrated the university and craft world sufficiently that *Glass Art Magazine*, in its "Guide to Glass Instruction," listed seventy educational programs, most of them offered within art departments. This expansion had a profound effect on the establishment of a critical mass of artists devoted to learning about, producing, and promoting studio

glass. Furthermore, in studying side by side with other art majors, studio glass artists were encouraged to develop high-art ambitions. Subjected to the same intellectual demands made of painting or sculpture majors, this new generation, although working in a traditionally craft-oriented medium, came to expect the rewards of the high-art world.

As the first glass teachers fanned out into universities and colleges, issues concerning glass curriculum and pedagogy came to the fore. The early glass teachers followed Littleton's personal teaching style and his preference for blowing. As a result, there was not much attention was given initially to philosophical inquiry.[41] Henry Halem, later professor of art at Kent State and founder of its glass program, remembers that his year-long study consisted solely of demonstrations by Littleton, after which individual students would struggle on their own to achieve similar results with blowpipes. "Harvey encouraged creativity and for us to learn from each other . . . Harvey didn't know much more than we did."[42] Mark Peiser, an artist and teacher, recalls that "what we did at first was the result of ineptitude, information [*sic*] and all. But the work had a vitality and an enthusiasm."[43] In all of these new university glass programs, the quest for technique and the need for new equipment shaped the coursework. The invention of basic hardware became an integral part of the glass experience.

During the first decade of formal art education, this lack of sophistication coupled with the difficulties inherent in working with hot glass resulted in formally naive work. Based on the bubbles that result when glass is blown on a blowpipe, the works displayed a lack of formal difficulty. Although the desire to make art was the professed goal, the complexity of glassmaking techniques and the need for some of them to be rediscovered mean that the end product was usually far from art. The first glass teachers had come to the medium because of its inherent qualities. Lacking a grounding in theoretical issues relating to art making, they paid little attention to issues of content.

Even with these limitations, part of what made these glassmaking opportunities so appealing was the impromptu and collaborative spirit engendered by the actual process of blowing glass. Glassblowing is a time-critical activity. The various tasks are broken down into discrete acts that are then carried out quickly by each specialist. This meant that each participant had a close relationship with all of the others on the team. Evident at the Toledo Workshops, this camaraderie became part of the glass lifestyle. The need for experimentation and teamwork while working in close quarters with the furnaces running twenty-four hours a day fostered deep and abiding collegial and interpersonal relationships.

Another aspect contributing to the cohesion of the studio glass community was the quest for alternative

Square Penetration, 1981. Henry Halem (United States, b. 1938). Vitrolite, 34 1/8 x 27 1/8 inches. Toledo Museum of Art, gift of Dorothy and George Saxe (1991.118)

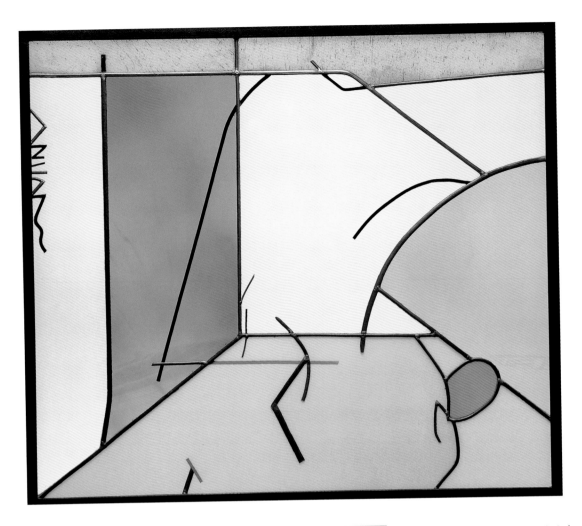

above: *Composition #55*, 1979. Robert Kehlmann (United States, b. 1942). Leaded glass with lead appliqués and steel; 34 x 38 ⁷/₁₆ x 1 inches. Toledo Museum of Art, gift of Dorothy and George Saxe (1991.97)

left: *"D" Black Form*, 1980. Joel Phillip Myers (United States, b. 1934). Blown glass, 7 x 6 inches.

An American Breakfast, 1970. Audrey Handler (United States, b.1942). Blown glass, cast silver, walnut; 7 $^{1}/_{2}$ x 10 $^{7}/_{8}$ x 14 $^{7}/_{8}$ inches.

Courage to be Vulnerable, 1982. Mary Bayard White (United States, b. 1947). Paint on glass, 11 x 9 inches. Location unknown.

lifestyles that arose in the 1960s; in this quest glass-making appeared particularly beguiling. Forming glass entailed a certain style of life, one that was compatible with many of the issues central to the counterculture—interest in communal living and the rejection of parental authority and the perceived restrictions of middle-class life.[44] It was the distinctive lifestyle associated with all craft-linked media and especially with glassmaking that led to the founding of the glass center at Pilchuck, near Seattle, in 1971.[45]

The Pilchuck Glass Center (later renamed the Pilchuck Glass School) is the premier place for artists to meet, work, and explore technique and content. It has also become a place for collectors to meet artists and to watch work being made. The center resulted from a collaboration between the glass artists Dale Chihuly and Ruth Tamura and the patrons John H. and Anne

Gould Hauberg. The Haubergs wanted to start a craft school associated with the Pacific Northwest Arts Center. Chihuly persuaded them to let him use land on a tree farm north of Seattle, where he could explore his innovative plan for creating a school that bridged the worlds of craft and art. Eventually the summer experiment became a residential summer school for glassmakers, the ambience set by notions of an alternative lifestyle free of the establishment values of the older generation. "We were hippies, Okay? People have to understand that. No watches, no underwear, no nothing," remembers Toots Zynsky of the early days at Pilchuck.[46] Learning to make art with glass, rejecting bourgeois rules, and living an antiestablishment lifestyle were irresistible and became part of the lore both of Pilchuck and the glass movement in general.[47]

NOTES

1. Similar changes were occurring in all crafts. By the late 1950s and early 1960s clay emerged from the cocoon of the crafts world (through the agency of Peter Voulkos and others) to gain recognition from the high-art world. Voulkos was honored as early as 1963 by the Art Institute of Chicago in its *Sixty-Sixth Annual American Exhibition: Directions in Contemporary Painting and Sculpture* and *Annual Exhibition 1964: Contemporary American Sculpture* at the Whitney Museum of American Art, New York. These exhibitions indicate wide acceptance within the high-art world for his ceramic sculptures. See Garth Clark, *American Ceramics: 1876 to the Present* (New York:

Abbeville Press, 1987); Elaine Levin, *The History of American Ceramics, 1607 to the Present: From Pipkins and Bean Pots to Contemporary Forms* (New York: Abrams, 1988); and Martha Drexler Lynn, *Clay Today: Contemporary Ceramists and Their Work* (San Francisco: Chronicle Books and the Los Angeles County Museum of Art, 1990).

2. Dan Klein, *Glass: A Contemporary Art* (New York: Rizzoli, 1989), 30.

3. The growth of a marketing and collecting network began in earnest between 1962 and 1975 but gained momentum after 1975.

4. Dr. Littleton's interest led to Corning's subsequent invention of its commercially successful Pyrex glassware. He is also credited with the discovery of the temperature at which glass melts, now known as the Littleton Point.

5. Harvey K. Littleton, *American Craftspeople Project: The Reminiscences of Harvey Littleton* (Columbia University: Oral History Office, 1988), 4.

6. Joan Falconer Byrd, *Harvey K. Littleton: A Retrospective Exhibition*, exh. cat. High Museum, Atlanta, 1984, 5.

7. Littleton, *American Craftspeople Project*, 8.

8. Ibid., 10.

9. Maija Grotell, although Finnish, trained at the Staatliche Bauhaus in Weimar and emigrated to the United States before World War II. Littleton credits her with instilling in her students the notion of pottery as an art form. This Bauhaus sensibility, which broadened the definition of art and promoted education, informed Littleton's philosophy deeply. Ibid., 18–19.

10. He received his master of fine arts degree in 1951. While coming to see that craft materials could be used for art, Littleton continued to produce orientalizing, functional vessels of stoneware and porcelain executed in the tan, brown, and taupe colors typical of the period.

11. Ibid., 15.

12. Dido Smith, "Offhand Glass Blowing," *Craft Horizons* 24, no. 1 (January/February 1964): 23.

13. Labino and Littleton differed dramatically in their beliefs about the transfer of knowledge between clay and glass. Labino believed that clay had no relation to glass because clay is crystalline and relatively solid and glass is amorphous and liquid. Littleton, whose perspective was less scientific, felt that the technology used in making ceramics was appropriate for glass. This difference, among others, would deeply affect the movement in the following years.

14. Ibid., 53. Also see Susanne K. Frantz, "The Evolution of Studio Glass Collecting and Documentation in the United States," in Davira S. Taragin, ed., *Contemporary Craft and the Saxe Collection* exh. cat. Toledo Museum of Art, Toledo, Ohio (New York: Hudson Hills Press, 1993), 21–22. At this time Littleton attempted to get support for this research but was unsuccessful.

15. Susanne K. Frantz, *Contemporary Glass: A World Survey from the Corning Museum of Glass* (New York: Abrams, 1989), 46.

16. It was at this conference that the high-art world theorist Rudolph Arnheim stated that for the crafts "the search for form can be successful only if it is also conducted as a search for content." This linking of form to content would become a central issue for glass in the next decade. See Charles Sawyer, "Education of the Craftsman: Its Changing Role," *Craft Horizons* 23, no. 3 (May/June, 1963): 52. Harold Rosenberg, an art historian and a socialist who supported craft because of its perceived link to the masses, attended the conference in 1961 and served as a panelist. Dwight MacDonald was there too. The attendance of these people underscores the early connection that crafts had to a socialist sensibility, a connection that, together with other craft-linked associations, would have to recede if glass were to be accepted by the urban high-art world. See American Craftsmen's Council, *Research in the Crafts: Papers Delivered at the Fourth National Conference of the American Craftsmen's Council* (New York, 1961); and Erika Doss, *Benton, Pollock, and the Politics of Modernism: From Regionalism to Abstract Expressionism* (Chicago: University of Chicago Press, 1991), for discussions of this connection as it relates to painting and sculpture.

17. American Craftsmen's Council, *Research in the Crafts*, 29.

18. Smith, "Offhand Blowing," 22.

19. Byrd, "A Conversation with Dominick Labino," *Dominick Labino: Glass Retrospective*, exh. cat. Western Carolina University, Cullowhee, North Carolina, 1982, 9. Between 1939 and 1982, Labino received sixty patents for work on formulas for high-quality, stable glass, reflections of his research into glass composition, furnace design, and devices for glass forming. His chief accomplishment was the invention of silica fiber for use in jet aircraft, which eventually led to his designing a machine that forms glass fiber into insulation for pipes. Three varieties of his glass fibers were used as insulation in the National Space Agency's Apollo space capsules. Daniel E. Hogan, *Dominick Labino: Decade of Glass Craftsmanship, 1964–1974*, exh. cat. Toledo Museum of Art, Toledo, Ohio, 1974, n.p.; and Boris Nelson, "Dominick Labino: A Renaissance Man in the 20th Century," *The Sunday Blade, Toledo Magazine* (Aug. 22, 1982): 8.

20. Always inquisitive, Labino investigated the methods that the Egyptians had used to fabricate their core-formed glass vials and subsequently published his findings in the *Journal of Glass Studies*. See Robert Florian, "Dominick Labino: The Color of Glass Dictates Form," *Craft Horizons* 26, no. 4 (July/August 1966): 28–29; and Roger D. Bonham, "Dominick Labino," *Ceramics Monthly* 15, no. 9 (November 1967): 14.

21. Byrd, "A Conversation with Dominick Labino."

22. Ibid., 9.

23. The building in which the workshop was held is variously described as a shed or a garage. I will refer to it as a garage, as this was the description used by the Glass Art Society when it held its conference From Garage to Glory Hole in 1993 at the Toledo Museum of Art.

24 The attendees for the first workshop were the ceramists Clayton Bailey and John Stephenson, and Edith Franklin, Karl Martz, Tom McGlauchlin, William Pitney, and Dora Reynolds. The second workshop was attended by Clayton Bailey again, Erik Erikson, Robert Florian, Rosemary Gulassa, Sister Jeannine (O.P. Siena Heights College, Toledo), John Karrasch, the ceramist Howard Kottler, Elaine Lukasik, Octavio Medelin, Diane Powell, June Wilson, and Stanley Zielinski.

25. Edith Franklin, "Where were You in '62?" *Glass Art Society Journal* (1993): 16.

26. Littleton, *American Craftspeople Project*, 26; and Byrd, "A Conversation with Dominick Labino."

27. Franklin, "Where were You in '62?" 17.

28. Frantz, *Contemporary Glass*, 52.

29. Clayton Bailey, "Where were You in '62?" *Glass Art Society Journal* (1993): 18.

30. Old Crafts Find New Hands," *Life* (July 29, 1966), 34–39, and passim. Also included in the article were Lenore Tawney, Paul Evans, Paolo Solari, Wendell Castle, Otto and Peggy Holbein, Francesca Tyrnauer, Bill Sax, Dorian Zachai, Alice Parrot, and Peter Voulkos. Voulkos, singled out in the editor's note, was described as a sculptor, which indicates the distance at the time between clay and glass in terms of their acceptance as art mediums.

31. Toledo Museum of Art, *Glass Workshop Report* (June 1962), 1; quoted in Frantz, *Contemporary Glass*, 53.

32. Fritz Dreisbach, "Thirty Years before the Glory Hole," *Glass Art Society Journal* (1995): 62.

33. In college curricula during the 1940s clay was accepted before glass. See Martha Drexler Lynn, "Clay Leads the Studio Crafts into the Art World," in Davira S. Taragin, ed., *Contemporary Crafts and the Saxe Collection*, exh. cat. Toledo Museum of Art; Toledo, Ohio (New York: Hudson Hills Press, 1993), 90–99.

34. Beverly Copeland, "Glass Focus Interview: Mark Peiser," *Glass Focus* (December 1989/January 1990): 11.

35. Marvin Lipofsky, one of Littleton's first students, is credited with sharing the American openness to experimentation with European and Asian glassmakers through his travels to glass factories throughout the 1970s and 1980s. Conversation with Lipofsky, Asheville, North Carolina, May 5, 1995, as quoted in Martha Drexler Lynn, *Masters of Contemporary Glass: Selections from the Glick Collection* (Indianapolis: Indianapolis Museum of Art and Indiana University Press, 1997), 90–99.

36. Frantz, *Contemporary Glass*, 59.

37. Ibid., 57.

38. Roland Jahn, "Future of Education," *The Glass Art Society Journal* (1987): 82.

39. The states with the greatest number of glass craftsmen (California and Wisconsin) had the largest number of universities offering glass courses. Other schools in the United States that offered glass programs (inception dates in parentheses) include: Alfred University (1965), New York Experimental Glass Workshop (1979), Rhode Island School of Design (1966), Massachusetts College of Art (1974), and Penland School (1969). See Lee Nordness, *Objects USA* (New York: Viking Press, 1970), 13–14, passim; Rose Slivka, "The Art/Craft Connection: Personal, Critical and Historical Odyssey," in Marcia and Tom Manhart, ed., *The Eloquent Object: The Evolution of American Art in Craft Media since 1945*, exh. cat. Philbrook Museum of Art, Tulsa, Okla. (Seattle: University of Washington Press, 1987), 76–78, 98; Andrew Phelan, "50 Years at the School for American Craftsmen," *Ceramics Monthly* 43, no. 2 (February 1995): 51–56.

40. Tom McGlauchlin, "Panel: Where Were You in '62?" *The Glass Art Society Journal* (1993): 18.

41. The development of studio glass in Australia followed the same arc as it did in the United States but within a shorter time frame. One distinct step forward occurred when Klaus Moje, an artist who worked with kiln-forming techniques, moved from Germany to Australia and took over the program at Canberra. Instead of focusing on technique as a starting point for teaching, he would ask his students what they wanted to make and then guide them in acquiring the appropriate technique. Conversation with Moje, Asheville, North Carolina, 1995. For the complete story, see Noris Ioannou, *Australian Studio Glass: The Movement, Its Makers, and Their Art* (New South Wales: Craftsman House and G-B Arts International, 1995).

42. Henry Halem, "Glass Education?" *Glass Art Society Journal* (1993): 30.

43. Mark Peiser, "Reflections," *Glass Art Society Journal* (1995): 60.

44. The use of drugs was a key factor in taking clay from its utilitarian beginnings to becoming an expressive art medium. While at Otis Art Institute in Los Angeles during the mid-1950s, Peter Voulkos and his students worked around the clock, fueling their sessions with peyote and jazz. See Mary MacNaughton, "Innovation in Clay: The Otis Era, 1954–1960," in Mary MacNaughton, ed., *Revolution in Clay: The Marer Collection of Contemporary Ceramics*, exh. cat. Ruth Chandler Williamson Gallery, Scripps College, Claremont, Calif. (Seattle: Ruth Chandler Williamson Gallery, Scripps College, in association with the University of Washington Press, 1994), 53–57.

45. Opposition to the unpopular war in Vietnam led college-age men at this time to resist the draft. This fostered an anti-establishment ethos, and the choice of an "alternative profession" in the arts (and even more, the crafts) became a badge of independence and individuality. Being a hippie meant dropping out of conventional society and "living free," a choice that had received an unwitting boost from a legal loophole that permitted those enrolled in college to be deferred from the draft. Marvin Lipofsky freely admits that he prolonged his art studies and pursued a master of fine arts degree to avoid being drafted. This delay enabled him to accept an offer to found the glass program at the University of California, Berkeley, in 1964. Conversation, Asheville, North Carolina, May 5, 1995.

46. See Tina Oldknow, *Pilchuck: A Glass School* (Seattle: Pilchuck Glass School and the University of Washington Press, 1996), 59, 83–109.

47. The shift from the earnest craftmaker of the mid-1960s to the anti-establishment glass artist of the 1970s is reflected in attire. At the 1964 First World Congress of Craftsmen, the men are pictured wearing suits and ties, the women were in dresses and heels. Only the occasional piece of ethnic jewelry reveals that these were not bankers or other professionals. By the 1970s bandannas, jeans, boots, and T-shirts were the uniform of choice. See conference report: *The American Craftsmen's Council's First World Congress of Craftsmen*, Columbia University, New York, June 8–19, 1964, published in 1965.

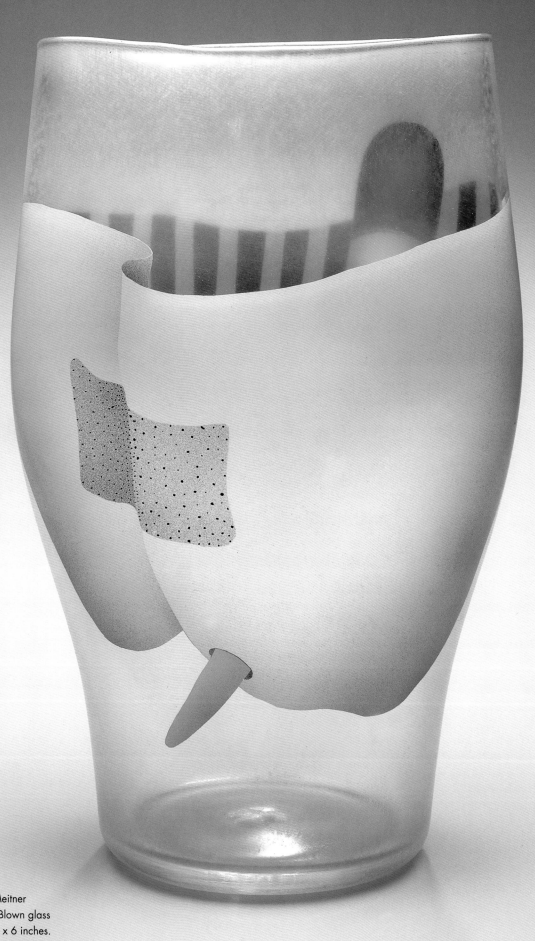

Untitled, 1984. Richard Meitner
(United States, b. 1943). Blown glass
and enamel; 14 ¹/₂ x 9 ¹/₄ x 6 inches.
Toledo Museum of Art, gift of Dorothy
and George Saxe.

Chapter 5

Marketing, Exhibitions, and Collecting—
Spreading the Word

Aftᴇʀ Woʀʟᴅ Waʀ II ᴄʀᴀꜰᴛꜱ ᴡᴇʀᴇ generally sold directly by the craftsman to friends, acquaintances, and those living within a local radius. This usually resulted in reasonable prices and a direct interaction between the maker and the consumer. Gradually, intermediaries appeared—gift or craft shops that sought to expand the retail market for these handcrafted items to a wider circle that came to include the anonymous general public. This system was augmented by a craftsman-initiated network of regional and seasonal fairs that returned to the direct sales interaction. By mid-century crafts had also appeared in the housewares sections of department stores as alternatives to postwar, mass-produced household goods.[1]

Next, multimedia craft shops appeared, often mirroring the selection of media seen in museum exhibitions of the period. By the 1970s the increase in the number of craftsmen and those who wanted to buy their wares resulted in the development of galleries dedicated to specific craft media—termed at the time *craft arts*. For clay, textiles, and wood, this process took several decades, with clay being the first medium to have a network of galleries dedicated to it. Studio glass moved through this process in less than a decade, and by 1972, there was at least one urban gallery dedicated exclusively to glass. This reflected the dramatic increase in the number of glass artists, as well as the development of a committed collecting public.

The direct marketing approach had distinct attributes. First, it occurred in unstructured settings in or around the artists' studios. Acquaintances would know of the work, as would colleagues, and might offer to purchase items as they were fabricated.[2] After Littleton and his followers began producing glass in their studios, they sold their wares at open houses, often staffed by family. Works were displayed on planks of wood or on the ground and priced at a few dollars each, reflecting the low demand for the material and its uncertain place among craft commodities. Littleton remembers that initially the traditional pricing practices for ceramics influenced the price structure for glass: "I've counseled my students in glass all along. When the pottery students were selling five dollar pots, the glass students were selling fifty dollar paperweights. . . . It got off on a different foot, because I thought they should not be giving it away."[3] The higher prices advocated by Littleton became the standard, justified by the higher cost of running a glass studio and spurred by the high-art ambitions developing within the movement.[4]

At the seasonal and weekend craft fairs items by hobbyists and nascent studio glass makers were shown side by side, displayed randomly on tables (see page 81). The hobbyists would participate only in fairs held nearby; the committed artisan would travel from location to location. Prices were low, and it was difficult to earn a living from these sales alone. Mark Peiser remembers managing to survive by selling his small handblown vessels for $7.50 each at local craft fairs in North Carolina during the late 1960s. Fortunately for

Michael Higgins at a craft fair, c. 1965. These events strengthened the craft community by providing an opportunity for craftspeople to congregate and exchange information for a few days while selling their wares from makeshift stalls.

him, by 1974 the price for one of his blown glass pieces had increased to $100.[5] This escalation continued. In 1989 Frances Higgins commented that "not too long ago we had a show at a place called Fifty/50 [in New York City]. We sold things that we sold in the '50s for $15. We got $1,500. for them."[6] In addition to the sales, the fairs helped to build community. In the early years proto-studio glassmakers such as Michael Higgins and Edris Eckhardt frequently participated in the fairs for the opportunity to congregate and exchange information while selling from makeshift stalls. In this way the community of craftsmen coalesced.

Juried exhibitions, such as the Midwest Designer-Craftsman Fair, which was inaugurated in 1954, also served as sales venues. While inclusion in exhibitions was coveted and conferred value, in fact, because there were so few studio glass artists the selection process was not always rigorous. Higher profile events also took place, such as the large, annual *May Show* at the Cleveland Museum of Art, where in 1956 Edris Eckhardt was honored with a special award for her glasswork. By the 1950s regional and seasonal shows sponsored by the American Craft Council (ACC) served as both exhibition venues and wholesale and retail marketing centers, and they were the most prestigious available.[7] Each of these shows helped to expose the emerging studio glass to a widening public.

Museum shops and bookstores also promoted sales—even before studio glass entered the museums'

permanent collections. Speaking before a professional practices panel at the First Annual Conference of the American Craftsmen's Council in 1957, Edris Eckhardt noted that "some of the things that have happened in Pittsburgh have taken place in Cleveland because of the policy and activity of the director of Cleveland Museum. . . . [W]e have several galleries which show the works of craftsmen. . . . Last May more than seven thousand dollars worth of arts and crafts were sold to the general public. . . . We also have a sidewalk Annual at which we sell."[8]

How to sell ones wares was an ongoing issue among craftsmen and was reflected in the range of panels devoted to the subject at the various craft conferences. With the early artists seeking to move beyond their position as hobbyists and to earn a living, all strategies for creating revenue were explored from informal sidewalk sales to formal galleries.[9]

During this period studio glass, along with other crafts, appeared in upscale department stores such as Bonniers in New York, Gump's in San Francisco, and Bullock's in Los Angeles. Locally produced craft items were presented in the housewares department alongside decorative items and tableware made in Europe (usually Scandinavia). The ceramists Gertrud and Otto Natzler remember retailing their works (see *Brown Crater Bowl*, page 41) alongside those of Glen Lukens, a proto-studio glass maker, at Bullock's on Wilshire Boulevard in Los Angeles. Collectors in Los Angeles recount that they purchased plates and bowls made of slumped glass by Lukens, who experimented with warm-glass techniques while he was a ceramics teacher at the University of Southern California.[10]

One of the most important craft outlets during the 1950s was America House, which offered handcrafted pieces ranging from traditional to contemporary crafts. Founded by Aileen Vanderbilt Webb, America House opened as a retail outlet in 1941 at 44 West Fifty-third Street. It was operated by the American Craft Council in New York, which had begun in 1939 as the American Craftsmen's Cooperative Council. The shop's stated mission was a simple one: "To obtain greater recognition for the creative work of outstanding American craftsmen. The vitality of the crafts movement in the United States [will be] revealed in the presentations and sales the year round." The advertisement that included the statement ended with: "Catalogue on request."[11] Eventually this shop led to part of the larger publishing and museum structure of the American Craft Museum (founded in 1956 as the Museum of Contemporary Crafts and now the Museum of Arts and Design) and *American Craft* magazine (formerly *Craft Horizons*).

America House had a direct effect on the expansion of studio glass. During the first World Congress of Craftsmen, held at Columbia University in New York in 1964, Joel Philip Myers's work was exhibited in the window of America House across the street from the conference.[12] While glass was being discussed as a potential art form, American House was offering a concrete example and a venue for sales. The significance of Webb's attempt to establish a retail outlet for handcrafted work in New York City cannot be overlooked. New York, then in the early years of its infatuation with European abstraction and modernism, was not as receptive to crafts as suburban and rural locales were. By establishing this venue for crafts, Webb trumpeted their existence and initiated the formidable task of expanding their availability.[13]

Painting and sculpture galleries also began to take an interest in the so-called new medium of glass.[14] Lee Nordness, the owner of the Lee Nordness Gallery, began to show works by studio glass artists in 1969. Known for his painting and sculpture exhibitions in

the late 1950s, he opened a larger space to celebrate the gallery's tenth anniversary in 1968. Proclaiming that glass artists were "America's leading object makers," Nordness displayed their work next to painting and sculpture. Unfortunately, this breakthrough in artistic parity did not start a trend among New York art galleries, and the next significant developments in the marketplace took place in galleries elsewhere. The displays in these galleries combined presentations of individual items, as is done in fine-art-galleries, alongside mock-ups of living rooms decorated with handcrafted works. This blending of high-art display and domestic decoration expresses the confused identity of studio glass (and all crafts) vis-à-vis art. [15]

Galleries that specifically showed studio glass began to appear in the 1970s. Among these were the Habatat Gallery (with its first location in Dearborn, Michigan, joined later by a second in Boca Raton, Florida). Opened in 1971 by Ferdinand Hampson and Thomas Boone, Habatat started as a multimedia craft gallery and did not focus on glass until a few years later. In order to create excitement about the medium, an annual invitational exhibition series was inaugurated at the gallery in 1973 and showed the work of twelve glassmakers. An account of the gallery's second annual *Glass National* in 1974 described opening night as crowded with collectors buying fast and furiously, even the modestly priced $175 pieces. In 1978 Tom Patti's work sold for nine hundred dollars; by 1984 his pieces cost between four thousand and eighteen thousand dollars.[16] In 1970 Appalachian Spring, a gallery in Georgetown, in Washington, D.C., offered for sale a decanter by William Bernstein for $26 and a miniature vase by Mark Peiser for $17.[17] These are not on a par with the prices garnered by painters, but they were an improvement over those fetched by earlier Peiser's work, for example, and reflected the status as a "collectable" that glass was achieving.

In New York the Contemporary Art Glass Group (founded in 1971 and later to become Heller Gallery) evolved, under the guidance of Douglas Heller and Joshua Rosenblatt, into the first and only gallery in New York dedicated to studio glass. These galleries and others that sprang up in Los Angeles and Chicago became the marketing venues of choice for glass artists.[18] By the late 1970s a staggering number of galleries featuring glass had opened, changed names, and closed their doors. By the 1990s there were a few leading glass galleries and many others selling lesser works made of glass.

In the early years patrons of these galleries and their exhibitions were often drawn from the members of the newly formed artist's group, the Glass Art Society, which grew out of an affiliation of glassblowers who were also involved with the National Council on Education in the Ceramic Arts (NCECA). In 1971 after the NCECA conference in Toronto, a group of glassblowers was invited to Penland School of Crafts in North Carolina by the director William Brown. A flyer rendered in the style of the day was produced and a small grant from the American Craft Council enabled the eighteen participants to attend a workshop held between April 4 and 6, 1971. Fritz Dreisbach, Mark Peiser, and William Bernstein led the workshop and elected Mark Peiser chairman of the group. The next year another workshop was held and twenty glassblowers attended. The participants decided to organize themselves formally into a nonprofit entity and elected Henry Halem as the first president of the newly minted Glass Art Society (GAS). The choice of this name and its acronym was not accidental. The mostly male, hot and dirty world of the glassblower and the faintly scatological contemporary colloquialism for a good time, made the choice a natural. [19]

American House, January 1946. Items for sale were presented within a faux-domestic setting that stood proudly in contrast to the chilly modernist presentations that could be seen around the corner at the Museum of Modern Art.

Glass Art Society board members, 1978–1980, at Asilomar, California. Left to right: Dan Dailey, Marvin Lipofsky, Jon Clark, Henry Halem, Audrey Handler, Michael Taylor, Sylvia Vigiletti.

Volto, 1974. Mark Tobey (United States, 1890–1976). Cast glass, with applied glass trailings; 15 x 8 ¼ x 7 ¼ inches. Toledo Museum of Art, gift of Dorothy and George Saxe (1991.116)

Flyer for GAS #1 meeting of the Glass
Art Society at Penland School, North
Carolina, April 5–7, 1971. Created and
drawn by Fritz Dreisbach.

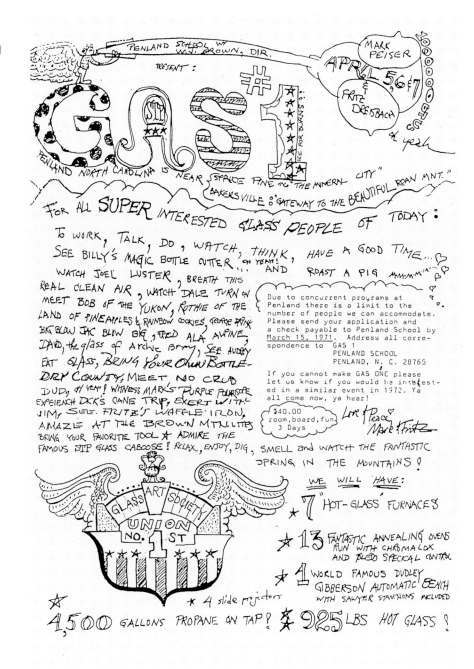

WRITING ABOUT STUDIO GLASS, 1941–1975

If the support structures of the marketplace and the collecting community were to develop, information about studio glass had to reach a wider public, beyond those people directly in contact with the artist. From 1962 to the end of the 1970s there were few periodicals and fewer books devoted exclusively to studio glass. For the glass practitioner, potential collector, or scholar of the 1950s and 1960s, only the multimedia craft magazine *Craft Horizons* provided any information. Founded in 1944 and renamed *American Craft* in 1979, this periodical has long been the most influential

magazine for glass and other craft media.[20] Initially intended to provide information for hobbyists who made crafts during their leisure hours, the early issues focused on technique and provided descriptions and practical tips rather than incisive analysis or critiques. For example, in 1955, Earl McCutchen, an instructor at the University of Georgia, wrote an article about fusing glass scraps in a kiln; in 1956 Dido Smith reported on Edris Eckhardt's experiments to re-creating Roman gold glass; and, in 1960 Frederick Schuler, a chemist, offered a two-part series on ancient glass forming.[21] A parallel in the high-art world was the painting-oriented

American Artist of the same period, which provided tips on how to execute watercolors and render figurative images.[22] The essays in *Craft Horizons* gave tantalizing hints about glass technology, but were often based on speculation about the techniques, not actual knowledge. Addressing the how-to aspect of craft, the magazine helped to embed a hobbyist sensibility within craft making. This practical approach was successful with clay and textiles, but not for glass, which requires specialized tools that, at the time, could be found only in factories. Not surprisingly then, there were three times as many articles on other craft media as on glass.

After the workshops held at the Toledo Museum in 1962, the situation improved, and more reliable articles began appearing regularly. In 1963 Dido Smith wrote about Littleton, and he, in turn, reflecting on his exposure to European glassmakers, published an article about the work of his friend Erwin Eisch, the Bavarian glass artist. Coverage increased during the 1970s, but the number of articles about glass was still significantly fewer than the number of articles about ceramics. In 1979 when *Craft Horizons* became *American Craft*, it was also redesigned with a more contemporary image and full-page color illustrations and

Vessel with Prunts, 1977. Robert Levin (United States, b. 1948). Blown glass; 6½ x 3¼ x 3¾ inches. Mint Museums, Charlotte, North Carolina; museum purchase from the 1978 Biennial of Piedmont Crafts, Collector's Circle Fund (1978.12)

advertisements. With these changes the visual appeal of glass became apparent, and this helped to develop a collecting public. The magazine certainly did expand awareness of early studio glass activities but offered no critical or theoretical insights or any framework for assessment.

Early books about glass offered technical advice, a general history of glass, or the occasional survey of contemporary work. Information about glassblowing was available only in industrial manuals, among them

Samuel R. Scholes's reference for engineers and technicians, *Handbook of the Glass Industry* (1941), which Littleton had consulted for his early work. *The Art of Glassmaking* by Sydney Waugh (1947), who was a designer for Corning Glass, presented glassmaking in laymen's terms and supplied illustrations. But it was filled with declarations that helped to perpetuate the fiction that glass could be made only in large factories. Kay Kinney's book *Glass Craft: Designing, Forming, Decorating* (1962), written for amateurs (the same audience, the glass hobbyists, who subscribed to *Craft Horizons*), offered, for example simple instructions about making objects from sheet glass heated in a kiln (slumping). Also in 1962 Ada Polak published her slender but still useful history of glass entitled *Modern Glass*.[23]

Fay Tooley's *Handbook of Glass Manufacture* (1953) and Million K. Burlyez's *Encyclopedia of Working with Glass* (1968), both essentially industrial texts, did offer practical advice, but these, and Polly Rothenberg's *Complete Book of Creative Glass* (1974), all made clear the need to solve technical issues before the movement could address concerns of content. Consequently, when an account of the seminar activities of the second Toledo workshop, including technical data, material resources, and guidelines for glassblowing, was published, the report made a significant contribution.[24]

Next to emerge were the surveys of the artists and their work. In the early 1970s the Laguna Beach Museum of Art published a series entitled *Southern California Designer Craftsmen*, about the work of many craft artists, some of whom later dropped out of the field. Typical of the surveys was *Contemporary Art Glass* by Ray and Lee Grover (1975), in which brief sketches of ninety-eight artists were placed alongside pictures of their work.[25] In their choice of artists the Grovers enhanced the prestige of American studio glass by linking it to the larger international studio movement. When examined now, this text, too, reveals the high attrition rate of the artists during the second decade of the movement.

The two most influential books of the period were written by Harvey Littleton and Dominick Labino.[26] In *Visual Art in Glass* (1968), Labino surveyed the history of glassmaking for the layman from a technological

Green Loop (from the Green Loop series), 1978. Harvey Littleton (United States, b. 1922). Hot-worked glass, cased; 16 ¾ x 13 ½ x 5 inches. Indianapolis Museum of Art, gift of Marilyn and Eugene Glick (IMA 2000.416)

point of view, using illustrations from Diderot's *Encyclopédie*. Labino's sense of glass history and focus on technique is implicit in the organization of the book, and he devoted only one chapter to recent developments in twentieth-century American glass, and covered the important Toledo workshops in a four-page epilogue.

Three years later Littleton wrote *Glassblowing: A Search for Form* (1971). Focused on glassblowing methodology, the book is primarily dedicated to the nature of glass and to descriptions of tools for forming, techniques, and safety guidelines—each topic accompanied by photographs. In the preface Littleton stated that the "book is both a guide and a revivalist mani-

festo" for the artist who wishes to explore the artistic potential of glass made within a studio setting.[27] This claim is the most often quoted part of the book, but more pages were devoted to sharing technical data than to extolling the importance and potential of glass art. For the next decade this work served as the primary text for how to blow glass in a studio setting and the most coherent statement in support of the medium.

EARLY EXHIBITIONS AND EARLY COLLECTORS

Within a world as compact as that of the glass community, it is possible for a few exhibitions and a few collectors to exert a profound influence, and this was particularly true during the decade following the Toledo workshops. In those years several key exhibitions—some multimedia and others devoted exclusively to glass— were mounted. Early collectors began to emerge, and their motivations and styles of collecting provided a blueprint for those who would later enter the field.

Most of the studio glass exhibited in museums during the 1950s and 1960s was included within larger survey shows. There were, however, a few exhibitions of glass only, chief among them the international survey exhibition *Glass 1959* mounted by the Corning Museum of Glass and opening at the Museum of Contemporary Crafts in New York.[28] This exhibition remained the most significant, until the multimedia *Objects: USA* exhibition of 1969. Funded and organized by the S. C. Johnson Company of Racine, Wisconsin, the exhibition was curated by Lee Nordness of Lee Nordness Galleries, New York City, and Paul J. Smith, then director of the Museum of Contemporary Crafts. The exhibited objects were selected from the Johnson Collection of Contemporary Crafts, included all craft media, and represented the work of twenty-four glass artists. Objects were assembled to "focus attention on the quality and originality that have taken the crafts revival out of the realm of folk art and into the world of contemporary art."[29] The exhibition's most significant contribution was its 360-page, hardbound catalogue wherein Nordness presented a coherent history of American craft that sought to place it within a framework of social cause and effect. By today's standards the entries for the artists look thin, but for the time it could be considered a scholarly publication; and the exhibition succeeded in increasing the audience for glass and directly spurred the development of a glass collecting community.[30]

Exhibitions by two museums with a long factory-based commitment to glass also expanded interest. The Corning Museum of Glass and the Toledo Museum of Art took advantage of their connections to industry to provide financial support for maintaining and expanding their permanent collections of glass, as well as undertaking active exhibition programs that supported scholarship relating to glass from all ages. Early exhibitions at the Corning Museum included works made by proto-studio glass artists, among them, fused-glass pictures by Ruth Maria Kilby in 1966 and kiln-fused pieces by Edris Eckhardt in 1968. Labino was honored in 1969 with a retrospective exhibition of his work after 1964. In 1969 and 1970, Andre Billeci and Eric Hilton, both members of the faculty of Alfred University, received solo exhibitions and Robert Willson of the University of Miami, Florida, exhibited his hot-worked glass sculpture at Corning in 1977 as part of a three-year international tour (see page 144). These exhibitions and the development of a permanent collection of historical glass helped to provide studio glass with historical context, museum validation and an expanded audience.[31]

In 1966 the Toledo Museum of Art mounted the first *Toledo Glass National* survey show, and exhibition of the work of forty-two glassblowers and one warm-glass artist, Edris Eckhardt. In 1968 the second *Toledo Glass National* included the work of fifty-seven glassblowers and traveled nationally. By 1970, when it was time for the third survey, the growing number of glassmakers forced the museum to change the format to an invitational with only eleven artists presented. After this show completed its traveling schedule, the series was discontinued.

In 1972, instead of a fourth *Toledo Glass National*, The Toledo Museum of Art in conjunction with the Museum of Contemporary Crafts in New York City co-organized the traveling invitational *American Glass Now*. Displaying the work of thirty-three glassmakers, the exhibition illustrated the advances in glassmaking that had occurred in the previous decade. Technically more varied and accomplished, the improved craftsmanship permitted additional formal and content possibilities, with glass moving from the vessel toward a sculptural identity, being used with other media, and being fabricated in larger scale. As these trends continued, glass was brought into contention for a position within the high-art world.

The development of a collecting community was spurred by such exhibitions as the Museum of Contemporary Crafts' *The Collector* (1974), which presented six private collections. Among the objects exhibited were works chosen from the collection of Sy and Theo Portnoy of Scarsdale, New York. The Portnoys had begun collecting and later selling glass after seeing the *Objects: USA* exhibition. The institutional attention that placed emphasis on the collector over the artist proved compelling to other would-be collectors of glass.

Regional exhibitions also exerted an influence on the development of the collecting audience. In 1958 the California lampworker John Burton (1894–1985) had a one-person exhibition at the Seattle Art Museum. Two significant survey exhibitions of studio glass occurred in 1966. The *National Invitational Glass Exhibition* at San Jose State College was a transitional show in which the work of some proto-studio glass artists (John Burton, Edris Eckhardt, Earl McCutchen, and Priscilla Manning Porter) was shown along with that of the new generation of glassblowers (Robert Fritz, Dominick Labino, Marvin Lipofsky, Joel Philip Myers, and Norman Schulman). This exhibition made it clear that the drama of glassblowing easily overshadowed all other forming methodologies.[32] In 1974 Western Carolina University in Cullowhee held a regional biennial exhibition that would eventually be known as *North Carolina Glass.*

With this increase in visibility after 1962, interest in contemporary glass as a collectable grew. Attracting attention initially because of its visual and technical novelty, the beautiful medium stimulated even the untrained eye. With technical execution still inconsistent, many early works were casually crafted, but even inadequately crafted works elicited enthusiasm from glass collectors as the visual appeal of the material became equated with aesthetic merit. Thus objects whose technical execution might have been considered unacceptable in another medium came to be deemed appropriate for display in museums and sale in galleries.[33]

As usually happens with new areas of collecting—before orthodoxies have been established—collections were built more as accumulations than as expressions of connoisseurship. During the early period of studio glass this tendency was more the result of the quality of work available than of an untrained eye. An example is the collection amassed by John and Anne Gould Hauberg between 1968 and 1972. What might appear to the casual observer as a group of shapeless glass bubbles is in fact a rare collection of early pieces

made during the first years of the Pilchuck Glass Center. The Haubergs, who had discovered glass in 1971[34] and were the founding supporters of Pilchuck, had developed their taste through exposure to high art, spurred by Anne's art education and a friendship with the painter Mark Tobey.

The first buyers of studio glass came from a variety of backgrounds. Some were glassmakers, others came to collecting from other media—either craft or high art—and still others first saw work in exhibitions or galleries. Typical of this group was Robert Florian, a high school art teacher, who created a collection while participating in workshops at the University of Wisconsin and at San Jose State College (now California State University at San Jose), where he was an event photographer. Harvey Littleton also amassed a collection of historic glass that includes studio glass made by visiting artists in his studio. This type of collection has personal relevance and the influence of friendship can be seen in its quality.

Other collectors included glass within contemporary craft collections that they sought to make encyclopedic. Paul and Elmerina Parkman of Washington, D.C., also received their initial introduction to crafts through the *Objects: USA* exhibition in 1969. In time they became supporters of the Renwick Gallery and involved with the craft field through a broad range of educational and acquisition activities. The Parkmans are unusual in their passion for the medium and represent a typical arc in the glass community, beginning as accidental enthusiasts, they became knowledgeable and devoted supporters of all institutions and organizations that relate to the craft world; while they had a passion for crafts, collecting for them came to lie "beyond acquisition" of the object.[35]

For many collectors newly opened studio glass galleries were by far the greatest influence. Hilbert and Jean Sosin of Michigan first encountered glass in 1971 at the Habatat Gallery. Jean Sosin remembers, "I was overwhelmed by the beauty of the glass around me. That evening, filled with excitement, I told my husband that I wanted to learn about and collect this new art form. From that day on, I stopped collecting prints and devoted my energy to glass."[36] Once again, the visual impact of glass had transformed an art collector into a

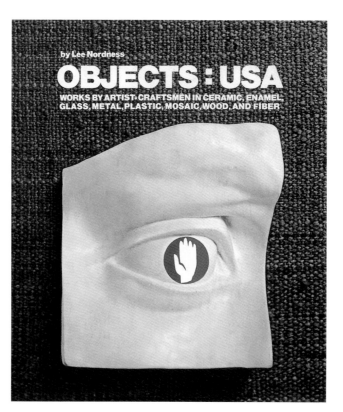

far left: *Fancy Feet*, 1973. Cyndi Von Der Embse. Blown glass stoppered bottle; 8 x 3 ½ x 3 ½ inches. Catalogue of exhibition and sale at the Laguna Beach Museum of Art in 1973.

left: Cover of catalogue for *Objects: USA*, by Lee Nordness, 1969.

The shop at the Egg and Eye (later the Craft and Folk Art Museum, Los Angeles), 1965.

top: Museum opening, Los Angeles. Craft and Folk Art Museum, 1965. From left to right: Edith Wyle, Rodessa Moore, Guy Moore, Bette Chase, and Stephen Wyle; ceramics by Beatrice Wood in case.

middle: Opening and sale at the Egg and Eye, c. November 1965.

bottom: Bess Littleton, Harvey Littleton's wife, selling his ceramic pots from a booth in the 1950s.

top: Announcement, Richmond Art Center, Richmond, California, showing one of a *Pair of Vessels*, 1965, by Marvin Lipofsky (see also *Pair of Vessels*, p. 58)

bottom: *First Doll, Portrait/The Chinaman*, 1980. Flora Mace (United States, b. 1949) and Joey Kirkpatrick (United States, b. 1952). Blown glass, wire, and glass threads; 10 ¼ high, 5 ⅞ inches in diameter. Toledo Museum of Art, gift of Dorothy and George Saxe.

glass collector. By 1977 Hilbert Sosin, after seeing a glassblowing demonstration by Herb Babcock, then head of the Glass Department of the Center of Creative Studies, had become committed as well.

The Sosins' collection of vessels and works of selected artists in depth is exemplified by their group of twelve works by Richard Ritter, covering the period 1971–1984. As is usual with couples who collect, each piece is selected jointly, with Mrs. Sosin reporting a "gut reaction" to the work and Mr. Sosin intrigued by technique. But the Sosins also took the unusual step of collecting ephemera relating to the artists and their exhibitions and strove to become knowledgeable about the history of glass as well.

In 1981 they formed the Studio Glass Collectors Group to encourage the Detroit Institute of Art to collect glass for its permanent collection.[37] Many early collectors founded such groups and encouraged museums to acquire and show glass, hoping to expand the profile of the medium. This assertive approach, whereby museums were brought to the medium by collectors, is a hallmark of the glass world and expresses the commitment felt by collectors, as well as their interest in preserving their investment.

STUDIO GLASS AND THE MUSEUM OF MODERN ART

Even though the forms produced by the early glass artists were not sophisticated in content or execution, some significant high-art museums were eager to display the new medium and even to add it to their permanent collections—this, it should be noted, somewhat later than the acceptance of clay and textiles.

In 1963, one year after the Toledo workshops, the Art Institute of Chicago displayed studio glass by Harvey Littleton. The next year he had a one-person exhibition at the Museum of Contemporary Crafts in New York, and that in turn led to his work entering the permanent collection of the prestigious Museum of Modern Art. These events had profound implications, and the story surrounding the MOMA acquisition highlights the ongoing challenges to the effort to place studio glass in a museum context.

In preparation for the exhibition at the Museum of Contemporary Crafts, Littleton submitted work for consideration that was the result of an

> irrational act of fusing and finishing a form that I smashed in an act of displeasure. . . . The piece lay in the studio for some weeks before I ground the bottom and brought it in the house. It aroused such immediate antipathy in my wife that I looked at it much more closely, finally deciding to send it to an exhibition. Its refusal there made me even more obstinate, and I took it to New York to show with other more established forms included in my exhibition at the Museum of Contemporary Crafts in January 1964.[38]

Even with the encouragement of Peter Voulkos (whose work was already in significant museum collections nationally), the piece was rejected for exhibition. Littleton remembers, "they said it was pornographic or something." But he showed it to the "people in the [Museum of] Modern [Art] in the Design Department [and] they were just having that addition built in '64, and they hadn't bought anything in a number of years, so they were desperately running around trying to buy things."[39] He also recalls that they wanted to buy a second one, but that did not happen.[40] So, in spite of being rejected by the artist (and his wife) and then by the Museum of Contemporary Crafts, Littleton's nonfunctional vase was purchased, not donated, by the Design Department for inclusion in the Museum of Modern Art's permanent collection.[41]

Further, Littleton remembers that the museum acquisition committee initially held that the design department could not buy the piece because, although it was glass, it did not have a hole in it. Without a hole it could not be given a utilitarian classification and so, technically, would be outside the Design Department's purview and within the category of art—as a piece of sculpture. This somewhat dubious logic reflected the museum's guidelines, which privileged painting and sculpture but did permit the acquisition of works from the "allied arts of architecture, film, photography, industrial design, manual industry, dance and theater design."[42] Craft-based works were only to be considered when related to industry or technology, not as artworks. As the curator R. Craig Miller observed,

Alpine Landscape #67,
1977. David Huchthausen
(United States, b. 1951).
Blown and cased glass, with
interior decoration; 8 inches
high, 6 inches in diameter.
Indianapolis Museum of Art,
gift of Marilyn and Eugene
Glick (IMA 2000.487)

300° Rotated Ellipsoid, 1980. Harvey Littleton (United States, b. 1922). Cased glass; 15 1/8 x 6 5/8 x 7 3/8 inches and 3 1/2 x 6 7/8 x 3 1/4 inches. Toledo Museum of Art, gift of Dorothy and George Saxe.

"During this time, MOMA evolved a distinct policy in that they were only interested in craft when it showed a new development in technology or material which could perhaps be applied to industrial design. Craft was not excluded per se from the museum, but its status was very much that of a "second cousin." [43] This,

Bottle with Internal Form, 1968. John Nygren (United States, b. 1940). Blown glass; 11 ¾ x 5 ¾ inches. Mint Museums, Charlotte, North Carolina; museum purchase from the 6th Annual Piedmont Craft Exhibition (1969.3)

of course reflected the general high-art view of craft-based work. The fact that Littleton's piece was acquired after being rejected first by the artist and his wife, and then by those who were familiar with crafts seems to hint at curatorial naïveté on the part of the museum staff and to exemplify the dangers of limited expertise and a mystifying acquisition policy.

"TECHNIQUE IS CHEAP"

The central controversy animating the first decade of studio glass was whether technique or art ambition was more integral to the growth of the movement.

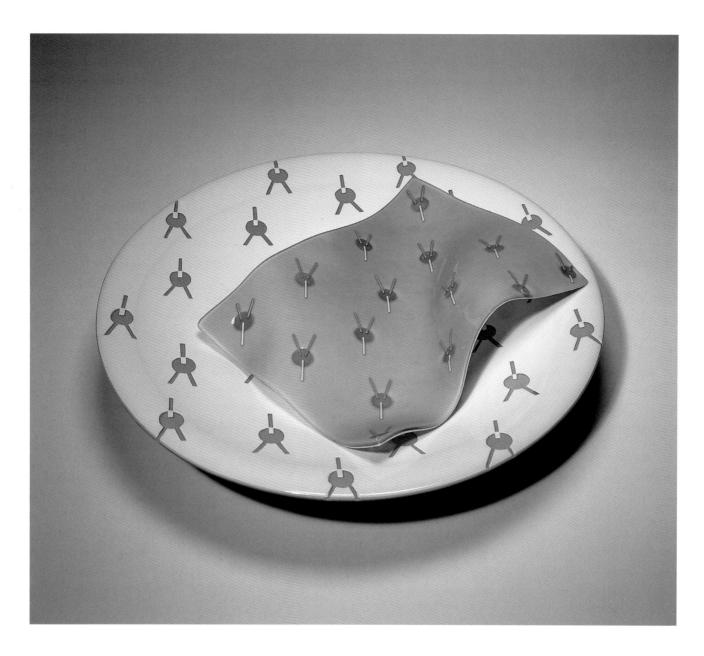

above: *Plate with Napkin*, 1982. Molly Stone (United States, b. 1950). Blown glass; 4 inches high, 14 ¾ inches in diameter. Racine Art Museum, gift of Dale and Doug Anderson (1994.2)

right: *Globe Form*, 1985. Robert Palusky (United States, b. 1942). Blown glass, cold-carved and polished; 11 ½ inches high, 14 ½ inches in diameter. Racine Art Museum, gift of Maxine Gano Mayo (1999.06)

These two competing goals were loosely personified by Dominick Labino on the technical side and Harvey Littleton on the art-making side. This growing tension was evidenced by the shift in formal vocabulary from vessel-based works to sculptural ones. Initially studio glass made in the 1960s related formally to utilitarian, vessel-based contemporary ceramics. This is not surprising: Littleton was trained as a potter, most of the other participants in the Toledo workshops had backgrounds in clay, and many of the new university glass departments grew from existing ceramics programs. Furthermore, the very act of glassblowing favored the vessel as it was technically easier to realize. Bubbles of glass created on the end of a blowpipe are by definition vessels, having once held the air that formed them.[44] To remove this utilitarian taint from blown glass took conscious action and an ambition to communicate content beyond issues relating to containment. It was this goal that spurred the interest in works that were not blown, for they could be more easily fashioned as sculpture.

During the first decade or so, the need to conquer technique had obscured the issue of content. The perceived controversy was couched in either/or terms, but in reality it was a procedural question, not a matter of value. To make glass, you had to know the technique; with that in hand, you could attend to content. But studio glass emerged during a time when the high-art world had eschewed technical skill in favor of casually crafted paintings and sculptures. Additionally, the valuing of objects became controversial as content was separated from material and physical manifestation. As avant-garde, nonobject-based, conceptual art took center stage in urban galleries, objects were devalued. This made the "how to" of glass production seem antiquated next to the art-linked "what." The unavoidable focus on technique during the early years threatened to bar studio glass from acceptance by the object-wary high-art world.

While understanding the necessity for technical competence, Littleton had always favored glass for art production. It is therefore ironic that he chose to work with blown glass, which required more skill than any of the other methodologies and made him initially dependent on technically knowledgeable colleagues such as Labino. Additionally, he had the chance to make sculptural (that is, art) clay, an avenue that had been opened by Peter Voulkos among others, but he did not. Instead, Littleton focused on blowing, but grew impatient with the apparent preoccupation with skill that he saw around him, commenting, at the National Sculpture Conference in Lawrence, Kansas, in 1972, that "technique is cheap." Wishing to position himself as part of the art and sculpture community, Littleton tried to shift the discourse and the activity of glassmaking from being skill based to being content centered. By calling for a break from the craft of glass (and its expression through the essentially utilitarian vessel) and a move toward sculpture, which he equated with art, Littleton dismissed those whose focus was technology.

This attitude represented a turnabout of sorts, as previously Littleton had positioned technique as the primary concern of glassmakers, holding that the main barrier to studio glass had been the lack of a small furnace.[45] He had also lamented the loss of glassblowing skills that diminished because of repetitive factory practice. In the beginning, certainly, studio glass could not progress outside the factory until it could physically be made in a studio. In reality, the two potentially competing notions were better placed in sequence, with technical issues to be addressed first and matters of art to be confronted second. Although Labino also strove to make art from glass, he continued for a number of years to insist that glass artists needed to understand the physical nature of their material. With a different emphasis, Littleton alienated many around him by declared that "technique must never be an end in itself."[46]

Littleton's provocative denigration of technique defined the next two decades of the movement. Artists were drawn either to Littleton's or to Labino's sensibility. Littleton was correct: for glass to be considered a contender in the high-art world—his longtime ambition—it would have to be content driven, with skill a necessary handmaiden. But technique was necessary too, and this would have made Labino also correct and an equal partner in the early development of the glass movement. Littleton's attitude became and remained, however, the predominant philosophy because it expressed the mounting art ambitions of glass artists who had been trained in university art schools. It can be argued that it eventually allowed glass to challenge the boundaries of the high-art world. Sadly, this perception of either/or led Littleton and Labino to go their separate ways, each attached to his competing vision of studio glass. Labino would skillfully fabricate vessels for the rest of his life, and Littleton would move to sculptural forms and eventually into printmaking using glass plates.

As the studio glass movement entered the late 1970s, technique did recede as a central concern but not because one personality won over another or because other fabrication techniques regained favor. Technique ceased to be a focus because it had largely been conquered by the late 1970s, a result of Labino's inventions. But by that time Littleton's statement of 1972 had left a bitter taste and was read as a direct criticism of all who strove to attain technical proficiency.

Some believed that the shift was driven, not by Littleton's commitment to content in glass, but rather by the material rewards that awaited those who gained high-art world acceptance for their product. Henry Halem, an early studio glass artist and former professor of art at Kent State University, noted that "art is not a product, but for some reason many of us treat it as if it were. To me the person who best exemplifies the idea of glass as a product is Harvey Littleton. He makes no bones over the fact that it is money that concerns him most and, as a result, treats his glass as a product. He is not alone in having confused priorities."[47] The tension between emphasis on the technical and ambition for art persists, and the question of Littleton as the putative leader of the glass movement still fosters controversy. But as glass artists became familiar with the material, their work naturally became predominately sculptural and studio glass became a content-driven production that was poised to challenge the high-art world establishment.

NOTES

1. Today these regional craft fairs present less sophisticated works than those considered in this book. Contemporary high-art glass has moved into urban, single-medium galleries. For a discussion of the general phenomenon as it affects musicians and some plastic artists, see Howard S. Becker, *Art Worlds* (Berkeley: University of California Press, 1982), 93–130, 286–343. For a discussion of lower quality crafts and their market, see Joel Samuel Yudklen, "The Viability of Craft in Advanced Industrial Society: Case Study of the Contemporary Crafts Movement in the United States" (PhD diss., Stanford University, 1987).

2. The Marer Collection of ceramics in the Scripps College, Claremont, California, was created in a similar manner. Fred Marer spent time with the ceramists at the Los Angeles County Art Institute (later Otis Art Institute), providing coffee and encouragement. When the works came out of the kiln, he would buy them for a few dollars. See Mary MacNaughton, ed., *Revolution in Clay: The Marer Collection of Contemporary Ceramics*, exh. cat. Ruth Chandler Williamson Gallery, Scripps College, Claremont, California (Seattle: Ruth Chandler Williamson Gallery, Scripps College and the University of Washington Press, 1994); and Kay Koeninger and Douglas Humble, eds., *Earth and Fire: The Marer Collection of Contemporary Ceramics, Catalogue of the Permanent Collection* (Claremont, California: Galleries of the Claremont Colleges, 1984).

3. Harvey K. Littleton, *American Craftspeople Project: The Reminiscences of Harvey Littleton* (Columbia University, Oral History Office, 1988), 21. Prices for works made by those not accepted by the glass gallery system are still low. A 7½-inch glass plate made by Glen Lukens in the 1950s was estimated to be worth about one hundred dollars in a collectors guide book in 1997. In contrast his clay pieces sell for many thousands of dollars. See Donald-Brian Johnson and Leslie Pina, *Higgins: Adventures in Glass* (Atglen, Pa.: Schiffer Publishing 1997), 60; and accession records of the Los Angeles County Museum of Art for glass objects M.90.1, M.90.40 and M. 83.235 and clay objects M.87.1.85 and M.90.82.31.

4. Issues revolving around the pricing of work have long been a subject to dispute in the craft movement. William Straite Murray (1881–1962) contested Bernard Leach's penchant for pricing his vessels inexpensively. Murray believed that his vessels were art and as such should be priced on par with paintings. Murray's timing was unfortunate as he took this stand in 1929. When the Depression resulted in a downturn in the market, his high prices ruined his business. See Ian Bennett, *British Twentieth-Century Studio Ceramics*, exh. cat. Christopher Wood Gallery, London, 1980.

5. Mark Peiser, correspondence with the author, 1995. In comparison, records from Betty Parson's New York gallery indicate that by 1952 Rothko's paintings were selling for three thousand dollars, up from their prices of between seventy-five and four hundred dollars in 1947. See Deirdre Robson, "The Market for Abstract Expressionism: The Time Lag Between Critical and Commercial Acceptance," *Archives of American Art Journal* 25, no. 3 (1985): 19–23.

Also see Oakland Museum, *1974 California Ceramics and Glass Competitive Exhibition in the Oakland Museum* (1974), for prices for clay and glass.

6. Frances Higgins, quoted in "Glass Focus Interview with Frances Higgins," *Glass Focus* (October/November, 1989): 9. Littleton also remembers that just after World War II his ceramic pots sold for twelve dollars each. See Littleton, *American Craftspeople Project*, 21.

7. Open to members only, these shows occurred in six regions across the nation. They lasted until the late 1970s. The organization of regional shows was abandoned because ACC felt that single-media organizations were more effective than was its multimedia approach. Sam Maloof (a pioneering woodworker and ACC board member emeritus), conversation, Alta Loma, California, March 1996.

8. Edris Eckhardt, "Professional Practices in Enamels and Glass," *Asilomar: First Annual Conference of the American Craftsmen's Council* (New York: American Craftsmen's Council, 1957), 144–45.

9. The Gallery Shop at the Brooklyn Museum of Art is an example of an early museum shop. By 1958 worldwide crafts (folk art) were displayed for sale. Carl Fox, the manager of the shop, noted that "even in this country where there is no broad folk craft tradition, we have found fine pieces in New Hampshire, Vermont, Connecticut, Massachusetts, North Carolina, New Mexico—and we have yet to cover all of the states or the remaining forty-two. What riches lie ahead for us and the museum visitor?" Carl Fox, "Brooklyn Museum's Craft Shop," *Craft Horizons* 18, no. 6 (November/December, 1958): 17. For mid-level artisans who work in glass, these regional fairs still provide a market outlet. They also serve to educate the public about handcrafted items. The number of glass artists during the period from 1962 to 1975 increased, and eventually their production supported independent retailing.

10. Martha Drexler Lynn, "Clay Leads the Studio Crafts into the Art World," in Davira S. Taragin, ed., *Contemporary Crafts and the Saxe Collection*, exh. cat. Toledo Museum of Art; Toledo, Ohio (New York: Hudson Hills Press, Inc. 1993), 90–99. Lucke Thorensen, conversation with the author, 1990, about her donation of a glass plate made in 1940 by Glen Lukens to the Los Angeles County Museum of Art (M.90.49).

11. America House sold high-quality crafts made in other locales. Webb had a passion for the arts, and her father had served on the board of the Metropolitan Museum of Art. Raised with impressionist paintings at home, Webb, like many craft devotees to come, was educated in the high arts but chose to support the crafts because of their perceived connection to fundamental American values. In the 1920s after her marriage to Vanderbilt Webb, she studied painting under Cecilia Beaux, enameling under Kathe Berl, and ceramics with Maude Robinson. By the 1930s she had adopted the elevation of crafts in America as her life's work and established Putnam County Products in New York to provide a marketing outlet for the dairy products and crafts produced by her neighbors. Advertisement, *Craft Horizons*, late 1940s. Doubtless there are other galleries, now forgotten, that had no appreciable impact on the national movement.

12. The works shown were made at Blenko Glass Company and actually represented the studio impulse executed in what was really a factory setting.

13. The issue of urban versus rural is important to studio glass. It was also important to other media at the time. For a detailed study of its effect on the Saint Louis art market during these years, see Stuart Plattner, *High Art Down Home: An Economic Ethnography of a Local Art Market* (Chicago: University of Chicago Press, 1996), esp. 6–47, 164–93; and Erika Doss, *Benton, Pollock, and the Politics of Modernism: From Regionalism to Abstract Expressionism* (Chicago: University of Chicago Press, 1991).

14. The term *new medium* has a specific art historical meaning. Ironically, it is not a meaning that applies to glass. Indeed, it has been known to decorative arts experts and classical scholars since ancient times. The high-art world's embrace of glass can in part be tied to its general acceptance of media other than painting and sculpture during the 1960s, due in part to the rapidly expanding demand for art goods.

15. Typical of this period, these display strategies and their mixed message continue today in craft galleries and gift shops outside the large urban centers of New York, Chicago, and Los Angeles.

16. Ferdinand Hampson, *State of the Art* (Dearborn, Mich.: Habatat Galleries, 1984): 7.

17. Paul and Elmerina Parkman, "The Rise of Glass Art: A Personal View," *Glass Art Society Journal* (1991): 44. In 1972 Sally Hansen changed the name of her Sarah Eveleth Antiques gallery to Glass Gallery and featured works by Harvey Littleton and Robert Fritz.

18. While galleries and museum exhibitions legitimized the new glass and spurred the market, most works made and collected in the 1960s and early 1970s were vessels. Many collectors, however, came to favor the increasingly prevalent abstract and figurative work and to consider the vessel passé. As they became more interested in emulating fine art collectors, they avoided pieces that evoked the utilitarian roots of their medium.

19. For a complete history of the Glass Art Society, see the *Glass Art Society Journal* (1995): 102–15.

20. The title change signaled that the craft movement in general had an American presence within the worldwide craft community. It is ironic that this change coincided with the period when craft became less identified with nationalities as it became internationalized through conferences and educational exchanges among artists. This cross-pollination among fledgling studio groups around the world is a key factor in the coalescing of the American movement. In 1998 *American Craft* redesigned its cover graphics with the word *American* diminished to a third of the size of the typeface used for *Craft*. The publication now seems poised to recognize that its field is contemporary world craft.

21. Earl McCutchen, "Glass Molding: Experimenting on a Low Budget," *Craft Horizons* 15, no. 3 (May/June 1955): 38–50; Dido Smith, "Gold Glass: An Ancient Technique Rediscovered," *Craft Horizons* 16, no. 6 (December 1956): 12–15; Frederick Schuler, "Ancient Glassmaking Techniques," *Craft Horizons* 20, no. 2 (March/April 1960): 33–37; and "Ancient Glass Blowing," *Craft Horizons* 20, no. 6 (November/December 1960): 38–41.

22. *American Artist* encouraged the adoption of art activities as leisure-time occupations. Published in New York by Watson-Guptill Publications, Whitney Library of Design, which also produces *Architectural Forum, Gift and Table Ware Reporter, Industrial Design,* and *Interiors,* the periodical never entered the high-art discourse. Indeed it represents the hobby impulse that appeared during the 1930s. As Steven M. Gelber noted, hobbies were promoted as therapeutic in nature—both for society and for the individual. Hobbies taught discipline, instilled focused behavior and "redeem[ed] idleness. . . . The word 'hobby' became a strategic term used less to be descriptive than to carry weight of authoritative approval when applied to individual activities. In other words the term 'hobby' as used in the Thirties was more an ideological construct crafted to distinguish between 'good' and 'bad' pastimes, than the natural category of leisure activity" ("A Job You Can't Lose: Work and Hobbies in the Great Depression," *Journal of Social History* 24, no. 4 [winter 1991]: 741–66). This quality of good versus bad is also seen in the craft community, among whom the practice of craftmaking in and of itself is held to bestow a mantle of righteousness not shared by people who are not craftsmakers; see Rose Slivka, *The Eloquent Object: The Evolution of American Art in Craft Media since 1945* (Seattle: University of Washington Press, 1987).

23. Kay Kinney, *Glass Craft: Designing, Forming, Decorating* (Philadelphia: Clinton, 1962); Ada Polak, *Modern Glass* (London: Faber and Faber [1962]); also see Ada Polak, *Glass: Its Tradition and its Makers* (New York: G. P. Putnam's Sons, 1975).

24. *Glass Workshop Report,* Toledo Museum of Art, Toledo, 1962.

25. Ray and Lee Grover, *Contemporary Art Glass* (New York: Crown, 1975).

26. Dominick Labino, *Visual Art in Glass* (Dubuque, Iowa: William C. Brown, 1968); Harvey K. Littleton, *Glassblowing: A Search for Form* (New York: Van Nostrand, Reinhold, 1971).

27. Littleton, *Glassblowing,* 6.

A reviewer of Littleton's book states that Littleton's "aim is to present the philosophy of an author who is a key figure in the second half of the twentieth century." In the same review Littleton is taken to task for loose terminology relating to *devitrifying* versus *weathering. Craft Horizons* 32, no. 3 (June 1972): 10, 69.

28. American artists received early recognition in Europe, often before they garnered it in the United States. In 1974 the Victoria and Albert Museum in London honored Labino with a ten-year retrospective exhibition that was co-organized by the Toledo Museum of Art and the British firm Pilkington Glass. The exhibition traveled to Toledo in 1975.

29. Unattributed flap copy from the catalogue for *Objects: USA* (New York: Viking Press, 1969).

30. The crafts presented were enamel, ceramics, glass, metal, jewelry, plastic, mosaic, wood, and fiber. Next to wood, glass was the smallest section. Each artist was highlighted with pictures of one or two works and an artist's statement.

A contemporary reviewer of the exhibition exalts the craftsmen as "pacesetters" who "emphasize the newest directions and inventions of the creative leaders in the major medium categories." See Robert Hilton Simmons, "The Johnson Collection: Objects USA," *Craft Horizons* 29, no. 6 (November/December 1969): 24–27, 66.

31. Equally important to both private collectors and institutions was Corning's establishment of an international slide collection in 1977. Entitled *Contemporary Glass* (changed in 1980 to *New Glass Review*), its list of objects and their makers was made available to the public on microfiche. In 1980 the format changed to a printed volume, and the *New Glass Review* evolved into a valuable documentary periodical about museum acquisitions and new artists.

32. Glassblowing has a live-action appeal that benefited from the 1960s interest in art making staged as happenings. Much of the success of the early glass work at Pilchuck Glass Center is related to this phenomenon. See Tina Oldknow, *Pilchuck: A Glass School* (Seattle: Pilchuck and the University of Washington Press, 1996), 105 passim.

33. It can be argued that this tolerance of casual craftsmanship, on the surface the opposite of what craft is about, was the result of the acceptance of the Funk sensibility, especially in clay, that occurred during the early and late 1960s. For artists working in craft media, Robert Arneson's imperfectly formed typewriters, toilets, and bottles helped break the focus on fine craftsmanship.

34. Anne Gould Hauberg had studied under the artist Mark Tobey and had wanted to open a Mark Tobey Museum of Northwest Arts and Crafts. The museum, located on a hilltop with a view of Puget Sound and the Olympic Mountains, was also to be an art center. But Tobey was not interested in a rural setting, and the project was dropped. This left the way open for a fruitful connection between Chihuly and the Haubergs in the early 1970s. For a complete account of this see, Oldknow, *Pilchuck: A Glass School,* 48–51; and Lloyd E. Herman, *Clearly Art: Pilchuck's Glass Legacy* (Washington: Whatcom Museum of History and Art, 1992), 17–18.

35. Paul and Elmerina Parkman, "Beyond Acquisition," *Glass Art Society Journal* (1989): 61.

36. Jean Sosin, "Glass Collectors in the USA," *Neues Glas* 2 (1986): 204–207.

37. Ibid. During this period collecting painting and sculpture had become a high-profile activity engaged in by nationally prominent and wealthy collectors such as Nelson A. Rockefeller, Joseph H. Hirshhorn, Norton Simon, and Giovanni Agnelli. Much has been written about the patronage of the wealthy; for an article about the four collectors mentioned, which was written during the period under examination, see Malcolm N. Carter, "The Magnificent Obsession: Art Collecting in the '70s," *ArtNews* 75, no. 5 (May 1967): 39–45, and Francis V. O'Connor, "Notes on Patronage: The 1960s," *Artforum* 11, no. 1 (September 1972): 52–56.

In contrast the glass collecting community consisted of successful middle-class professionals like Hilbert Sosin, a certified public accountant based in Michigan. They were able to join the game by collecting art that sold for a fraction of the cost of works by the old masters or of avant-garde paintings.

38. Littleton, *Glassblowing*, 130.

39. Ibid., *American Craftspeople Project*, 31.

40. Ibid.

41. Ibid., 32. For a perceptive discussion of contemporary art trends that may have affected the acquisition, see Benjamin H. D. Buchloh "Conceptual Art 1962–1969," *October* 55 (winter 1990): 37–143. The relative significance of a gift and a purchase is important. A gift means that the curator felt that it was appropriate for the item to enter the collection; a purchase means that precious acquisition funds were paid for the work, indicating a deeper level of enthusiasm.

42. James T. Soby, "The Collection of the Museum of Modern Art: Four Basic Policies," *Art in America* 32, no. 4 (October 1944): 235.

43. R. Craig Miller, "Betwixt and Between: Contemporary Glass in American Art Museums," *The Glass Art Society Journal* (1991): 28.

44. The quality of the glass also affects the tension. Until the late 1960s most glass blown in American studios was derived from the #475 fiberglass marbles used at the Toledo workshops, rather than being mixed from raw ingredients. The resulting work displayed a characteristic pale green tint that limited the visual effects and, hence, the content that could be attained.

45. Littleton, *Glassblowing*.

46. Ibid., 84.

47. Henry Halem, "Beyond Technique: Henry Halem," *Glass* 39 (winter 1989): 11. Littleton stated in his oral history that the "tragedy of the [Bernard] Leach philosophy" is that in taking the stance of the humble and poor craftsman, the artist did not himself to grow and "get ahead." Littleton, *American Craftspeople Project*, 22.

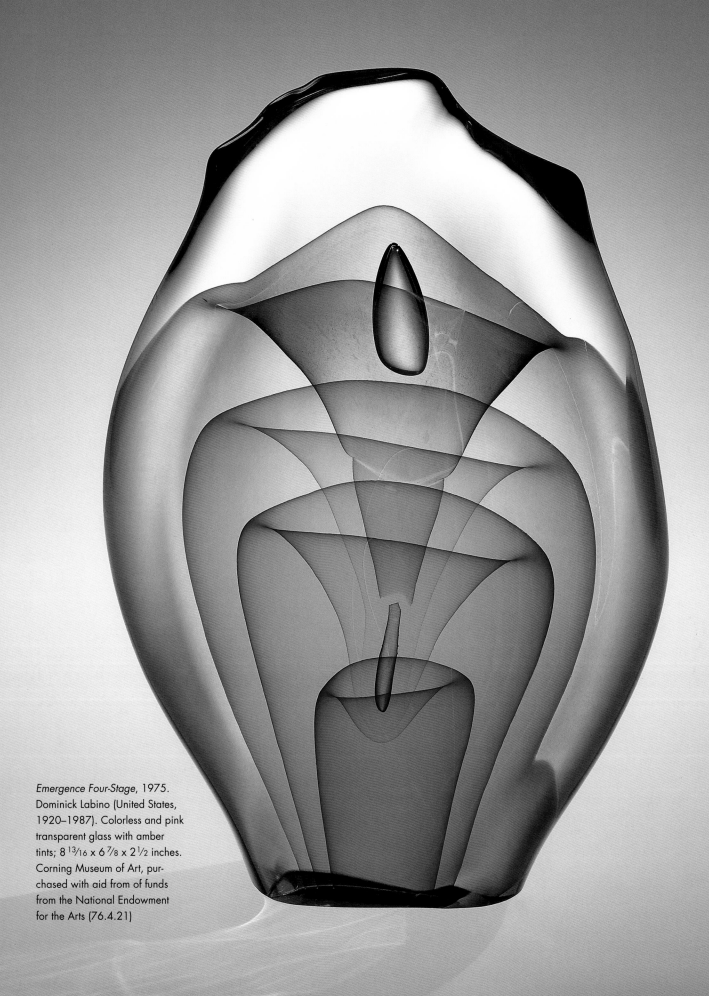

Emergence Four-Stage, 1975.
Dominick Labino (United States,
1920–1987). Colorless and pink
transparent glass with amber
tints; 8 $^{13}/_{16}$ x 6 $^{7}/_8$ x 2 $^{1}/_2$ inches.
Corning Museum of Art, pur-
chased with aid from of funds
from the National Endowment
for the Arts (76.4.21)

Chapter 6

Dealers, Galleries, and Auctions—
Creating the Market

THE ARTIST, said Douglas Heller, one of the earliest dealers to treat studio glass as high art, is "a visionary seer, a person with special gifts whose talent and training enable him or her to make the invisible manifest to the rest of us. The artist is a messenger. The dealer assists by maintaining the gallery which functions as a meeting place for those seeking the artist's message."[1]

It was the dealers who shaped the expanded market for glass as it moved from regional fairs to multimedia craft shops to dedicated galleries and, eventually, to sophisticated art galleries that accorded studio glass the status of painting and sculpture.[2]

STUDIO GLASS DEALERS AND DEDICATED GALLERIES

The progression began with the development of a group of viable galleries that recognized glass as an interesting medium. Passionate respect for the glass artist and the realization of the need for a marketing mechanism to operate between glass artists and the buying public also provided the impetus for the founding of glass-only galleries.[3] Studio glass galleries are typically small businesses that have owner-directors and a few low-salaried assistants to help with packing and installation. A gallery, as the curator-turned-dealer Charles Cowles noted, "is a business and the business should make money. The Art Dealers' Association does not consider a person for membership until he has been in business for five years, because ninety-five percent of all galleries—and this is a statistic quoted by the Art Dealers' Association—go out of business in

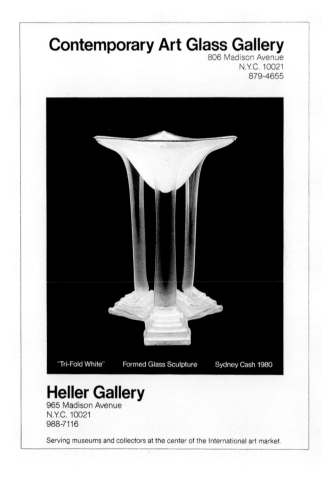

Contemporary Art Glass Gallery
806 Madison Avenue
N.Y.C. 10021
879-4655

"Tri-Fold White"   Formed Glass Sculpture   Sydney Cash 1980

Heller Gallery
965 Madison Avenue
N.Y.C. 10021
988-7116

Serving museums and collectors at the center of the International art market.

Advertisement for the Contemporary Art Glass Gallery and the Heller Gallery that appeared in *Glass* magazine in 1983.

under five years."[4] Complicating the chances of a gallery's success is the fact that traditional economic rules do not apply to art markets or galleries. The market for studio glass was and continues to be even more idiosyncratic. It was, after all, an untried medium with hobbyist roots, lacking a history of validation. This made it, like high art, "a little corner of the speculative market—albeit a highly specialized one."[5]

To ensure success, dealers relied on practices that date back to the early eighteenth century.[6] At that time a class of dealers emerged who operated in a manner paralleling the commission system used by the church, state, and aristocracy to secure artworks. As dealers became middlemen in the transactions that moved art from the artist's studio into the hands of private or state collectors, their role became central, and it soon developed its own structure, customs, and mechanisms—often unwritten.

Selling art requires a compelling vision of the commodity presented, which must be supported by a mythology constructed specifically to enhance that commodity. The sociologist Diana Crane writes that "the business of selling art is a most unusual one. The nature of the commodity itself—it has been described as 'dealing in myths'—is responsible for this."[7] The visual appeal of studio glass, its forming methodology, and its brief contemporary history made it fertile ground for such a mythology. Indeed, the dealers accepted the carefully crafted narrative used by Littleton and his followers, and others, to relate the tale of the so-called invention of studio glass at the 1962 Toledo workshops. Although mediated and incomplete, this history appealed to collectors because, as the cultural historian James Clifford has noted, "collecting presupposes a story; [and] a story occurs in a 'chronotope.'"[8] The little-known history of contemporary glass provided a perfectly formed time and space narrative focusing on the heady days in Toledo when a band of adventurous artists wrestled art from amorphous molten glass. This in turn led to the triumphant inclusion of glass in art school curricula where it began its ascendancy to high art. As a tale of American can-do spirit, grafted onto the valorous goal of art creation, the events provided a powerful narrative that succeeded in rousing passion and beguiling prospective buyers.

To sustain the mythology, dealers took pains to make their gallery spaces look more like theaters than shops. Glass-only galleries borrowed the aesthetic of avant-garde high-art galleries, with their generally windowless spaces and spare modernist architecture

intended to focus attention on the works displayed. Spotlights beamed down on individual artworks, which were carefully placed on raised pedestals with protective vitrines (see page 99). These strategies highlighted the presence of each piece, separating it from its audience and muting the external world that did not privilege glass. The attempt to create a closed system lent cachet to membership in this world and reinforced a sense of scarcity, which is necessary for the selling of all art. With this rarefied environment in place and the mythology understood, "the 'commodity' [was ready] to succeed on its own merits—to sell itself."[9]

Dealers had to be proactive in their marketing. Focusing on a three-part strategy for selling that, again, was modeled on high-art practice, they sought to increase visibility and status for the medium, to differentiate themselves from other glass dealers in the minds of artists and collectors, and to develop stables of top-quality artists to supply work to the collectors.

Exhibition schedules change regularly. The exhibitions, usually featuring the current work of a single artist and usually marked by an opening party, established a set pattern of attendance—recurrent attendance being critical to educating the collectors and, besides, as Ruth Summers of the former Kurland/Summers Gallery in Los Angeles, commented, "people did not just drop by, they needed to have an occasion to come in for."[10] To broadcast the opening event and the availability of art works, the gallery published illustrated announcements just like those sent out by high-art galleries. Printed in runs of fewer than a thousand, these announcements became the first regular documentation of studio glass (see page 97). They usually included the artist's name, a picture of a work offered for sale, the dates of the exhibition (sometimes unfortunately omitting the year), the time and date of the opening party, and, interestingly, basic technical data. With these gallery cards, dealers became the primary suppliers of information about the artists and the medium and focused attention on the "gee whiz" appeal of glass that emanated from its technical virtuosity. Dealers were providing an attractive commodity, presenting it in a compelling manner, and significantly, directing their audience toward technique as the point of entry for understanding the medium.[11]

Aqua Bowl #2, 1984. Mary Ann (Toots) Zynsky (United States, b. 1951). Slumped glass threads; 5¼ inches high x 15 inches in diameter. Racine Art Museum, gift of Barbara S. Rosenthal and Kenneth W. Juster (1996.43)

To augment gallery announcements, dealers soon began to publish slim brochures and multipage publications, sometimes generously called catalogues.[12] Although not scholarly or theoretical, these publications were the first to document in an extended form the works being produced.[13] Over time gallery publications came to include commissioned essays about the artists, essays that ranged from puff pieces to, occasionally, serious, objective evaluations. But, essentially the catalogues were sales tools.[14]

The form and function of the exhibition opening were almost equally important. A festive, partylike event, the opening was a social occasion with business as its intent. Gallery sheets listed the titles and the asking prices for the works exhibited, and wine and nibbles spurred conviviality. As an added enticement, the artist was usually present, providing a chance for all to meet and claim to know him.[15] Especially committed supporters would be invited to see the pieces before the opening in order to have first chance at the best ones. Works sold in this manner were then indicated on opening night as either a sale —with a red dot next to the pedestal number—or as a hold—with a green (or half of a red) dot. This system of notation was calculated to increase the buzz as people speculated about who had purchased what.[16]

To expand their market, glass dealers needed to differentiate their wares from those of others who were also selling studio glass.[17] Between 1975 and 1990, they took a two-pronged approach. First they distinguished their presentations from the makeshift stalls or pseudo-domestic settings of craft fairs and multimedia craft shops. Then, to attract the art crowd, they present predominantly content-driven works, which became possible because artists had began to expand their repertoire beyond technical accomplishment.

Galleries need to develop distinctive sensibilities, which was difficult while talented makers were few. Several galleries would have to vye for the best artists, and the artists, in turn, would select who they wanted to show with—often on the basis of personal connection. The quality of the relationship between the artists and the dealer often determined which gallery secured the best works from a given artist. The artist's perceptions about the abilities of a dealer to present his work to prestigious collectors tended to give urban dealers an edge over their regional confreres. In Los Angeles, Ruth Summers worked around this issue by sponsoring a number of new artists. Her strategy succeeded (to an extent)[18] because glass collectors were always on the lookout for the next, new talent and the dealer was an indispensable link in the system.[19]

All the dealers worked to assemble a stable of top artists. This involved spending time in selecting and grooming the up and coming ones before introducing them to the public. The ability to find and champion new talent involved continual contact with recent graduates from the glass schools, as well as with established artists. In practical terms, new artists were found through tips from other artists and teachers or because the artists, with a packet of slides, introduced themselves and their art to the dealers. To groom a new artist, especially in a medium not yet completely accepted, required a commitment of time and resources, as well as an excellent eye. For the studio glass artist, as well as for high-art artists, by "the 1980s, the development of artists' careers and reputations was increasingly tied to dealers' complex promotion and marketing schemes." Indeed, as the dealers / gallery matrix became the dominant form of marketing, "it was difficult for artists to establish themselves outside of the dealer-gallery system."[20]

Dealers often sought sole representation for their top producers, but exclusivity had advantages and disadvantages for both sides. Exclusive representation with an East Coast dealer might mean no exposure, and no sales, for the artist on the West Coast. In a world as small as that of studio glass, a dealer who showed only a select few artists might find himself unable to expand his audience; not all potential collectors liked or could afford all the work offered by the most elite group of artists. This was not a problem during the early years when a desirable piece could be purchased for a few hundred dollars, but, as works began to cost thousands of dollars, some collectors were priced out of the market. "One-of-a-kind artists like Dale Chihuly . . . discovered that younger collectors need to be cultivated. The way that Chihuly approached this market was by offering work that sold for less than $3,000."[21] By the late 1990s prices had escalated into the low six figures for the best known makers, thereby cutting out a significant number of early buyers and potential new buyers. Chihuly and others continue to produce items in a number of price categories.

THREE GLASS-ONLY GALLERIES

During the 1970s and 1980s a number of galleries dedicated solely to studio glass emerged. Three major galleries at the time were Habatat Gallery, in Dearborn, Michigan, Heller Gallery, in New York City, and the now-defunct Kurland / Summers Gallery in Los Angeles.[22] Each of these was influential as it expanded the audience for glass and successful in distinguishing itself from other glass-only galleries and fostering new talent. All three supplied vital conduits between artists and collectors, both public and private.

In 1971 Ferdinand Hampson, his sister Linda, and her husband Thomas J. Boone opened Habatat Gallery in Dearborn, Michigan, as a multimedia crafts gallery. The selection of Michigan was a natural outgrowth of the already established Michigan Glass Month activities, which centered around Littleton and his followers. Habatat instituted the first *National Glass Invitational* two years after opening. The idea came to Hampson and the Boones while returning from California after having seen a glass exhibition at the Richmond Art Center in the San Francisco Bay Area (see page 81) that included blown works by, among others, Robert

DAN DAILEY

April 25 – May 31, 1985

KURLAND/SUMMERS GALLERY
8742 A Melrose Avenue, Los Angeles, CA 90069
213/659-7098

Photo "Sick as a Dog"
Buy this Sick Dog for only 6,500.00 DELUXE

Ruth T. Summers of Kurland/Summers Gallery in Los Angeles, 1989. Summers took over the Ivor Kurland Gallery in 1982 and successfully created a community of artists, collectors, and museum professionals who support studio glass in Los Angeles.

Gallery announcement for an exhibition and sale of work by Dan Dailey at Kurland/Summers Gallery in Los Angeles in 1985. Announcements of this sort were printed up in small quantities and served as the first sustained publication of images of American studio glass.

Installation shot at Kurland/Summers Gallery, Los Angeles, November 1988.
Display strategies were the same as those used in neighboring high-art galleries.

Opening party for the Ivor Kurland Gallery, October 14, 1981. Left to right: Steve Smyers, Randy Strong (?), and John Kurland. Kurland died in 1982 a few weeks after hiring Ruth Summers. She carried on the business under the name Kurland/Summers Gallery until 1993.

Opening party for Ivor Kurland Gallery in Los Angeles in 1981. Left to right: Narcissus Quiagliata, Marvin Lipofsky, and Kyoto Fugita.

Installation shot at Kurland/Summers Gallery, Los Angeles, November 1988.

Fritz, Marvin Lipofsky, and Richard Marquis. The first Habatat invitational included work by twelve artists from California and the Toledo area. With the appearance of being juried, all works were for sale, the most expensive item being a vessel by Charles Lotton for four hundred dollars.[23]

In the 1976 and 1977 exhibitions the works displayed were predominantly of blown glass (conforming to Littleton's definition of true studio glass) or stained glass (a cold-working technique that had long been popular with craftsmen), representing two groups working in glass: craftsmen who enjoyed the medium and craftsmen who produced concept-driven work, the camps mirroring the contemporaneous split between Dominick Labino and Harvey Littleton.

In time more content-driven material became available, and this shift became the subject of the *10 Concepts in Glass* exhibition that Habatat mounted in 1979. With work by Howard Ben Tré, Steven Wein-

berg, William Carlson, Dan Dailey (see page 118), and Mary Shaffer (see page 146), among others, the exhibition marked the glass artists' transition from vessel-based forms to sculptural ones. At that time, Habatat became a dedicated glass gallery, showing both artist-made studio glass and high-end production glass. After relocating to a new, larger space in Lathrup Village, Habatat was able to separate production works from unique, more sculptural material. This distinction underscored the art of the unique material and differentiated Habatat's offerings from those of other glass galleries.

The Habatat Galleries were leaders in publishing information about studio glass.[24] In 1981 Habatat and Bowling Green University copublished a catalogue entitled *Emergence in Glass*, for an exhibition of the

CFTBLUECLEARKSG 1984, 1988. Joel Philip Myers (United States, b. 1934). Glass; 16 x 21 1/8 inches.

work of fifty-seven new artists and forty-three better-known ones. To document the growth of glass from 1974 to 1984, Habatat published *Glass: State of the Art* (1984). Next followed *Insight: A Collector's Guide to Contemporary American Glass* (1985), a hardcover publication aimed at providing guidance for collectors. This book offered glimpses into the creative process through the words of the artists themselves and was astutely positioned as an unabashed collection-building tool. Next came *25 Years: Glass as an Art Medium* (1987) and *Glass: State of the Art II* (1989), both of which reinforced the notion of glass as an art medium. In the early 1990s Habatat highlighted the rapid ascension of glass with *The Annual Invitational Exhibition 1973–1992: A Tradition in the Evolution of Glass,*

publishing works by the pioneers in glass from the 1960s to the early 1980s. With publications that educated, enticed, and guided the hungry collectors, Habatat was the best source (in both quantity and quality) of written information about studio glass for the general public and would-be collectors.

In 1972 a gallery named the Contemporary Art Glass Group opened. A joint project of the brothers Douglas and Michael Heller and Joshua Rosenblatt, it developed into the first dedicated glass gallery in New York, the high-art capital of the United States. Like many new galleries, it operated on a shoestring, moved

several times, and changed its name. After the first two years the owners rented a very small gallery space on Madison Avenue. When they wanted to put on larger exhibitions, they leased a space in Lever House, where they presented two early exhibitions, *Contemporary Art Glass '76* and *Glass America 1978*.[25] In 1978 they moved their business to Soho, the up-and-coming center for avant-garde galleries at the time, and in 1982 they changed the name to Heller Gallery.[26]

Heller quickly came to represent content-driven glass artists. Most dealers understood that vessels were easy for new collectors to comprehend, but Doug Heller "had no thoughts of pandering to the market—to the best of [his] knowledge, there was no market."[27] The Heller brothers also introduced European masters such as the Czech artists Stanislav Libenský and Jaroslava Brychtová and the Swede Bertil Vallien to eager New Yorkers. Convinced of the potential of glass for art making and seeing the role of the gallery as that of a meeting place for the artist and collector, Heller combined an eye for sculptural work with increasingly high prices. Conscious of the implications of referring to studio glass as a "movement," which would imply parity with other art forms, Doug Heller prefers to describe it as a "phenomenon" and sees it as having important links to the established studio glass traditions of Germany and Czechoslovakia.[28] Another gallery in which fine studio glass was shown during this period was the Charles Cowles Gallery, which had established a reputation first in the world of painting and sculpture.

Untitled Vase Form, 1981. Steve Tobin (United States, b. 1957). Blown glass; 9 inches high, 7 inches in diameter. Racine Art Museum, gift of Dale and Doug Anderson (1993.08)

In Los Angeles the marketing of high-quality studio glass occurred a bit later and was originally undertaken by John Kurland, a transplanted New Yorker.[29] A successful writer who had relocated to Santa Cruz and had begun to collect glass himself, Kurland opened his Ivor Kurland Glass Gallery in 1981. As he had little experience in the business of running a gallery, he hired Ruth Summers in February 1982. Summers, who had previously worked at the Greenwood Gallery in Washington, D.C., provided the business expertise and the knowledge of the field that Kurland lacked.

However, a few weeks after hiring Summers, John Kurland died. Summers, feeling a responsibility to the artists who had placed work with Kurland, wanted to keep the gallery running. Through a chance meeting in late April 1982 with Gloria and Sonny Kamm, who were local collectors, Summers secured financial backing for the gallery. By May 1982 the Kamms had become Summers's business partners and the gallery was renamed Kurland/Summers.

Like the founders of Habatat and Heller before her, Summers was ambitious for the medium and quickly moved to improve the level of work she presented. Consciously striving to create an art gallery, she began scheduling new exhibitions every six weeks, each with printed invitations, a gallery catalogue, and a price list annotated with red dots. State-of-the-art low-voltage lighting was installed, and artworks were placed on white pedestals and covered with vitrines. Realizing that artists and collectors would benefit from museum validation, Summers wooed curators at the local Los Angeles County Museum of Art by offering to educate them about studio glass. The entertainment of artists, collectors, and curators became a regular component of the gallery's activities. Summers also developed new talent and was known for her willingness to commit herself to artists for the long run.

The gallery was successful, but by the early 1990s Summers sensed a new pattern among collectors, who seemed now to value art less than they did the bragging rights that came from coercing the gallery into a price reduction.[30] After twelve years Kurland/Summers closed on April 15, 1993. Ruth Summers reformulated her business and became a private dealer of new and secondary-market studio glass for a time before becoming executive director of the Southern Highlands Handicraft Guild in Asheville, North Carolina. Like many in the financially challenging field of art dealing, she found the vagaries of the marketplace disheartening.

NOTES

1. Douglas Heller, "About Galleries," *Glass Art Society Journal* (1988): 32.

2. Lawrence Alloway, "Network: The Art World Described as a System," *Artforum* 11, no. 1 (September 1972): 28–36. See also Raymonde Moulin, *The French Art Market: A Sociological View*, trans. Arthur Goldhammer (New Brunswick, N.J.: Rutgers University Press, 1987), particularly his discussion of "the actors," that is, the art dealers, art critics, collectors, and painters (artists) who make up the art market, and whose counterparts in the studio glass movement are the focus of this book as well. See also Thomas E. Crow, *Painters and Public Life in Eighteenth-Century Paris* (New Haven, Conn.: Yale University Press, 1985), specifically his detailed discussion of the audience for art, which expanded from a specialized group to the more general public. This same pattern is seen in studio glass.

3. This passion for art was a limited commodity. During the 1940s only about twenty galleries specializing in American art existed. In 1968 the first high-art galleries opened in Soho, New York, and by 1978 seventy-seven were in business. There was one studio glass gallery in New York, Heller Gallery, which opened in 1972. On September 25, 1971, four significant high-art galleries opened at the 420 West Broadway building: André Emmerich, John Webber, Leo Castelli, and Ileana Sonnabend. Both Emmerich and Castelli would be important to the studio glass world in later years. Interestingly, high-art galleries such as Emmerich, Blum-Helman, and Max Protetch showed clay in the early 1980s but not glass. See Diana Crane, *The Transformation of the Avant-Garde: The New York Art World, 1940–1985* (Chicago: University of Chicago Press, 1987), and Sharon Zukin, "Art in the Arms of Power: Market Relations and Collective Patronage in the Capitalist State," *Theory and Society* 11 (1982): 423–51.

4. Laura de Coppet and Alan Jones, eds., *The Art Dealers: The Powers behind the Scene Tell How the Art World Really Works* (New York: Clarkson N. Potter, 1984), 246.

5. Martha Rosler, "Money, Power, Contemporary Art," *Art Bulletin* 79, no. 1 (March 1997): 21.

6. Andrew McClellan "Watteau's Dealer: Gersaint and the Marketing of Art in Eighteenth-Century Paris," *Art Bulletin* 78, no. 3 (September 1996): 439–53. McClellan notes that scorn for art dealers was already established by the

eighteenth century. The term *dealer's shop*, for example, referred to a group of works assembled with the dealer's eye substituted for the collector's (p. 443); (a *dealer's collection* is the equivalent in studio glass).

7. Crane, *Transformation of the Avant-Garde*, 111.

8. James Clifford, "On Collecting Art and Culture," in Russell Ferguson, et al., eds., *The Predicament of Culture: Twentieth-Century Ethnography, Literature, and Art* (Cambridge, Mass.: Harvard University Press, 1988), 236. Clifford takes his term from Mikhail Bakhtin, who wrote in 1937 about the effect of time and space on the structure of novels; time and space, said Bakhtin, have parity, and fictional locales provide the structure for their power relationship to become visible. For glass one can argue that the need to break free of the assumption that glass can be made only in the factory intensified the power issues surrounding the Toledo workshops in 1962 and caused this "reality" to be fictionalized and mythologized for the benefit of the movement.

9. Crane, *Transformation of the Avant-Garde*, 111.

10. Ruth Summers, conversation, February 6, 2000.

11. Controlling the information, dealers successfully focused interest on easily comprehensible matters, for example, how a work was formed, and not on theoretical issues. Control of this kind can be likened to what Irving Sandler describes as the insider process of the painting world in New York during the mid-1940s. See Irving Sandler, "The Club," *Artforum* 4, no. 1 (September 1965), 27–31.

12. The production of in-house publications by dealers began in the late nineteenth century in Paris when Paul Durand-Ruel produced a review of the Barbizon and impressionist painters shown in his gallery. See A. Deirdre Robson, *Prestige, Profit, and Pleasure: The Market for Modern Art in New York in the 1940s and 1950s* (New York: Garland, 1995), 90.

13. As part of a larger discussion of the formation of the art market and the commodification of art, Andrew McClellan ("Watteau's Dealer," 443 and passim) credits the French dealers with instituting two marketing tools that survive today in the high-art world and were adopted by the glass world: the public auction of artworks and the publication of sales catalogues for auctions (p. 445). He also credits Watteau's dealer, Edme-François Gersaint (1694–1750) with inventing the sales catalogue, which began as a newspaper or flyer. Unlike the contemporary sales catalogue, Gersaint's were filled with personal asides relating to the works presented. The auction and sales catalogues for auctions have been instrumental in the commodification of American studio glass.

14. The development of supporting literature relating to American painting and sculpture went through a similar stage. See Wanda Corn, "Coming of Age: Historical Scholarship in American Art," *The Art Bulletin* 70, no. 2 (June 1988): 188–207; and Elizabeth Johns, "Histories of American Art: The Changing Quest," *Art Journal* 44, no. 4 (winter 1984) 338–45.

15. For a discussion of the interaction of the market and cultural artifact, especially the dynamics of the group and the artifact as a conversational tool, see Gary Alan Fine, "Popular Culture and Social Interaction: Production, Consumption, and Usage," *Journal of Popular Culture* 11, no. 2 (fall 1977): 381–84.

16. Martha Drexler Lynn, "Panel: Gallery Dealers in Glass," *Glass Art Society Journal* (1993): 51–54.

17. Crane (*Transformation of the Avant-Garde*, 110–18) notes that in the high-art world of painting and sculpture, dealers differentiate themselves by championing a new style or medium, for example, by moving from acrylics to photography. Because studio glass is a medium-linked expression, such shifts were not possible. But when artists moved from hot-blown glass to warm- and/or cold-glass techniques, or from vessel-based works to content-driven pieces, this could provide the differentiation necessary.

18. Ruth Summers recounts that, because Heller and Habatat Gallery were representing most of the major East Coast talent, she had to work to develop her own group. Sadly, she found that after launching these artists, they would be lured away by other galleries. Summers, conversation, February 7, 2000.

19. For the importance of the dealer in this equation, see Anne M. Wagner, "Courbet's Landscapes and Their Market," *Art History*, 4 no. 4 (December 1981): 410–31. Here the improvement in the market share for Courbet's work after his death was credited to the work of dealers. This type of dealer-based power was also operative in the studio glass world. See also Robson, *Prestige, Profit, and Pleasure*, 77–85.

20. Krystyna Warchol, "Artists Entering the Marketplace: Pricing New Art," in *On the Margins of the Art Worlds*, ed. Larry Gross (Boulder, Colo.: Westview Press, 1995), 72. This relationship between artist and dealer also obtains in European art galleries. For a comparable case, see Karl Max Kober, "Art Exhibition and Art Galleries: Their Role in Art Appreciation and the Perception of Art," *Journal of Popular Culture* 18, no. 3 (winter 1984): 125–44.

21. Wendy Rosen, "The Changing Marketplace for Glass," *Glass Art Society Journal* (1999): 86.

22. A partial list of the galleries that showed glass in the 1970s would include Appalachian Spring and Third Spring Galleries, Washington, D.C.; Helen Drutt Gallery, Philadelphia; The Elements Gallery, Greenwich, Connecticut; Fairtree Gallery, New York (a sister gallery to Galeria Del Sol in Santa Barbara); Foster/White Gallery, Seattle; The Hand and the Spirit, Scottsdale, Arizona; Holstein Gallery, Stockbridge, Massachusetts; Mindscape Gallery, Evanston, Illinois; Theo Portnoy Gallery, New York; The Works, Philadelphia; and Yaw Gallery, Birmingham, Michigan. A partial list of the galleries that opened in the early 1980s would include American Glass Gallery, Santa Monica; Contemporary Artisan (renamed Elaine Potter Gallery), San Francisco; Del Mano Gallery, Brentwood and Pasadena, California; Glass Veranda, Boston; Greenwood Gallery, Washington, D.C.; Maurine Littleton Gallery,

Washington, D.C.; Meyer, Breier, Weiss, San Francisco; Oktabec Gallery, Los Angeles; Judy Youens Perception Gallery, Houston; Betsy Rosenfield Gallery, Chicago; Snyderman Gallery, Philadelphia; and William Traver Gallery, Seattle. Many of the galleries showed work in various media and many survived for only a few years. In 1991 Leo Kaplan/Modern, New York, began to represent studio glass artists.

23. The other artists included were Herb Babcock, Bon Biniarz, Dick Huss, Kent Ipsen, Don Johnson, Gilbert Johnson, James Lundberg, Thomas MacGlauchlin, Mark Peiser, Richard Ritter, and William Warehall. Dominick Labino was invited but declined the invitation. Habatat displayed his work anyway and Labino did not speak to Boone or Hampson for five years.

24. For complete information about the first two decades of Habatat, see Linda Boone and Ferdinand Hampson, *The Annual Invitational Exhibition, 1973–1992: A Tradition in the Evolution of Glass* (Farmington Hills, Mich.: Habatat Galleries, 1992); Ferdinand Hampson, *Insight: A Collector's Guide to Contemporary American Glass* (Huntington Woods, Mich.: Elliot Johnston, 1985); Ferdinand Hampson, et al., *The 22nd Annual International Glass Invitational* (Farmington Hills, Mich.: Habatat Galleries, 1994);

Ferdinand Hampson, ed., *Glass: State of the Art II* (Huntington Woods, Mich.: Elliot Johnston, 1989); and *Emergence in Glass, 1981: A National Invitational Exhibition* exh. cat. (Bowling Green, Ohio: Bowling Green State University, 1981).

25. Marvin Lipofsky's *Venini Series—Split Piece* (1975) and Mark Peiser's *The Wheat Piece* from the Paperweight Vase series (1978) were shown in the exhibition of 1978 and eventually were purchased by Marilyn and Eugene Glick and donated to the Indianapolis Museum of Art in 1995.

26. For more on this pattern, see Crane, *Transformation of the Avant-Garde*; and Zukin, "Art in the Arms of Power," 423–51.

27. Heller "About Galleries," 32.

28. Heller, conversation, New York City, January 19, 2000.

29. Four other establishments in Southern California sold glass: Del Mano Gallery in Brentwood and Pasadena; Eileen Kreman's Design Recycled in Fullerton; and Oktebec on Melrose Avenue in Los Angeles, which specialized in Czech glass and dubious Gallé pieces.

30. Summers, conversation, February 6, 2000.

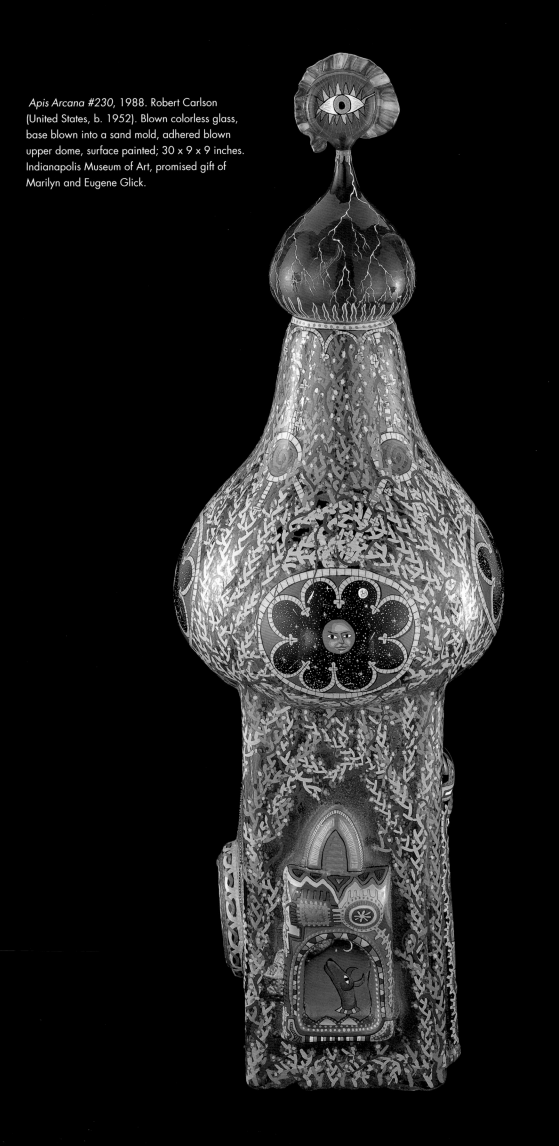

Apis Arcana #230, 1988. Robert Carlson
(United States, b. 1952). Blown colorless glass,
base blown into a sand mold, adhered blown
upper dome, surface painted; 30 x 9 x 9 inches.
Indianapolis Museum of Art, promised gift of
Marilyn and Eugene Glick.

Chapter 7

A Measure of Success—
Escalating Prices

IN THE EARLY DAYS, studio glass artists feared that their work would be described as mere craft merchandise. The threat was real because most of the work made during the 1970s was small in scale, vessel-based and relied on visual appeal, with little evident conceptual content. Such objects did not warrant high-art prices. Nonetheless, as the ambitions of studio glass artists grew and as they began to produce more abstract, complicated sculptural work, they increasingly sought to be paid on a parity with sculptors in other media and to be shown in galleries with painters and sculptors, or at least in galleries of the same quality. The quantifiable effect of association with a high-art gallery is revealed in Patterson Sims's observation that the difference between an artist who was represented in a less-prestigious gallery and one represented by a high-art gallery in New York was about "ten thousand dollars."[1]

While both the artists and dealers desired the better remuneration, escalating prices were of concern to glass collectors. Almost as soon as glass began to be transformed into an art commodity, collectors began to reminisce fondly about how they had started their collections with modest investments. Writing in the *Glass Art Society Journal* in 1981, Ferdinand Hampson, the owner of Habatat Gallery, noted that the previous two years had seen a dramatic price increase for most studio glass and that prices for the top artists had increased by 100 percent.[2] He attributed the rapid climb to the increasing numbers of collectors, who reflected the expanded public exposure to glass due to museum exhibitions. With more collectors chasing fewer works, prices naturally rose. While this development validated the investment side of collecting, it also threatened to drive some collectors out of the market.

The opening of a new exhibition in a gallery is typically the moment for the dealer and artist to increase prices.[3] The appropriate amount of the increase is determined through a delicate process of evaluating the response from collectors, curators, and the press, and assessing the artist's ability to foster interest and sustain future attention. For glass the sheer cost of manufacturing makes the basic cost of production of the artwork higher than it is in other media, including painting. All of these considerations are balanced by the need to keep the price within the reach of the collectors. The reputation and location of the gallery also affects the price. Urban galleries can charge more than rural ones. As the movement matured, collectors often preferred to purchase from a New York gallery for the added prestige and as an excuse for going to New York.

The long-standing high-art practice of providing discounts to purchasers also influences the retail price in galleries. As the marketing of studio glass became more like the marketing of high art, glass dealers, to their dismay, were routinely asked for discounts. "A lot of young collectors," said Charles Cowles, in the mid-1980s, "have come to expect a discount and don't want to buy unless they receive one. If a collector asks me for a discount he is asking me to take money out of my pocket, or even worse, out of the artist's pocket. Its dishonest, ultimately, to the artist."[4]

These courtesy discounts could also be used to play one dealer against another. Among the works in any given series by an artist, there might well be aspects that were similar. Some collectors would consider the related works as equivalent and expect an equivalency of price. While permitting bargaining, this practice brought with it the danger of reducing profit margins to the point where dealers were driven out of business and collectors' access to new work diminished.

Between 1970 and 1990, the prices for studio glass kept increasing. In 1972 the average price for a studio glass piece was $150. By 1990 an emerging artist's work might bring over a thousand dollars, while works by established artists would bring many thousands of dollars. As expected, the prices, although lower than those for some paintings, placed the "customer for craft [outside] the mainstream population. Less than 4 percent of the entire population are potential customers for works priced [at] five hundred dollars and up."[5] By the end of that time, large-scale works by the best-known artists commanded prices as high as eighty-five thousand dollars (and have since risen to the low six figures). This escalation threatened to take the "poverty code out of craft," further separating studio glass from other media still associated with the crafts world.[6] On the financial level, at least, by the 1990s, studio glass had joined high art.

PUBLICATIONS, EXHIBITIONS, AND CRITICAL REVIEWS

When Ferdinand Hampson stated that prices had increased 100 percent as a result of the increased exposure afforded glass, he was alluding to the importance of museum exhibitions in the acceptance of glass as an art form. Interest from museums influenced dealers and the collecting community and facilitated the commodification of glass by providing increased exposure for the medium through exhibition catalogues and the attention of the high-art press.

Of seminal importance to the commodification of glass was the exhibition *New Glass: A Worldwide Survey* mounted by the Corning Museum of Glass in 1979. Organized in conjunction with the Victoria and Albert Museum in London and supported by funds from the Pilkington Group, the National Endowment for the Arts, Owens-Illinois, and Owens-Corning, the exhibition was a juried presentation of 275 objects made by 196 glassmakers, designers, and companies drawn from 28 countries. The jurors were Franca Santi Gualteri, editor of *Abitari*, representing a housewares design sensibility; Russell Lynes, who offered a cultural history perspective; Werner Schmalenbach, the director of the Kunst Museum in Düsseldorf, who brought an art historical bias; and Paul Smith, then the director of the Museum of Contemporary Crafts in New York, who provided an arts and crafts sensibility. Unlike its predecessor, *Glass 1959*, the exhibition included more studio-made glass than production pieces. Russell Lynes noted that "in the [*Glass*] 1959 exhibition about ninety percent of the glass was 'factory work' and ten percent [of the] glass was conceived and made by craftsmen working as individual artists. This time the percentages are almost reversed and so are the intentions of the makers."[7]

The exhibition opened in Corning, New York, and toured to the Toledo Museum of Art, Toledo, Ohio, the Renwick Gallery of the National Collection of Fine Arts, Smithsonian Institution, Washington, D.C., and the California Palace of the Legion of Honor in San Francisco. It then traveled to the Victoria and Albert Museum in London, the Musée des arts décoratifs in Paris, and to Japan, marking the first time American studio glass was shown there. At the last minute another venue was added: the Metropolitan Museum of Art in New York. This addition was of particular importance to the still-young studio movement. The exhibition, which was an edited version of the original, was accepted because the curator, Penelope Hunter-Stiebel, was interested in studio glass. Discussing his predecessor, R. Craig Miller, commented that "one of her most important acts was to show the 1979 Corning exhibition, *New Glass: A Worldwide Survey*, at the Metropolitan. Many contemporary observers such as Helen Drutt, as well as Michael and Douglas Heller have cited this New York venue as a major turning point in winning acceptance for contemporary glass among collectors."[8] Doug Heller described it as "a landmark exhibition in many ways" and felt that the

top left: *Untitled*, 1983. Sydney Cash (United States, b. 1941). Sandblasted plate glass sculpture slumped on a wire armature; 11½ x 5¼ x 6 inches. Indianapolis Museum of Art, gift of Marilyn and Eugene Glick (IMA 2000.447)

top right: *Cloistered Block with Cactus and Spirits*, 1988. Paul Stankard (United States, b. 1943). Cast glass, lampwork; 4¾ x 2½ x 3 inches. Indianapolis Museum of Art, gift of Marilyn and Eugene Glick (IMA 2001.88)

left: *Convexed Green with Gray*, 1979. Thomas Patti (United States, b. 1943). Glass; 3 x 3¾ x 3¾ inches. Mint Museums, Charlotte, North Carolina; gift of Bob and Mindy Jones (1988.142)

Female Bust with Leaves, 1989. Richard Jolley (United States, b. 1952). Hot-worked colorless glass, with cane drawings, sandblasted; 13 ½ x 10 x 7 inches. Indianapolis Museum of Art, gift of Marilyn and Eugene Glick (IMA 2000.496)

validation from the Met could not have come at a better time or from a better institution.[9] Ferdinand Hampson also credits it as the "single-most important exhibit that occurred in glass in years."[10]

The lavishly illustrated 288-page catalogue also garnered attention from private and institutional collectors. Although essentially a picture book with brief biographical data on the artists and statements from each juror, the catalogue provided enticing illustrations and some basic information. George and Dorothy Saxe, who were collectors in California, recall seeing the catalogue at a friend's house, leafing though it, and being attracted to the medium. And indeed, for a time, this publication served as a guidebook for many collectors.

Glass was also starting to attract notice from the high-art press, although it was not necessarily favorable. The third *Americans in Glass* exhibition held at Leigh Yawkey Woodson Museum, Wausau, Wisconsin, in 1984 was the subject of a feature-length article, "Decorative Arts 'Americans in Glass': A Requiem?" by Robert Silberman, which appeared in *Art in Amer-*

ica in March 1985, illustrated with twenty images of glass from the exhibition. The article reflected jurors' statements questioning the future of the medium. Silberman described glass as "almost fatally attractive," but went on to quote J. Stewart Johnson, the design curator at the Museum of Modern Art, who had suggested that the exhibition itself might prove to be a "requiem" for glass due to its lack of quality.

The article was condescending and critical, but Silberman did perceptively highlight a concern facing the studio glass movement: the issue of the good glass artist as distinguished from the good artist. He questioned the notion that studio glass artists should be assimilated into the fine arts world lest they lose "the distinctive history of glass."[11] Many people in the glass community actively sought this inclusion, but Silberman believed that it would mean abandoning something inherent in the medium. Such sensitivity and awareness of the long history of glass was rare in the high-art world.[12]

In 1987 a multimedia exhibition from Oklahoma took center stage in the craft and glass worlds, and it, too, garnered an important critical review. The Philbrook Museum of Art in Tulsa mounted an exhibition entitled *The Eloquent Object: The Evolution of American Art in Craft Media since 1945*. It was curated by the husband-and-wife team of Marcia Manhart, the executive director of the Philbrook, and Tom Manhart, a ceramist and dealer. Funded by Mobil Oil Corporation, the National Endowment for the Humanities, and the National Endowment for the Arts (in addition to state and local agencies), the exhibition united curatorial validation with the interests of galleries and artists.[13]

Considered a lavish example of the craft survey shows common during the period, the exhibition presented items made in all craft media and was more comprehensive than insightful. One hundred and forty-two artists were represented by one item each. The catalogue reflected the current thinking about crafts—ranging from opinions formed in the 1960s (expressed by Rose Slivka, the retired editor of *Craft Horizons*) to high-art world perspectives that sought to define craft one dimensionally (voiced by the critic Lucy Lippard and the curator Mary Jane Jacobs). In an effort to equate craft with art, the curators placed artists either from the high-art world or accepted into it—Robert Arneson, Peter Voulkos, Judy Chicago, Stephen DeStaebler, and John Mason—alongside many who were known only within the craft community. Among those presented, twelve were studio glass artists.[14]

Although the exhibition did not travel nationally—which would have increased its effect—it did receive a notable, albeit stinging, critique from the high-art press. Derek Guthrie, the publisher of *New Art Examiner*, wrote a review entitled "'The Eloquent Object' Gagged by Kitsch" for his magazine: "The stale smell of brokered consensus permeates the book and dominates the exhibition. . . . The objects are selected and arranged primarily to carry the intellectual pretensions of the curators and so to prove that craft objects have indeed evolved beyond their lowly origins."[15] Ironically, this review focused attention on crafts in much the same way that similarly disparaging reviews stimulated the recognition of new art movements in the nineteenth century. By (faintly) praising John Perreault's catalogue essay and even devoting space to a review, Guthrie implied that there was something worth talking about in the craft arena. Indeed, the intensity of his comments seemed to indicate that crafts (and studio glass) were perhaps gaining on the high arts and needed to be beaten back.

In 1989 the Corning Museum of Glass published catalogue of its permanent collection, *Contemporary Glass: A World Survey from the Corning Museum of Glass*, written by Susanne K. Frantz (then the museum's curator of contemporary glass),[16] that made a significant contribution to the marketing of glass and the history of the movement. The first book to focus on glass and the first to acknowledge the Toledo workshops and the work of proto-studio glass artists active before the early 1960s, it was also the first to present American studio glass with the intellectual rigor usually reserved for high-art media. Presented in coffee-table format and lavishly illustrated (Frantz had the advantage of drawing on Corning's vast holdings of glass and the extensive archival and primary information in its library), the book marries the visual appeal of glass to the scholarly form of a permanent collection catalogue.

Before 1970 contemporary avant-garde art of any media was seldom auctioned by the large national and international auction houses—and studio glass not at all.[17] This was because the auction market is considered a wholesale market and the dollar amounts realized would generally be lower than the retail prices asked by galleries. In such an event, the market would tip downward, and collectors might begin to search the auction markets for works at lower than retail prices. By the 1990s, however, the auction market in the contemporary art field had had become more of a retail (primary) market (selling to the end user). So, while the primary market offers objects sold for the first time at a set retail price by the maker to the final user (usually through a dealer or shop owner to a collector), the secondary market offers objects that are resold by dealers or auction houses to collectors or resellers for a price that is not predetermined. In this way sales of contemporary art on the secondary market can affect the gallery retail market because, when a contemporary work is resold, it does not have an established retail value or many prospective purchasers, and may decrease in value. Thus an uncertain secondary market can spook collectors and undermine the primary market.[18] However, the importance of the growth of a secondary market to the success and wide reception of American studio glass cannot be overestimated. Donna Schneier, a consultant to Sotheby's auction house for fine craft and a dealer who focuses on the secondary market, has aptly stated: "If you don't have a secondary market, you don't have a primary market."[19]

The secondary market for studio glass—like that for high art—exists in two forms: dealers who resell work through their galleries (referred to as "backroom sales") and public auctions held by dealers or dedicated auction houses. The two types differ significantly. Backroom sales are private and the prices known only to the dealer, artist, and buyer. Auctions are public, and although the purchaser may not be known, the price paid becomes part of the public record and could undermine retail gallery sales.

The secondary market for studio glass began in the back rooms of craft and dedicated glass galleries. The buyers were usually collectors who wanted to upgrade or augment their current holdings and the sellers had usually purchased early pieces and wanted to cash in on their prescient selections. Because resales are often undertaken to trade a good piece for a better one, the best works may not appear in this market. Unlike the developed market for old masters (which is in reality a secondary market), contemporary material tends to move down in price and quality at this secondary level, leaving the primary (dealer) market with an enduring edge.

With good work, such sales can reveal the strength of a market (a piece by Harvey Littleton that originally sold at retail for fourteen hundred dollars was resold by Heller Gallery in 1994 for seventy-five hundred dollars).[20] The difference in price was influenced by the increased viability of the studio glass movement, Littleton's advancing age, the fact that he ceased making glass in the early 1980s, and the imprimatur of the gallery as New York's leading venue for studio glass. Other factors that affect resale prices include the quality of the specific work and the prestige of the previous owner (provenance). In the unusual event that a fine piece of studio glasswork does come back on the market, its price can exceed the original retail price.

In the studio glass world, auctions are either public sales (hosted by dealers or national auction houses) or charity fund-raising opportunities. Auctions mounted by galleries or dedicated auction houses in both regional and urban settings, can be semipublic or very public affairs, and range from strictly business events to those with a charitable purpose. One semipublic charity auction dedicated to studio glass was held at the Pilchuck Glass School in 1978. A spur-of-the-moment affair, put on at the end of the school season, the auction was a response to the impending loss of financial backing from Pilchuck's cofounder John Hauberg and was essentially a private event with only board members and staff attending. Sensing the potential for sustained revenue from auction sales, however, the school organized a more formal, festive, and public auction at the Pilchuck lodge the following year, with the artist Patrick Reynteins, dressed in a kilt, presiding as auctioneer. Large items sold for as much as a thousand dollars, and the sale netted nine thousand dollars.[21] The works were sold by auction, but, in reality, the event was more akin to the activity of the primary market, as the works were new and were moving from the artist to the collector for the first time. Doug Anderson, a collector, commented that "although it is generally admitted that charity auctions are not 'real life,'. . . they [do] play a part in convincing the commercial auction houses that there [is] a market for this material."[22] Pilchuck's use of the auction format did not immediately produce a stampede of national or international studio glass auctions.

Large international auction houses such as Christie's and Sotheby's did become interested in studio glass by the late 1980s. With art values high and the market seemingly insatiable, glass seemed ready for their attention. The first national auction of American studio glass was held on February 13, 1989, in New York at Christie's and consisted of 160 items, most made after 1985. The sale was not prompted by the desire to test the secondary market but rather was a result of a court order that impelled the American National Bank of Cleveland to sell its corporate collection as part settlement of an embezzlement case involving its Ohio owners, Ted and Kay Evans. Despite this, the mood surrounding the event (always important to the success of an auction) was euphoric and to the expressed relief of Kathleen Guzman, the president of Christie's East and a specialist in decorative arts and lower end fine arts, all but three lots sold well.[23] But, although the low estimates were exceeded and the auction netted over half a million dollars, the hammer prices made retail gallery prices appear inflated.[24] This did not please the glass community. Including as it did works of uneven quality and in poor condition, the auction exposed second-rate material to the public and potentially threatened to damage future primary and secondary markets. Indeed even though the results were respectable, this attempt to make glass a staple of the auction scene proved premature.

Auctions were, however, still an attractive vehicle for fundraising. With the inherent drama of competing bids winding higher and higher, auctions provided several elements that appealed to collectors: an art-related entertainment, the thrill of the chase, and the potential for owning a unique object. Burnished with the virtue of raising funds for a worthy cause, charity auctions led the development of the secondary market for studio glass. By adding the charitable aspect to the equation (and the inducement of a tax benefit), modest hammer prices could be construed as no threat to the still wobbly retail market.

On April 10, 1989, Christie's held an auction of studio glass entitled "Masterworks of Contemporary Glass" to benefit the New York Experimental Glass Workshop (later UrbanGlass) in Brooklyn, New York. Eighty-nine pieces of contemporary work were offered and the auction was accompanied by a full-color catalogue. The idea had been proposed by William Warmus, formerly the curator of contemporary glass at the Corning Museum of Glass and at the time the editor of *New Work*, a glass magazine, and the sale was managed by Dan Klein, an opera singer-turned-modern-glass-dealer who had formerly been the director of twentieth-century decorative arts for Christie's in London.[25] A collector of mid-century, high-end production glass and studio glass, Klein first auctioned studio glass through Christie's London in the 1980s. Although this was not mentioned in the glowing introduction to the catalogue, the idea was initially met some resistance from Nancy McClelland of Christie's New York: "it would be over my dead body," she said, that Christie's would sell glass on Park Avenue.[26]

Nonetheless, the sale proceeded, with interesting results. A piece by the Italian studio glassmaker Gianni Tosi sold for twenty-six thousand dollars, twice the retail price for his work. It turned out that it was the last of a series and two collectors wanted it to complete their holdings. Another work, *Buddha* (1988), by the German artist Erwin Eisch exceeded its estimate of between four and five thousand dollars and sold for sixty-two hundred dollars to Marilyn Glick, who subsequently donated it to the Indianapolis Museum of Art. This price was achieved in part because Eisch's work was relatively scarce on the American market, and because he was associated with the high-art Spur group in Munich and had helped to found the related Radama group.[27] In contrast, works by Harvey Littleton and David Huchthausen sold well below their estimates, which made collectors concerned that their beloved glass would turn out to be an unwise financial investment.

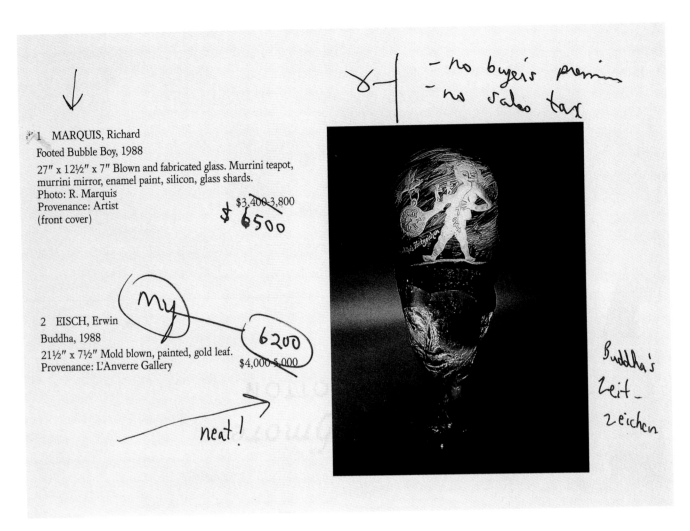

Handwritten annotations on the catalogue page:

— no buyer's premi[um]
— no sales tax

1 MARQUIS, Richard
Footed Bubble Boy, 1988
27" x 12½" x 7" Blown and fabricated glass. Murrini teapot, murrini mirror, enamel paint, silicon, glass shards.
Photo: R. Marquis
Provenance: Artist
(front cover)
$3,400-3,800
$6500

my

2 EISCH, Erwin
Buddha, 1988
21½" x 7½" Mold blown, painted, gold leaf.
Provenance: L'Anverre Gallery
$4,000-5,000
6200

neat!

Buddha's Zeit-zeichen

Page from catalogue of auction held by Christie's in New York, April 10, 1989. Pictured is *Buddha*, 1988, by Erwin Eisch (German, b. 1927), with original auction notes by Barry Shifman, the curator of decorative arts at the Indianapolis Museum of Art. Exceeding the estimate, Eisch's piece was bought for $6,200 by Marilyn Glick, who subsequently donated it to the Indianapolis Museum of Art (1989.56)

Despite the results, Christie's continued to auction glass but chose to change the manner in which it was presented.[28] On October 4, 1989, the firm held an auction of "The Martin and Jean Mensch Collection of Contemporary Glass," which was included as part of a sale of contemporary paintings, drawings, and sculpture. This practice of placing studio glass in among other contemporary artworks became the custom and it seemingly conferred high-art status to studio glass.[29] The results of this sale were good, but the art market suffered a recession beginning in 1990, and demand for all contemporary arts decreased. Even though studio glass had not proved to be a money maker, the large, international urban auction houses did not completely abandon it. In 1995 Dan Klein expressed his faith in the future of the secondary market: "Its going to be a great market, but the question is when. I may not be around to see it."[30]

STUDIO GLASS PERIODICALS, 1975–1990

As the market for studio glass grew so did the market for periodicals about it. Several magazines devoted to studio glass were founded between 1975 and 1990. These joined the available gallery announcements, dealer catalogues, and museum exhibition catalogues, but were distinctive in providing a steadier stream of information. Magazines also presented dealers with a vehicle in which to publish glossy color images of their wares, thereby contributing to the commodification of glass.

The earliest craft magazines were aimed at practitioners and provided how-to advice rather than discussions about content or aesthetics. By the early 1970s, however, glass had inspired a group of specialized publications. *Glass Arts Magazine* (renamed *Glass* in 1977) was founded in 1973. Presented as a bimonthly,

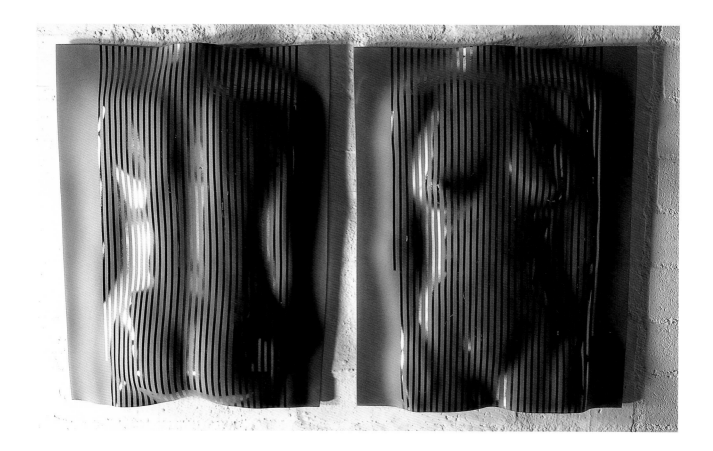

Torso Series, ca. 1980s. John Gilbert Luebtow (United States, b. 1944). Kiln-formed and etched glass; 26 x 19 x 4 inches. Collection of the artist.

the first issues were produced by the glassmaker Albert Lewis from his studio in Oakland, California. Offering a comprehensive range of technical information, the magazine promoted communication among glass artists and provides evidence of the close relationships between teachers and practitioners and of the primary concern with technique that marked the early years of the movement. In 1977 the magazine initiated the Fragile Art competition and attracted six hundred entries. But, by 1980 the number of submissions for the competition had fallen to one hundred and seventy-five, indicating that other outlets for glass artists had developed. By 1983 the publication, which had described itself as "the art magazine that's readable," ceased publication.[31]

Another magazine, *Glass Studio*, devoted to studio production and the current technical accomplishments of glass, first appeared in 1978 and continued intermittently until 1983. A third periodical, *New Work*, was published by the New York Experimental Glass Workshop (later named UrbanGlass). First issued in 1980 (and renamed *Glass* in 1990—but with no connection with Albert Lewis's *Glass* magazine), it mirrored the increasing art ambitions of the field and focused on aesthetic issues. As the publication arm of an urban glass studio that offered classes to professional glassmakers, it provides a record of the tensions between the high-art world and the glassmaking community.

Still being published is the quarterly, bilingual *Neues Glas*, which is available by subscription in the United States (it is published in Germany and distributed by German Languages Publications of New Jersey). Most articles are (partially) translated into English, but they offer a useful way to compare the work of American glass artists with that produced by Europeans who have a longer history of glassmaking. During the 1980s the magazine was edited by Dr. Helmut Ricke, a noted German glass scholar and curator at the Düsseldorf Museum, who brought his own rigorous academic standards to bear on it. Read by artists and collectors alike, *Neues Glas* offers a reasoned perspective that helped to balance the less-sophisticated writing found at that time in the American studio community. With its high standards of critical analysis, it continues the

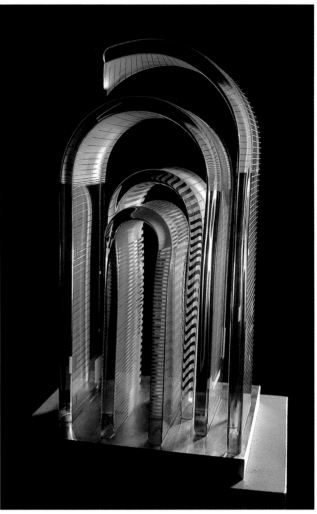

Series Crystalex-Hantich #11, 1982. Marvin Lipofsky (United States, b. 1938). Blown glass; 12 x 16 inches.

Glass Sculpture, 1983. John Gilbert Luebtow (United States, b. 1944). Kiln-formed and etched glass; 22 x 12 x 12 inches. Collection of Ruth T. Summers.

long-standing European, and particularly German, interest in historical glass, and by extension, contemporary glass.

In 1987 a periodical created specifically for collectors of studio glass collectors emerged. *Glass Focus* is still the official newsletter of the Art Alliance for Contemporary Glass, an association of collectors. Sporting no lavish pictures or advertising and presenting no scholarly perspective, the newsletter, which runs to between eighteen and twenty pages, carries primarily extensive listings of galleries (which pay for being included) and verbatim interviews with artists, collectors, and dealers. Articles in *Glass Focus* concentrate on collectors and established artists—those most likely to be included in the collections of the association's members. Initially available by subscription only, it is now a benefit of membership in the Art Alliance. It is given free of charge

to museum curatorial staff who indicate an interest in adding contemporary glass to their collections.[32]

Although these publications often had color photographs, advertisements for galleries, and articles about artists, few attempted to place glass within a critical framework. With text limited to biography, description, and technical information, they provided beautiful pictures and little theorizing. All of these magazines were available only by subscription and, hence, were not widely accessible to the general public, which relies on newsstands for its reading material.

Beginning in 1976 the Glass Art Society published *The Glass Art Society Newsletter* to document the activities of its annual conferences. An important publication, the newsletter was renamed *The Glass Art Society Journal* in 1979.[33] As studio glass-making became more sophisticated, the *Journal*'s emphasis on

Lillies of the Valley PWV 034 (from the Paperweight Vase series), 1976. Mark Peiser (United States, b. 1938). Blown and cased glass; 8 ½ inches high, 5 inches in diameter. Indianapolis Museum of Art, gift of Marilyn and Eugene Glick (IMA 2000.64)

technical knowledge and the review of educational programs gradually gave way to discussions of the interrelationships among art, craft, and design. The *Journal* continues today and is a primary resource for dealers, collectors, and curators.

CROSSOVERS FROM GLASS TO HIGH ART

When established artists chose to work with glass, and thus temporarily joined the studio glass world, and a select few glass artists moved into the purview of the high-art galleries, the commodification of glass art was spurred and its presumed validity as an art medium confirmed.

For the established artists, the use of glass was predicated mainly on its optical features. Artists such as Vito Acconci, Nicolas Africano, Larry Bell, Lynda

Benglis, Laddie John Dill, Donald Lipski, Italo Scanga, John Torreano, James Turrell, and Christopher Wilmarth, among others, have used glass both with other media and by itself,[34] but they cannot be classified as studio glass artists because they only visited the medium, as it were, and relied upon others for fabrication. Their identity as artists does not lie within glass or the studio community. Nonetheless, their use of glass hastened its acceptance as an art medium. This crossing over to glass even briefly introduced the notion that the boundary between glass and high art was permeable and spawned the idea that studio glass artists could cross the other way into the realm of high art—which they did.

The first steps occurred when these visitors approached the glass community in order to acquire a better understanding of how to work with the medium and how to appreciate its expressive potential. Nicolas Africano, Laddie John Dill, Donald Lipski, John Torreano, and James Turrell attended workshops on glass-forming technology held at Pilchuck Glass School. Christopher Wilmarth was a second-session artist-in-residence at Pilchuck in 1984, as was Lynda Benglis in 1984 and 1985, when she explored the production of glass knots using cast glass (see page 154). Larry Bell, Donald Lipski, and Italo Scanga, among others, attended Glass Art Society conferences and made presentations at them.[35]

Fewer glass artists made the journey in the other direction, from the studio world to the high-art world, but the attempts were more significant. Between 1975 and 1990 the most visible traveler was Dale Chihuly. Chihuly's acceptance in the high-art world was signaled when he began to be represented by the Charles Cowles Gallery, New York. Cowles had been born in Los Angeles and had been exposed to modern art from an early age though his father, Gardener Cowles, who was a trustee at the Museum of Modern Art in New York for thirty years. After studying journalism at Stanford University, Cowles landed a job at the new high-art magazine, *Artforum*. After moving the magazine to Los Angeles in 1965 and then to New York in 1967, Cowles learned much about the contemporary art scene from his friendship with Leo Castelli, the legendary New York high-art dealer.

Ocean-Linear Beach-Grass (from the
Oceanic series), 1979. Dan Dailey
(United States, b. 1947). Glass
blown, sandblasted, acid-polished,
and cast; 11½ x 10 ⅝ x 5 ¾
inches. Racine Art Museum, gift of
the Brillson Foundation in memory of
Michael Baer Brillson (1995.113)

After ten years at the magazine, Cowles was persuaded to take a job as founding curator of the modern department at the Seattle Art Museum. Completing a five-year stint with the museum, he returned to New York and took over André Emmerich's former gallery space at 420 West Broadway. With his credentials established in the world of museums and collectors and in the community of dealers and critics, Cowles had sufficient standing to introduce art made of unsanctified materials to the high-art world of Manhattan.

His choice of Chihuly as the centerpiece of his move into glass was understandable; a rising star, Chihuly was easily the best known of the studio glass artists. His appealing color-saturated works and his own aggressive marketing of them revealed him to be an artist with compelling talent, a flair for showmanship, and high-art ambitions.[36] Also, while at the Seattle Art Museum, Cowles had worked with Chihuly during the course of curating an exhibition, *Carpenter, Chihuly, Scanga 1977,* of the artist's work, along with that of Italo Scanga and Jamie Carpenter. Easily matching Chihuly's ambition, Cowles championed his work and quickly charged between twenty-five and thirty thousand dollars for Chihuly's table-sized pieces and more for his larger works. By showing the glass alongside painting and sculpture and asking such prices, Cowles moved Chihuly across the boundary that separated glass from high-art. Cowles went further (and differentiated himself from other glass galleries) by avoiding the word *glass* in exhibition titles, substituting instead *sculpture,* a strategy he also used for exhibitions of work by Howard Ben Tré.[37]

Chihuly's introduction to the New York high-art world in the mid-1980s moved glass to another level, placing it on a par with painting and sculpture and garnering for it notice in the high-art press—even though, in fact the press was more interested in the gallery than the glass. The combined status of Chihuly and Cowles created the success of both. In time well-respected art critics (such as Carter Ratcliff and Kim Levin, among others) would write for glass-centered magazines such as *New Work* and Robert Silberman would review studio glass exhibitions. All of this gave currency to the belief that glass could and should be included within the high-art universe.

Other benefits flowed from these crossovers. They helped to attract an audience for glass that was different from the one that frequented studio glass galleries. These collectors were accustomed to paying higher prices for artwork and were comfortable with large-scale pieces. They were also less likely to be seduced by the inherent physical properties of glass.

Much of Chihuly's appeal to the high-art world lay in the fact that his work could, apparently, be linked to that of artists who were already accepted. Henry Geldzahler, the curator of twentieth century art at the Metropolitan Museum of Art, placed Chihuly within the American color field school of painting and connected his work to the "veils of Morris Louis, the chevrons and stripes of Kenneth Noland, and the large stained chromatic landscapes of Helen Frankenthaler."[38] These connections were useful to Chihuly, but were not without a price for studio glass as a whole.

When glass is validated in terms usually reserved for painting and sculpture, it has then to conform to standards that discount its long history and essential materiality. If glass needed to play by the rules of painting and sculpture, it risked loosing its unique value. This was what Robert Silberman feared for glass as it eagerly adopted high-art marketing practices and sought commercial parity. The price for success seemed to require the suppression of its distinct identity as a medium.

NOTES

1. Patterson Sims, "Material Culture/Cultural Material: Parallels in American Arts and Crafts—1945 to the Present" (paper presented at the symposium *A Neglected History, Twentieth-Century American Craft*, American Craft Museum, 1990). The comment was made in reference to a photographer who had moved from the Light Gallery to Sidney Janis Gallery, New York City.

2. Ferdinand Hampson, "New Interest in Glass Sends Prices Soaring," *Glass Art Society Journal* (1981): 38–40.

3. Krystyna Warchol, "Artists Entering the Marketplace: Pricing New Art," in *On the Margins of the Art Worlds*, ed. Larry Gross (Boulder: Westview Press, 1995), 85.

4. Charles Cowles, quoted in Laura de Coppet and Alan Jones, eds., *The Art Dealers: The Powers Behind the Scene Tell How the Art World Really Works* (New York: Clarkson N. Potter, 1984), 248–49.

5. Wendy Rosen, "The Changing Marketplace for Glass," *Glass Art Society Journal* (1999): 85. In support of the fluctuating valuation of contemporary art, Diana Crane notes that "value is attributed entirely on the basis of evaluations of quality by experts, including critics, museum curators, and, to some extent, eminent collectors. However, the criteria which they use to evaluate quality change as styles change, and these evaluations are often inconsistent. The correlation between early evaluations of artworks and their eventual value can be very low. The early reviews of Abstract Expressionism were very poor although the Museum of Modern Art purchased some of these works as soon as they were shown. Within five years, the values of some of these paintings had more than tripled." Diana Crane, *The Transformation of the Avant-Garde: The New York Art World, 1940–1985* (Chicago: University of Chicago Press, 1987), 112.

6. Lois Moran, editor of *American Craft*; quoted in Davira S. Taragin, "Studio Craft Comes of Age," *Contemporary Crafts and the Saxe Collection* (New York: Hudson Hills Press and the Toledo Museum of Arts, 1993), 17.

7. Russell Lynes, *New Glass: A Worldwide Survey* (Corning, N. Y.: The Corning Museum of Glass, 1979), 25.

8. See R. Craig Miller, "Betwixt and Between: Contemporary Glass in American Art Museums," *Glass Art Society Journal* (1991): 30. Helen Drutt was an influential dealer in Philadelphia.

9. Tina Oldknow, *Pilchuck: A Glass School* (Seattle: Pilchuck and University of Washington Press, 1996), 166.

10. Ibid.

11. Robert Silberman, "Decorative Arts 'Americans in Glass': A Requiem?" *Art in America* 73, no. 3 (March 1985): 52.

12. Ibid., 47–53.

13. Marcia and Tom Manhart, eds., *The Eloquent Object: The Evolution of American Art in Craft Media since 1945*, exh. cat. Philbrook Museum of Art, Tulsa, Okla. (Seattle: University of Washington Press, 1987).

14. The artists were Hank Murta Adams, Howard Ben Tré, Dale Chihuly, David Huchthausen, Kreg Kallenberger, Dominick Labino, Marvin Lipofsky, Harvey Littleton, Tom Patti, Richard Posner, Mary Shaffer, and Therman Statom—the leading glass artists of the day.

15. Derek Guthrie, "'The Eloquent Object' Gagged by Kitsch," *New Art Examiner* 16, no. 1 (September 1988): 26. Guthrie uses the Greenbergian cudgel of "kitsch" to deny the validity of crafts as an art medium. Indeed, other articles in the issue were devoted to deflating the potential for clay as an art medium.

16. A catalogue of this type documents the items that are part of the permanent collection of a museum. In contrast, exhibition catalogues present a thesis about a set of works, either owned by the museum or on loan to it for this purpose. Frantz's book stands in sharp contrast to Dan Klein's *Glass: A Contemporary Art* (New York: Rizzoli, 1989), which contains factual errors, does not recognize the role of the proto-studio glassmakers, and includes unattributed photography pirated from private collectors and museums. As is typical of early documentation of art phenomena, neither author applies a theoretical methodology, choosing instead to present a transparent history.

17. Diana Crane writes that "after that period, auction sales of these works became much more frequent. . . . Pop, Minimalist, Photorealist, and Figurative artists whose dealers were among the eleven leading gatekeeper galleries were more likely than other artists to have had works sold in the auction market." See Crane, *Transformation of the Avant-Garde*, 115.

18. Another method of purchasing art involves direct commissions. In an often intricate arrangement, the client contacts the artist (usually through the artist's dealer) to establish what the general form of a finished piece would take. After agreeing, the artist then produces the work. A number of studio glass pieces have been commissioned. Anne and Ronald Abramson, who are private collectors in Washington, D.C., underwrote the commissioning of architectural elements and sculpture that they then lent to public and private venues. Dan Dailey designed and fabricated a complete dining room suite with room panels, a table, and chairs for Bernie and Mimi West of Los Angeles under the guidance of Ruth Summers. Institutions have also commissioned pieces. The Los Angeles County Museum of Art commissioned a chair from Therman Statom in 1987, funding it with a grant from the museum's Black American Artists Fund (see page 122). By 1977 the process was sufficiently widespread to warrant publication in the *Glass Art Society Newsletter* of an attorney-authored sample "commission agreement" between artist and collector. See Michael C. Skindrud, "Legal Problems and Protection for the Artist," *Glass Art Society Newsletter* 2, no. 1 (1977): 14–27.

19. Karen S. Chambers, "Secondary Market: Going, Going, Gone or Coming, Coming, Coming?" *Neues Glas* 4 (fall 1995): 42–43.

20. Ibid., 47.

21. Oldknow, *Pilchuck*, 167. In time the Pilchuck auction would become a major event and a reliable source of funds for the school.

22. Chambers, "Secondary Market," 43.

23. Ibid.

24. See Susanne K. Frantz, "The Evolution of Studio Glass Collecting and Documentation in the United States," in Davira Taragin, ed., *Contemporary Crafts and the Saxe Collection* (Toledo: Toledo Museum of Art and Hudson Hills Press, 1993), 21–89.

25. Dan Klein pegs the beginning of the commercialization of crafts to the successful sale of work by the ceramists Hans Coper and Lucie Rie in London in 1986. This opened up the notion that craft-based works could demand prices similar to those seen for paintings and sculpture. Dan Klein, "Buying New Glass the Second Time Around," *Glass Art Society Journal* (1987): 32–36.

26. Chambers, "Secondary Market," 44.

27. Holding that capitalism produces consumers who do not actively participate in public life, the Spur group thrived between 1957 and 1972 in Europe. Radama was aligned with the Movement for an Imagist Bauhaus. See Martha Drexler Lynn, *Masters of Contemporary Glass: Selections from the Glick Collection* (Indianapolis: Hudson Hills and the Indianapolis Museum of Art, 1997), 60–62, and passim.

28. In 1992 Sotheby's New York entered the glass market under the guidance of Barbara Deisroth, who believed it was a slowly developing market that would mature in ten or fifteen years. Christie's Guzman included glasswork in contemporary art sales, but she sold only the work of established glass artists who have crossed over and are familiar to collectors of contemporary paintings and sculpture. Studio glass has also been presented either in contemporary art sales or in decorative arts sales. Habatat Gallery also organized three auction sales, the first in 1994 with 90 percent of the lots consisting of work from the 1970s and 1980s.

29. Barry Shifman, conversation, 1995.

Included in this auction was an early studio piece by Joel Philip Myers entitled *Dr. Zarkhov's Tower* (1971), which was purchased by the Glicks for the Indianapolis Museum of Art.

30. Chambers, "Secondary Market,"49. Since 1990 the auction market has produced some good results. The cast-glass *Head I* (1957–1958) by the Czech glass artists Stanislav Libenský and Jaroslava Brychtová sold at Sotheby's in February 1994 for $14,950. Thirteen months later, in March 1995, it was auctioned again for $20,700.

Several years earlier the Heller Gallery had offered the work for $200.

31. Frantz, "Evolution of Studio Glass Collecting," 28.

32. The newsletter is written and edited by Beverly M. Copeland from her home in Morton Grove, Illinois. Originally named *The North Shore Studio Glass Newsletter,* the publication became affiliated with the Art Alliance for Contemporary Glass within a few months of its first issue and changed its name.

The Art Alliance for Contemporary Glass also provides financial support for museum exhibition brochures and eventually came to underwrite the biannual "Glassweekend" in the glass-factory town of Millville, New Jersey, where gallery personnel, collectors, and artists come together for a three-day conference: Potential purchasers meet the artists, have the opportunity to see them work, and can buy artworks from the big-name glass galleries. This event intended to bring the three components of the glass community together shows a sophisticated understanding of the relationships among the marketplace, collectors (public and private), and the artists.

Three important factors should be noted in relation to the Art Alliance for Contemporary Glass: The glass collecting communities in Ohio and Chicago were the first to organize themselves, the Alliance defines itself as an art society, and only established glass artists are featured in *Glass Focus*.

33. This is not to be confused with the *Journal of Glass History* published by the Corning Museum of Glass, which deals exclusively with historical glass.

34. Other artists who have used glass include Josef Albers, Arman, Alexander Calder, Joseph Cornell, Salvador Dalí, Marcel Duchamp, Felix Droese, Lucio Fontana, Barbara Hepworth, Wassily Kandinsky, Mario Merz, Henry Moore, Meret Oppenheim, Lucas Samaras, Robert Smithson, DeWain Valentine, and David Smith. In an astonishing stretch, the American Craft Museum even claims that Jackson Pollock worked in glass, the evidence being a single photograph taken by Hans Namuth Newton of Pollock painting on plate glass.

35. See James Turrell, "Light in Space," *Glass Art Society Journal* (1983–1984): 5–10; Melinda Wortz, "Larry Bell," *Glass Art Society Journal* (1986): 58–61; Neil Goodman, "Vito Acconci," *Glass Art Society Journal* (1986): 118.

36. Donald Kuspit, *Chihuly* (New York: Abrams, 1997).

37. At the time Howard Ben Tré was the only other artist to have crossed over into the high-art world by joining the Charles Cowles Gallery. Tom Patti, Dan Dailey, and Paul Stankard would eventually find high-art gallery representation.

38. As quoted in Kuspit, *Chihuly*, 42

Chapter 8

*Private and Public Patronage—
Displaying a Passion for Glass*

Glass appeals to the cool instincts of librarians, curators and collectors. The hermetic display case that seals in the objects, the glossy exhibition catalogue, the exclusive conference: all conspire to elevate, conserve, and purify the objects. Glass also appeals to hot, rough, intense personalities, to artists who sweat before the furnace. To collectors and writers who love argument and intrigue and cutting deals.[1]

—William Warmus

Chair on Base, 1987. Therman Statom (United States, b. 1953). Plate glass, paint, and blown elements; 58 x 24 x 26 inches. Los Angeles County Museum of Art, Black American Artists Fund (M 87.174a-b)

T HE CREATION OF A COMMUNITY of patrons dedicated to the advancement of the American studio glass movement was the second major achievement of the 1980s. Coinciding with the expansion of a network of dealers, the emergent collecting community comprised three distinct groups: private individuals, curators employed by public institutions, and corporations that owned collections, this last a blend of the private and the public.

All collectors, private or public, select from the same pool of works, but the criteria they use to make acquisitions differ; thus each glass collection is clearly distinguishable and has contributed in its own way to the increased acceptance of the medium.[2] Privately held studio glass collections preceded the development of public collections and the collectors at once resemble and differ from collectors of other forms of art. Their distinctive qualities have driven them to interact assertively with one another and with the validating institutions, creating a strong support base for glass and advancing its acceptance as an art form.

STUDIO GLASS COLLECTORS

The function of craft in this stage of the twentieth-century ought not to be the silly caperings after exaggerated effects of quasi-art funded by the ignorance of the nouveau riches anxious to become collectors.[3]
—Peter Dormer

The drive to collect is universal and is found in all cultures and all social strata. Consequently, the literature analyzing this impulse is extensive.[4] A. Deirdre Robson, the historian, observed that "the main reasons for collecting art are characteristically, status (whether involving social distinction or sociocultural conformity), cultural esteem or cultural capital (whether from connoisseurship or from association with "difficult" art forms), conspicuous consumption, decoration, investment and speculation, vicarious creativity and, finally, the more nebulous ideas of excitement, love of beauty or pleasure."[5] When applied to studio glass collectors, Robson's reasons can be distilled to yield five principal motivations: the desire for status (cultural capital), the wish to accumulate unique and opulent objects for domestic decoration (enjoyment of conspicuous consumption), the hope for increased monetary value (investment growth), the pursuit of excitement, and the "love of beauty or pleasure" derived from the activity itself and the works collected.[6] Robson omits mention of two other motivations that are crucial to the character of the studio glass community: the preference for contemporary (rather than historical) art forms and the desire to participate in the social life that unites glass collectors, artists, dealers, and institutional experts. These seven elements are clearly manifest in the activities of studio glass collectors and shape their interaction with the material.

As a general rule collectors of studio glass are middle-aged, married couples of significant means; usually they are self-made or the first generation to have inherited money.[7] The community boasts more Jewish people than people of other cultural groups. Collecting behaviors can be traced in many cases to childhood, and the move into glass generally occurs in the middle years when parenting obligations have receded and financial resources are secure.[8] Drawn from the college-educated, professional classes (lawyers, doctors, business executives, and so on), the glass-collecting couple typically elects to enter the field together as a shared leisure-time activity.

Their preference is for contemporary art. Studio glass, with its minimal theoretical underpinnings is well suited to those for whom historical material holds few attractions.[9] This preference is related to the inherent decorative potential of studio glass and the fact that it can be appreciated absent an understanding of historical precedents or the complexities of art history

and critical theory. This affinity for contemporary art over the historical can even be seen in "the way an individual handles glass . . . using both hands, tense under white gloves, and with infinite care; or lifting the object with outstretched hand in order to freely encourage a visitor to touch and explore. One attitude lives in and for the past, the other in the now."[10]

Because studio glass is a contemporary medium, collecting it requires only the ability to select the reputed best from an ever-changing array of newly fabricated works. This ability is more closely related to fashion-driven decisions than to the scholarship and connoisseurship associated with old master paintings. The narrow class of potential collectibles provides an immediacy that connects collectors to the work as an expression of something new and fresh, rather than old and venerated. As Dianne Sachko Macleod has noted, "the middle class propensity for buying the more easily understandable art by living artists" wins over the demands of historical material.[11] This predilection for contemporary material is clearly evident within the studio glass collecting community.

In order to join the community of collectors, several basic criteria must be met. First, prospective collectors need ample discretionary income to support the purchase of several works each year—a commitment of between fifty and one hundred thousand dollars annually. Second, to expand their knowledge and increase their holdings, they need to have the time and funds to travel to relevant museum exhibitions, conferences, and galleries. Serious collectors need to travel to as many glass-related exhibitions and events as possible and make regular visits to glass galleries across the country. Third, they must be willing to cultivate dealers, artists, and, eventually, museum personnel.

Sociable collectors often provide links between the gallery (marketplace provider), the museum (validating institution), and themselves (collectors as consumers). These links often lead to another of the collectors' functions: lending works from their collections to local and national exhibitions and opening their homes to visiting collectors and museum groups and sometimes hosting events for local museums.

Collectors are influenced—especially in a new field such as studio glass—by the galleries from which they

Sailing to Byzantium, 1986. Kéké Cribbs (United States, b. 1951). Sandblasted glass, gold leaf, wood, paint, pâpier mâché; 18 ¹³/₁₆ x 17 ⁷/₈ x ⁵/₈ inches, and 11½ x 29 ¹/₈ x 7 inches. Los Angeles County Museum of Art, gift of Maxine Mayo (M.90.9a-b)

purchase work. As in any emerging field, dealers train public and private collectors alike. This powerful position is a phenomenon found in all contemporary art circles, where bringing new talent to the marketplace (a gatekeeper function) is paramount. The resulting concentration of power within the selecting and marketing arm contributes to the several distinctive qualities manifest in the private and public collections of American studio glass.

The first motive for collecting of studio glass, the desire for cultural capital (status and prestige), is problematic, for although dealers and collectors lead the campaign to include glass in the high-art world, its position is tenuous.[12] Consequently, studio glass collec-

tors are by definition risk takers, and this in itself contributes a layer of cultural esteem beyond that attained from the collecting of other, already sanctified media. It should be noted that risk taking is not a trait usually associated with the middle class, but here the risk (again, ironically, related to the medium and not to the content of the art) places the studio glass collector on the cutting edge of the avant-garde. Consequently, the interest and passion for glass is transformed into evidence of perspicacity and bravery. All of these elements enhance the collector's personal cultural capital.

Meanwhile, the desire to display wealth through conspicuous consumption tugs collectors in a more mundane direction. Most glass collectors are married, and they display their collections in their homes, presenting thoughtfully constructed domestic interiors that showcase the glass. Evidence of this construction is seen in display practices where upscale and stylish residential furniture and objects are paired with elements borrowed from museums. The result is a domestic space coded with both social and cultural signs: the domestic coffee table boasts a Littleton, and the museum pedestals and vitrines flanking the designer sofa present Chihulys and Labinos. Bookcases have usually been taken over by glass and books moved to another, less central location. The domestic furniture implies intimacy, but the reverential strategies and museumlike structures establish an intentional distance between the viewer and object, underscoring high valuation, both monetary and social.[13] Expressive of what Macleod calls the "worship of art," this approach is typical of new, middle-class collectors, who present their artworks in domestic "private art galleries (some of which resemble the interiors of churches) [that] refer to the preeminent position held by art in society."[14] The collector's home is thereby transformed into a cultural-capital factory, uniting everyday life with art and status in the setting of a designed, middle-class home.[15]

Despite the domesticated setting, however, studio glass collecting is motivated in part by the desire for excitement, the thrill of the chase, the competitive aspect that animates the locating and procuring of the best. The competition is intensified by the small size of the community. Relative position is measured by the quality (often determined by the dollar amount paid) and frequency of acquisitions. Prestige is awarded to those who exhibit insight (the early purchase of an up-and-coming artist or selection of what comes to be acknowledged as the best of a given artist's current run), display cunning and the ability to negotiate (securing additional discounts from dealers), and receive extra attention from knowledgeable curatorial and other institutional staff. The early acquisition of work by important artists—purchased for a reasonable price—coupled with a genial phone call from the local curator or museum director signals success within the community.[16] The excitement is enhanced by retellings of collecting trials and triumphs: meeting the artist, getting to a first-name basis with leading dealers, negotiating purchases, and access to regular curatorial help, even for solving problems of display and shipping.

The desire for pleasure or beauty, derived from objects is, however, the most powerful, and complicated motive for the studio glass collector. Glass collectors—whether collecting ancient or contemporary glass—universally describe in glowing terms the visual impact that glass has on them. Indeed, it is this that initially ignites their passion for the medium, often to the exclusion of the merit of the work. The intense visual experience of glass, referred to by collectors and artists loosely as "its beauty" or the "wow factor," has little parallel in other crafts (or contemporary high arts). Interviews, articles, and museum catalogues are replete with passionate statements from collectors about the beauty of glass and their attraction to it. When describing the acquisition of his first piece of studio glass, the president of a leading West Coast university remembered with glowing eyes that it was "when [he and his wife] walked into the shop . . . it was so beautiful, [we] had to buy it!"[17] Similarly, a collector in northern California remembers that he "had never seen such colors before nor such forms, all made from such ordinary material."[18] This enchantment affects artists, too. Michael Taylor notes that "glass is rarely the vehicle, the medium, for thoughtful reflection. The sheer physical challenge of making anything in glass too frequently triumphs over content."[19] This attraction to the material of glass establishes a bond between the collector and the work that places understanding second to emotional response.[20]

The social interactions entailed in studio glass collecting also contribute to "pleasure—defined in a number of ways." The small, self-selected, upscale, risk-taking, glass-smitten community provides an interesting and consuming round of activities. One couple discovered studio glass and came to "love" the artwork and enjoy the company of the artists and collectors associated with it. Glass proved so compelling that they joined in all aspects of the community from assembling a collection to participating as gaffers at glass events. In time they became officers in one of the national studio glass collectors groups. For them studio glass provided a community of shared interests, a leisure-time activity (commensurate with their financial resources), and augmented status. The social pleasure of the glass collecting community helps to knit it into a formidable force.

Glass collectors, however, display at least one characteristic that separates them from other collectors:

September Cactus, 1987. Flo Perkins (United States, b. 1951). Blown and assembled glass; 17 x 12 x 7 inches. Racine Art Museum, gift of Dale and Doug Anderson (1994.128)

Leitungs Scherbe LS 282, 1982. David Huchthausen (United States, b. 1951). Sheet glass, Vitrolite, and agate glass blocks; 11 x 16 1/2 x 11 3/8 inches. Toledo Museum of Art, gift of Dorothy and George Saxe.

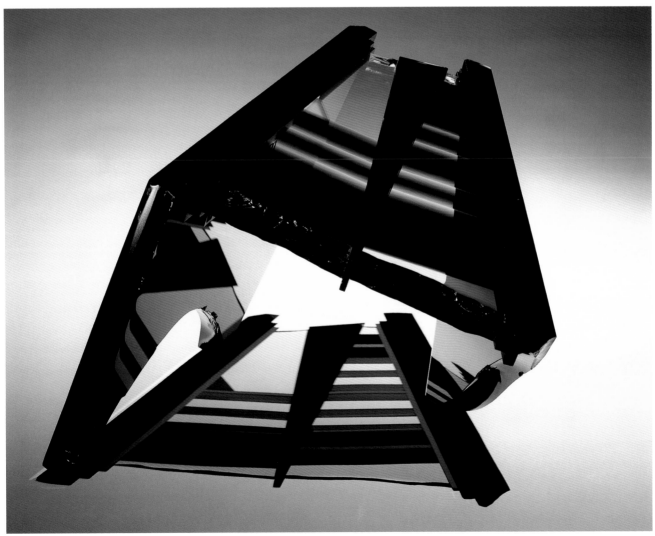

they are overtly ambitious for their medium. They feel keenly that glass is undervalued by the high-art world, and they have often turned their commitment to the medium into a focused and effective campaign for the acceptance of glass as a high-art medium. The concern (and irritation) about the valuing of glass is seen in a communiqué sent to glass collectors on the West Coast:

> We may not be doing something as important as cancer research or giving shelter to the homeless, but as far as art is concerned, Studio Art Glass [*sic*] is an incredible new movement in the art world and should be recognized and represented by the finest museums. . . . It is important that contemporary glass should not be dismissed by the so-called elite of the art world (that follow each other like sheep) as craft.[21]

The attitude seems tinged with embarrassment about "not doing something as important as cancer research" but, clearly feeling the limited acceptance for their chosen medium by the high-art world to be the result of snobbery, astute glass collectors embarked on an attempt, the like of which has never been under-

taken in the service of other craft media, to change the status of their medium, proselytizing aggressively for recognition from the art press and critics and for representation in museum collections. One leading group in this crusade is the Art Alliance for Contemporary Glass, an association of several hundred collectors who are devoted to glass and desire its recognition by the high-art world as a full-fledged art medium. With many members drawn from the most successful ranks of American business and well connected to museum boards, the alliance has not been shy in promoting glass as an important art medium whenever it could.

Two of the leaders, Dale and Doug Anderson, took the time to research and observe the mechanisms of cultural validation and apply them to glass. To that end they (and other members) employ several strategies to encourage increased appreciation of glass. One includes inveigling curators who show an inclination toward glass, along with selected journalists and critics, to attend the biannual "Glass Lovers Weekend" at the Creative Glass Center of America in Millville, New Jersey, the site of a nineteenth-century glass factory and museum of glass artifacts. The event permits curators to interact with their colleagues, to meet dealers, who are accompanied by their wares for sale, and collectors, who might donate to their collections, and to see studio glass without cost to themselves or to their institutions. As an additional attraction, curators are often invited to participate in résumé-building colloquia and to give presentations about their collections. As curatorial success is measured by ongoing acquisitions and expanding areas of expertise, this strategy has produced an increased interest in studio glass, even among curators who did not previously have active acquisition programs for crafts. The experience increases the curators' awareness of glass as an art medium and gives collectors access to the institutions and the staff responsible for validating their artworks.

PRIVATE COLLECTING

From 1975 until 1990 the collecting community grew rapidly as those who had assembled modest collections were joined by those with larger ambitions. Two additional categories of private collectors emerged during this period: the artist-collector and the blue-chip collector. Artist-collectors—artists who accumulate works made by their colleagues— are few in number.[22] An example of this style of collecting may be seen in the activities of the past director of a crafts school near Asheville, North Carolina, who amassed a collection of studio glass made by artists who came to work at his institution from the mid-1960s until his retirement in the early 1980s.[23] Although it was not formed with public display in mind, the collection was exhibited at Western Carolina University, Cullowhee, North Carolina, in 1984. Harvey Littleton also acquired pieces by artists who worked with him on his intaglio glass prints. Naturally, this very personal type of collection does not express a formalized collecting vision, nor, given the friendship-based nature of these assemblages, does it necessarily reflect a cool, discriminating eye.[24] Inclusion in such a collection is not generally listed on an artist's résumé; it does, however, provide an important internal validation from one artist to another.

The blue-chip collector combines passion for the medium, ample resources, and, most importantly, high-

art ambitions. It is collectors of this sort who proved to be effective proselytizers for glass. Gathering works by well-known glassmakers, purchased from the leading dealers across the country and in Europe, blue-chip collectors worked aggressively to win greater exposure for glass and eventually museum validation.[25]

The blue-chip collections of this period tended to resemble one another in size, motivation, and the artists represented. Generally comprising more than a hundred pieces of glass by the noted glassmakers of the period, they exemplify new money placed at the service of compelling personal goals and focused on new artistic expression. Ample financial resources teamed with newly acquired art expertise meant that blue-chip collectors learned as they went, taking advantage of the small size of the glass community and the unformed nature of the marketplace. This pioneering spirit turned out to be a virtue in the new field of American studio glass and helped compel its acceptance by the high-art world.

Typical of emerging blue-chip glass collectors were a couple in northern California who had profited from various business ventures and investments. They turned to collecting glass (and eventually other crafts) when it was suggested by a counselor as a way to ameliorate tensions in their marriage.[26] Craft had already exerted a hold over the woman; she later remarked that she was attracted to craft because she liked the "handmade objects—things you can touch and fondle and hold."[27] After seeing *Young Americans: Clay / Glass* (1978) and the Corning Museum of Glass exhibition *New Glass: A Worldwide Survey* (1979), the couple purchased the first glass piece, which they candidly admit "was acquired as a decorative accessory."[28] For them glass (along with their other craft-based holdings) initially filled three needs: for a shared leisure activity, a source of decoration for their home, and an expression of their material success.

In the brief span of two years they acquired more than 150 works by 70 American and European glass artists. They said of their collaborative process, we did "things very intuitively. Sometimes we can't explain why we like things. It gets us by the guts."[29] Here a sense of pleasure coupled with the direct visual appeal of glass cemented the connection between the collector

Spotlit Bowl (from the Profiles and Silhouettes series), 1982. Margie Jervis (United States, b. 1956) and Susie Krasnican (United States, b. 1954). Plate glass and enamel; 9 1/4 x 19 1/2 x 9 1/2 inches. Toledo Museum of Art, gift of Dorothy and George Saxe (1991.96)

right: *Sentinel III*, 1985. K. William LeQuier (United States, b. 1953). Plate and blown glass; 17 1/16 x 18 5/8 x 6 inches. Toledo Museum of Art, gift of Dorothy and George Saxe.

and the work. Eventually, the desire to experience a continued rush from the acquisition of new work compelled them to branch out into other craft media, when they found it difficult to discover new glass artists.

Like other blue-chip collectors, they were not interested in forming a historically based collection to chronicle academically the development of American studio glass. Instead they chose to purchase widely from the newest works on display at the leading glass galleries, notably Heller in New York, Habatat in Michigan and Florida, and Kurland/Summers in Los Angeles. By following their visceral reaction, their passion for the medium, and the forceful lead of the urban glass galleries, they (and others like them) created what some describe as "a dealers' collection," consisting almost exclusively of the work of the artists represented by the high-level galleries they frequented. For collectors to discover new talent without going through the dealer and gallery system is almost impossible. Although their knowledge of glass and glassmakers deepened, the influence on their collection of "certain American dealers" was evident in the strong examples in the collection by Bertil Vallien and Ann Wolff from Sweden."[30]

Indeed, many blue-chip glass collectors are described as having "a kind of checklist—and checkbook—connoisseurship, using a major exhibition catalogue or standard history book as a guide to be strictly followed."[31] This is not unusual for a new collecting area, which has yet to establish independent norms for classifying work. Many collections could initially be described as dealer's collections, but, over time, the addition of artworks in other craft media such as textiles and jewelry indicated a maturation in the collectors' understanding and a greater willingness to make independent judgments. Also, because relatively few outlets presented studio glass and the pool of artists is small, it was understandable that collections of this period would be remarkably uniform. This occurs, too, in other craft media, but is especially pronounced in the case of studio glass. As independent judgments came to enliven the collections, the collectors grew more confident and sophisticated.

By the mid-1980s several blue-chip collectors had built collections prominent enough to warrant museum exhibitions. The George and Dorothy Saxe collection

was displayed in 1986 at the Oakland Museum in Oakland, California. Entitled *Contemporary American and European Glass from the Saxe Collection* and curated by Kenneth R. Trapp, it traveled to the American Craft Museum in New York. The accompanying sixty-four-page catalogue presented seductive color images and an essay that placed the works within the continuum of craft and glass history. This was one of the first exhibitions for which the work was properly documented and it garnered enthusiastic public response, making it clear that glass could bring crowds to museums.

As the blue-chip collections grew and incorporated other media, it became evident that the next step should be to place the works in a permanent museum collection. Glass (and other craft objects) in domestic settings can and often did inspire extensive remodeling to display growing collections. The only long-term remedy to continual acquisition is to donate. Then the works could be seen by more people and the museums would provide institutional validation for the collection. There was no precedent for this, however, as no large collection of studio glass had at that time been donated to a top-tier museum. In an effort to find the right place for all or part of their holdings, collectors began conversations with curators across the United States. Unfamiliar with the unwritten rules of quid pro quo for donations, some collectors grew frustrated with what they felt was the lukewarm response to their proposed gift. They would eventually learn, through many conversations with museum directors and curators, that their request for extensive institutional recognition was unattainable, due in part to the lack of respect for the medium, which was in part an effect of the relatively low cost of amassing it. Even within the esoteric museum world, as within the business community, a hard-headed parity between dollars spent and status awarded prevails.

The Saxes were fortunate. In 1988 they met with Roger Mandle, the director of the Toledo Museum of Art, to discuss a possible donation. Then David Steadman, who was even more receptive to glass, became director (after leaving the directorship of the glass-centered Chrysler Museum in Norfolk, Virginia). A deal was struck. The plan included the donation of glass and pieces in other craft media to be selected by the museum's curatorial staff from the entire Saxe collection. As is usual in response to a significant gift, the museum committed itself to publishing a catalogue of the donated works. This gift would mark the single largest and most important acquisition of studio glass by a significant museum to date and would set a benchmark for other blue-chip collectors and top-tier museums.

Davira Taragin, the curator of decorative arts at the Toledo Museum of Art, challenged the convention of vanity catalogues by proposing one that would directly contribute to the sparse scholarship on craft. She assembled a team of scholars for each medium represented and asked them to discuss the patterns manifest in the Saxes' collecting. The resultant volume, *Contemporary Crafts and the Saxe Collection* (1993), marked the first time the commodification of American craft and the process of assembling a craft collection had been chronicled.[32] The transfer of sixty-three objects in glass and other craft-media from the Saxe Collection to the Toledo Museum of Art in 1990 made the museum's collection, because of its strong historical glass holdings, second only to that of the Corning Museum of Glass in its importance to the studio glass community. This acquisition and the appointment of Taragin as curator of glass returned Toledo to the head of the field after a twenty-year absence. Of equal interest for the acceptance of studio glass was the message conveyed by the Toledo Museum's presentations. The so-called minor arts and the high arts are displayed side by side in chronological groupings, a method that effectively insures that all the galleries are curated by more than one person. This strategy implies parity among art media and indicates the museum's willingness to accept glass as a legitimate art medium.

Another blue-chip collection was formed a bit later in the Midwest during the 1980s. Financed by success in the real-estate business, the collection also grew out of an interest in contemporary art purchased for domestic decoration. In this case, however, the historical glass that the collectors saw at their local museum was the impetus. Indeed, the first piece purchased for the collection was by the established glass artist Harvey Littleton. As for other first-tier collectors, acquisitions of glass provided an opportunity to secure a position of leadership in the collecting community and to engender social interaction. "We love having people come to our home to see the glass. Collectors, artists, students, teachers, museum staff and trustees come individually and by the bus load. I love to tell people about glass and the artists," wrote this Midwestern collector in 1995.[33] Once again, collecting glass provided a vehicle for social connection and increased cultural esteem.

As they built their holdings, some blue-chip collectors turned to curatorial expertise to augment that found in the dealer community. For the Midwest collection a local curator was contacted, as was Penelope Hunter-Stiebel, then curator at the Metropolitan Museum of Art, to help guide the collectors. Two galleries were also pivotal in providing works: Heller Gallery in New York and Habatat near Detroit. In time the collectors came to rely on Kurland/Summers in Los Angeles, which was then the leading West Coast gallery.

Making donations to a museum would seem a straightforward activity. It is, however, a complex and nuanced exchange, layered with coded meaning. First, although all collecting museums desire donations, each desires only the best the collectors have to offer. And the collectors want to receive attention from the most venerated institutions. Consequently, both parties engage in activities that permit each to maximize the opportunities. Given the relatively limited sources for studio glass at this time, the collections, both public and private, would be very similar. Therefore, if the proffered collection contained works that completed or complimented a museum's existing holdings, or presented significant artists in depth, it would be more attractive to a museum. Consequently, when donors consider placing a collection in a museum, they often change the personal focus of their acquisitions and adopt an institutional perspective in order to make the collection more appealing and thereby secure the best placement. This consideration can also lead collectors to contouring their collections to fit the acquisition goals of the desired museum. As part of the negotiation between donor and museum, the promise of a catalogue of the donated items is usually discussed. Because the field is new, such accompanying catalogues

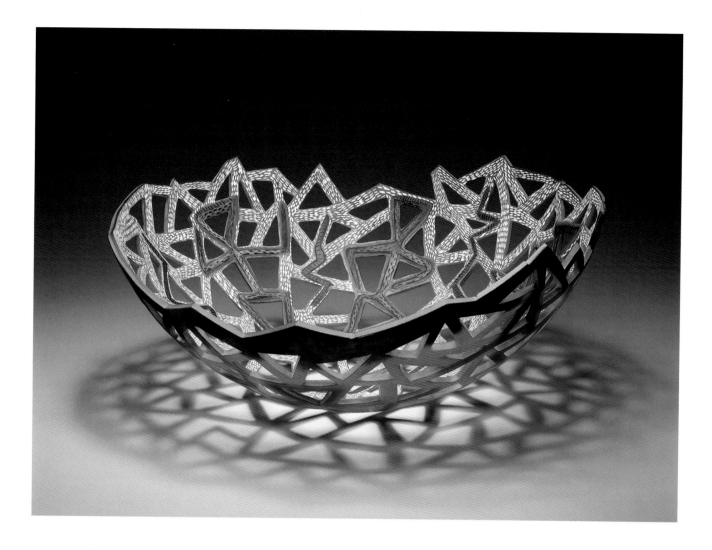

have often been the first publications to treat contemporary glass with the rigor regularly applied to historical material. The inducement of an exhibition of objects from the donation was less frequently used by the mid-1990s.

Over time some glass collectors found that their interest in glass waned—a result of the difficulty of finding new work, a rise in prices so as to exceed budgets, or of events such as divorce, or even natural disasters such as the earthquake in Northridge, California, in 1994. Some collectors run out of room, and prefer to curtail their collecting rather than open up space by donating to museums. Still others transfer their passion to other art media—often equally new media, such as photography or even other craft materials.

In addition to the blue-chip collectors there are those who assemble less comprehensive and more modest collections —evidence of the widening audience for glass and the greater availability of works. Often attracted to the visual delight glass provides and intrigued by the technical expertise necessary to form it, these collectors typically acquire fewer pieces and attempt a less encyclopedic range. Some segue into contemporary glass from historical glass (paperweights, ancient glass, and so on). An interest in glass that ranges from historical material through to contemporary works shows an adventuresomeness not associated with those who collect only historical glass, and it testifies as well to the compelling nature of the latter.

CORPORATE COLLECTIONS

The number of corporate art collections increased in the 1970s. Amassed as investments, executive toys, or expressions of corporate identity, they shared the char-

Wizard Teapot, 1985 (left), and *Murrine Teapot,* 1985 (right). Richard Marquis (United States, b. 1945). Blown glass with murrine canes; 12½ inches high, 6¼ inches diameter; and 6 inches high. Indianapolis Museum of Art, promised gift of Marilyn and Eugene Glick (IMA 299.124)

below: *Cityscape,* 1982. Jay Musler (United States, b. 1959). Glass and paint; 7 ½ inches high, 18 inches in diameter. Los Angeles County Museum of Art, gift of Daniel Greenberg and Susan Steinhauser

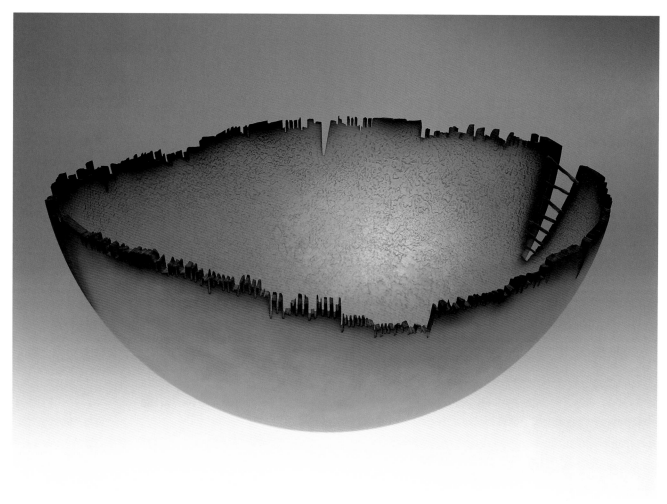

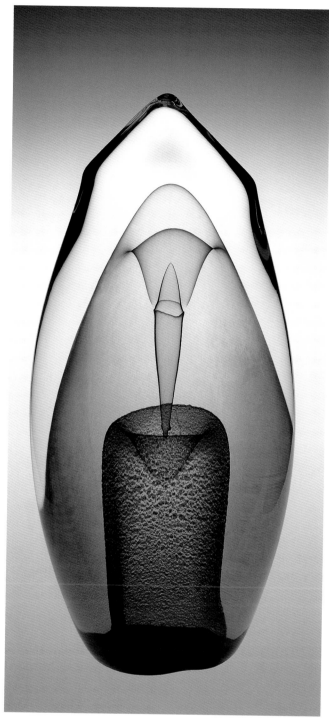

Untitled (from the Emergence series), 1982. Dominick Labino
(United States, 1920–1987). Clear glass with dichronic veiling
and cased crystalline iridescence; 8 ½ x 4 x 3 inches. Indianapolis
Museum of Art, gift from the collection of Marilyn and Eugene Glick
(IMA 1991.219)

Dr. Zarkhov's Tower, 1971. Joel Phillip Myers (United States,
b. 1934). Blown in six parts of red glass, applied gold lusters, glued,
and gilded metal base (replacement); 26 ½ inches high. Indianapolis
Museum of Art, gift of Marilyn and Eugene Glick (IMA 1991.223a-b)

On October 4, 1989, Christie's New York auctioned the Martin and
Jean Mensch Collection of Contemporary Glass, and this work from
that collection was purchased by the Glicks for the Indianapolis
Museum of Art.

acteristics of both private and public collections. Governed by a commercial entity and shaped either by a curator or an enthusiastic corporate executive, these collections were not subject to a public mandate for furthering education, or required to link to other holdings, nor to preserve cultural patrimony. Instead, they embodied personal tastes, while being cared for by professional curators and financed with quasi-private

Hand Forms, 1982. Joel Philip Myers (United States b. 1934). Blown glass, manipulated while hot; tallest: 10 x 5 ¼ inches; diameter of base 3 ⅝ inches. The Corning Museum of Glass (73.4.71)

corporate funds. Often as idiosyncratic as private collections, they tend to favor name artists (to preserve value) and are often seen decorating the walls and shelves of corporate headquarters. It was these collections that set the benchmark for pricing, when several were auctioned into private or institutional hands in the 1980s.[34]

Corporate collections devoted solely to studio glass were rare.[35] However, there were collections that included glass along with other material. One of the most significant, and one that included glass, was that assembled at the behest of S. C. Johnson & Son, Inc., Racine, Wisconsin. After serving as the basis of the influential *Objects: USA* exhibition, approximately one-third of the collection was donated to the American Craft Museum in New York in 1977. There it formed the core of the museum's permanent craft col-

lection. In the 1990s, the Racine Art Museum would take a leading position in collecting crafts; a jump-start donation in 1977 might have spurred it into the fray several years earlier.

There were so few corporate collections devoted entirely to glass in part because of the newness of the medium and its unproved bankability. The collections most likely to include glass were those formed in corporations that were close to glass-making centers. Links to its home base of Seattle and the world-famous Pilchuck Glass School inspired the Safeco Insurance Company's collection. The Prescott Collection of Pilchuck Glass resulted from the establishment of a "1 percent for art" program that was adopted by Seattle in return for permission to develop real estate. Works in this collection were commissioned and placed on display initially in the public spaces of the Pacific First Centre in 1989. Other collections, such as that of the Capital Bank of Houston, also included glass.

As glass attracted more collectors, support groups that catered exclusively to the collectors' interests began to develop, springing up regionally and nationally. An early manifestation of this trend was to be seen at the annual conference of the Glass Art Society in Tucson in 1983. At this event approximately twenty collectors and dealers, joined by a few glassmakers, discussed purchasing strategies and display practices as well as their complementary roles within the field. The event afforded an opportunity to establish a network for the exchange of information among peers and to focus on educational activities aimed at widening the audience for glass.[36]

The desire of collectors to gather more formally was an incentive for the nonprofit Creative Glass Center of America at Wheaton Village, Millville, New Jersey, to initiate its biennial "Glass Lovers Weekend" in 1985, an event accomplished in partnership with the Art Alliance for Contemporary Glass, a national collectors' group. Proceeds provided fellowships for glass artists at the center. Similar events were held annually and one, sponsored by the Edgewood Orchard Gallery in Fish Creek, Wisconsin, and beginning in the early 1980s, was a regional activity that attracted several hundred enthusiastic collectors. Events such as these, planned by and for collectors, developed more extensive connections among the collectors (and in some cases between the collectors and museum personnel) than were to be found any of the other craft communities.

By far the most important collectors' support group was the national Art Alliance for Contemporary Glass, which was formed in 1987. The name was carefully constructed to make it resemble groups dedicated to the support of contemporary painting and sculpture, and the organizers' ambitious goal was to expand the appreciation of studio glass among the general public and within the specialized museum world. The Art Alliance held its first national meeting in September 1989 at the Navy Pier in Chicago at the annual New Art Forms Exposition, the event that was later rechristened Sculptural Objects and Functional Arts (SOFA). To stimulate interest among the collectors, the Alliance instituted what was called a national "visitation network," whereby glass collectors would show their collections to traveling colleagues. This network was reserved for fellow collectors and generally excluded the public at large.[37]

Locally focused organizations sprang up as well. The Studio Glass Collectors' Group was founded in 1980, in part to encourage and support the acquisition of contemporary glass by the Detroit Institute of Art. The group promoted exhibitions and educational programs relating to studio glass. Other urban groups with similar goals were formed: the Metropolitan Contemporary Glass Group, founded in 1984, consisted largely of collectors in the vicinity of New York; the Contemporary Glass Group of the Delaware Valley was founded the same year; in 1987 the North Shore Studio Art Glass Group, based in suburban Chicago, was formed. All of these provided information, camaraderie, and spurred enthusiasm, ensuring a growing sense of community. As the collectors melded into a recognizable group, they came to discuss issues that related to their holdings. In time these conversations turned to the eventual disposition of their collections. The outgrowth of that was a pattern of donations of studio glass to top-tier and second-tier museums.

NOTES

1. William Warmus, "The Cool Fire of Venetian Glass," *Glass* 67 (summer 1997): 37.

2. In anthropology collectable commodities are distinguished as either *alienable* (mass-produced, with no prior social ties to influence the nature of their exchange or the relationship of those who traffic in them) or *inalienable* (those marked by social ties). Studio glass falls into the second category because of its use as a social marker. See James Carrier, *Gifts and Commodities: Exchange in Western Capitalism since 1700* (London: Routledge, 1995).

3. Peter Dormer, "Running to Fat," *Glass Art Society Journal* (1988), 23; first printed as part of "The Ideal World of Vermeer's Little Lacemaker," in Dormer, *Design after Modernism: Beyond the Object* (New York: Thames and Hudson, 1988): 141–44.

4. The literature purporting to explicate the practice of collecting (both motivation and activity) appears in a number of disciplines: art, art history, psychology, sociology, anthropology, and consumer studies, to name a few. For theories and observations that best apply to studio

glass collectors during the period 1975–1990, see "The Problematics of Collecting and Display, Part 1," *Art Bulletin* 77, no. 1 (March 1995): 6–24; and "The Problematics of Collecting and Display, Part 2," *Art Bulletin* 77, no. 2 (June 1995): 166–85. See also, Werner Muensterberger, *Collecting: An Unruly Passion* (Princeton, N.J.: Princeton University Press, 1994); Susan M. Peace, *Museums, Objects, and Collection: A Cultural Study* (Washington, D.C.: Smithsonian Institution Press, 1992); Joseph Alsop, *The Rare Art Tradition: The History of Art Collecting and Its Linked Phenomena Wherever These Have Appeared* (New York: Harper and Row, 1982); John Elner and Roger Cardinal, *The Culture of Collecting* (Cambridge, Mass.: Harvard University Press, 1994); James Clifford "On Collecting Art and Culture," in Russell Ferguson, ed., *Out There: Marginalization and Contemporary Cultures* (Cambridge, Mass.: MIT Press, 1990); 141–69; Russell W. Belk, *Collecting in a Consumer Society* (London: Routledge, 1995); and Mihaly Csikszentmihalyi and Eugene Rochberg-Halton, *The Meaning of Things: Domestic Symbols and the Self* (Cambridge: Cambridge University Press, 1981).

5. See A. Deirdre Robson, *Prestige, Profit, and Pleasure: The Market for Modern Art in New York in the 1940s and 1950s* (New York: Garland, 1995), 81, 257. Cultural capital is defined as the prestige of being associated with creativity without any guarantee of financial reward. The slippery notion of beauty and its impact on the art lover are discussed by Howard Becker in *Art Worlds* (Berkeley: University of California Press, 1982), 275–76.

6. Pierre Bourdieu investigated the sociology of high culture in *Distinction: A Social Critique of the Judgment of Taste* (Cambridge, Mass.: Harvard University Press, 1984). Beginning where Immanuel Kant left off in his *Critique of Judgment* (1790), Bourdieu, in defining a segmented cultural field, places writers as artists rather than as producers of commercial artifacts. He also describes the separation between the writing of text and the activity of evaluation and legitimation, with the critic acting as a "metaliterati." This important separation of roles does apply to studio glass, but it is the lack of a meaningful critical voice that has been noted by a number of authors and continues today. See also Chandra Mukerji, "Artwork: Collection and Contemporary Culture," *American Journal of Sociology* 84, no. 2 (1978): 348–65; and Helmut K. Anheier, Jurgen Gerhard, and Frank Romo, "Forms of Capital and Social Structure in Cultural Fields: Examining Bourdieu's Social Topography," *American Journal of Sociology* 100, no. 4 (January 1995): 859–903.

7. Although the nature of craft collecting is considered low-brow (or middlebrow at best) by the high-art world, all three constituencies—the artists, the dealers, and the collectors—are middle class. See Lawrence W. Levine, *Highbrow, Lowbrow: The Emergence of Cultural Hierarchy in America* (Cambridge, Mass.: Harvard University Press, 1989); Russell Lynes, *The Tastemakers: Shaping of American Popular Taste* (New York: Dover, 1980); Adrian Forty, *Objects of Desire: Design and Society, 1750–1980* (London: Thames and Hudson, 1986); and George E. Marcus, "Middlebrow into Highbrow at the J. Paul Getty Trust, Los Angeles," in Brenda Jo Bright and Liza Bakewell, eds., *Looking High and Low* (Tucson: University of Arizona Press, 1995), 173–98.

8. From the Web site for the Art Alliance for Contemporary Glass report of the Glass Weekend panel "Paths of Glass: Choosing Your Collecting Strategies," July 1999.

9. This is in contrast to those who collect historical production material (Scandinavian, Italian, Germany, American), which does require historical perspective and often fluency in a foreign language.

10. Warmus, "Cool Fire," 37.

11. Dianne Sachko Macleod, "Art Collecting and Victorian Middle-Class Taste," *Art History* 10, no. 3 (September 1987): 329. See Alsop, *Rare Art Tradition*, 33–85; and Ragnar Johnson, "Accumulation and Collecting: An Anthropological Perspective," *Art History* 9, no. 1 (March 1986): 71–83. Any collection is improved by deeper knowledge of the medium's history and cultural milieu, but only a few studio glass collectors approach this benchmark of sophistication, which would have been mandatory for the great British and German glass collectors of the nineteenth century. The contemporary glass collector may or may not have a connoisseur's eye, a library of reference books, or a wide knowledge of the other arts.

12. In social terms, as outlined by Pierre Bourdieu, the accumulation of a culturally significant collection endows the owners with cultural capital. This is true for collections of glass, but the existence of any lasting cultural capital in glass has yet to be proved. This does not prevent glass from operating as a symbol of status, related primitively to the dollars spent. Also its pretensions to art make it a marker that seems to broadcast intimate knowledge of arcane "arts." See Grant McCracken, *Culture and Consumption: New Approaches to the Symbolic Character of Consumer Goods and Activities* (Bloomington: Indiana University Press, 1988); and Steven W. Naifeh, *Culture Making: Money, Success and the New York Art World* (Princeton, N.J.: Princeton University Press, 1976).

13. In the course of discussing the issues of the fragility and reception of glass, Dr. Barry Glassner of the University of Southern California pointed out that glass was usually stored away from little fingers and presented behind glass doors as a precious (and presumably beautiful) commodity.

14. Macleod, "Art Collecting and Victorian Middle-Class Taste," 332.

15. The taxonomy of social display is well known to collectors. Indeed the "constellations of artifacts are structured, and culturally positioned, ways of communicating some kinds of critically important cultural information" notes Katherine C. Grier in *Culture and Comfort: Parlor Making and Middle-Class Identity, 1850–1930* (Washington, D.C.: Smithsonian Institution Press, 1988), xi. Grier discusses the way in which the display of objects in the Victorian parlor had clear symbolic meaning for the owners and visitors. This symbolic language can be seen in the selection of studio glass items displayed by private collectors.

16. See Russell W. Belk, "Possession and the Extended

Self," *Journal of Consumer Research* 15 (September 1988): 139–68.

17. Conversation with author, Pasadena, California, 1998.

18. Davira Taragin, "Selections from the George and Dorothy Saxe Collection at the Toledo Museum of Art," *Glass Art Society Journal* (1993): 129.

19. Michael Taylor, "Regional Glass Artists and Studios of Northwest New York State," *Glass Art Society Journal* (1991): 91.

20. The issue of the visual appeal of glass is tendentious. With beauty being in the eye of the beholder, any generalization linking glass and beauty as an absolute is difficult to make. But most collectors (and artists) mention that glass captivated them visually at some point and that this compelled their involvement. The artist Kreg Kallenberger freely admits this seduction, but he "works hard not to ride on the back of its beauty"(conversation with author, Asheville, North Carolina, 1995). Indeed, "glass—having an aesthetic all its own—certainly entails danger for the artist. It is all too easy to get carried away by the beautiful, but in the last resort simple decorative shine of the material." Christine Schroeder, "Metaphors in Glass: The Role of Glass in Contemporary Art," *Neues Glas* 1 (1996): 10–17.

21. Anne Cohen, president of the Glass Alliance of Los Angeles, to members, November 29, 1999.

22. It is a commonplace in arts that the first people to recognize the artistic potential of new artists are their peers, then their teachers, and then the dealers. Collectors, public and private, are at the end of the chain.

23. Private collectors can be either accumulators or collectors. Accumulators assemble large numbers of objects without a unifying conceptual framework; collectors have a unifying vision that determines the requirements for inclusion or exclusion. In the case of studio glass, this vision usually requires that collectors have representative works by each important artist shown in the New York galleries. In an interesting insight into the studio glass world, Jon C. Liebman, president of the Art Alliance for Contemporary Glass, uses a generous criterion for the definition of a glass collector: he applies the term to anyone who has a few pieces of glass and who is drawn to the medium. He does make a distinction between those who have a hundred thousand dollars or less to spend and those who have more. Liebman to author (e-mail), March 1999.

24. The clay artist Viola Frey calls her collection an "accumulation" and refers to it as a library of visual solutions. See Joyce Lovelace, "'I Don't Really Collect . . .' Tales of Artists' Possessions," *American Craft* 55, no. 6 (December 1995/January 1996): 40–45. See also, Jane Falconer Byrd, interview with Bill Brown, April 1984, in *The Bill and Jane Brown Glass Collection*, exh. cat. Chelsea Gallery of Western Carolina University, Culowee, N.C., 1984.

25. This period also coincided with the unprecedented expansion of the high-art market; the increased enthusiasm for contemporary art undoubtedly influenced glass collecting.

26. Another by-product of their collecting activity was their involvement with the American Craft Council; both have served as members of the board.

27. Jesse Hamlin, "A Passion for Collecting Crafts," *San Francisco Chronicle,* June 24, 1999, sec. E, p. 1.

28. Robert Silberman, "The Art of Craft: Contemporary Works from the Saxe Collection," *American Craft* 59, no. 5 (October/November, 1999): 78 n.1.

29. Hamlin, "Passion for Collecting Crafts,".

30. Silberman, "Art of Craft," 76. Bertil Vallien and Ann (Warff) Wolff are European glassmakers who produce both factory and studio work. Introduced to the American glass-collecting community by the urban galleries, both artists are represented by works in prestigious collections of American studio glass.

31. Ibid.

32. See Taragin, "Selections from the George and Dorothy Saxe Collection," 129–30; and idem, ed., *Contemporary Crafts and the Saxe Collection* (Toledo: Hudson Hills and the Toledo Museum of Art, 1993). A similar investigation was undertaken by the English Crafts Council in the publication *Building a Crafts Collection: Crafts Council Collecting, 1972–1985* (London: Crafts Council, 1985).

33. Martha Drexler Lynn, *Masters of Contemporary Glass: Selections from the Glick Collection* (Bloomington: Indiana University Press, 1997), 12.

34. Susanne K. Frantz, "The Evolution of Studio Glass Collecting and Documentation in the United States," *Contemporary Crafts and the Saxe Collection* (New York: Hudson Hills and the Toledo Museum of Art, 1993), 38. Other corporate collections include those of the Best Products Co, Inc., of Richmond, Virginia, and John Portman & Associates, Atlanta, Georgia. Two governmental agencies also created collections, the General Services Administration, Washington, D.C., and the Washington State Arts Commission, Olympia, Washington. During Walter Mondale's tenure as vice president, a collection of crafts was assembled under the guidance of Mrs. Mondale for Blair House, Washington, D.C.

35. It can be argued that the Corning Museum of Glass was originally a corporate collection maintained by a professional staff of curators.

36. In later years other attempts were made to create events for collectors in conjunction with the GAS conference, but it turned out that the interests of the artists and the collectors did not coincide. GAS catered to younger artists, and the collectors wanted to meet and socialize with established ones.

37. Letter to members of the Art Alliance for Contemporary Glass, August 19, 1996. To protect their privacy, collectors are listed by Zip Code and city only.

Beauty's Alter Ego as a Tornado,
1990. Ginny Ruffner (United States,
b. 1951). Glass, paint; 18 x 11 x 11
inches. Los Angeles County Museum
of Art, gift of Brendan Walters and
Ginny Ruffner (M.91.18)

Studio Glass in the Museums—
Validating the Collections

To SATISFY THE GOALS of the studio glass community (artists and collectors), glass had to enter public museums. One way to prime the process was for collectors to donate works to select museums.[1] By the mid- to late 1980s, many collectors were selling or giving away works to focus and upgrade their holdings. Others refined their collections to bring them into line with institutional practice and make them more appealing as a donation. Still others, discouraged by the increasing prices and scale of the newest work, were leaving the field altogether and wished to place their collections in perpetuity.

Soon collectors learned that just placing glass in a museum was not enough to accomplish their goals. A donation to the permanent collection (even if not on display) was of more significance than short-term inclusion in a temporary traveling exhibition. To ensure its acceptance by the art world, glass had to be represented in the permanent collections of first-tier museums.

Curators of public institutions are employed for the benefit of the public and have distinct duties that can affect potential donations. As connoisseurs and scholars, curators perform a teaching function, using the art objects in their collections as tools of instruction.[2] Through exhibitions and related catalogues, brochures, and scholarly writings, the curator's knowledge can provide a framework for presenting the material in a coherent manner, often guiding the public with fresh interpretations and insights. Thus curators are required to embrace knowledge that is broadly historical and more culturally attuned than that necessarily required

by dealers or individual collectors. Curators are also charged with creating permanent collections that reflect the focus of their institutions. If the institution is a glass museum—the Corning Museum of Glass, for instance—only material related to glass is appropriate. Consequently, if a proffered collection does not afford an opportunity to realize some aspect of the institution's goals, it may be turned down. Unlike private collectors, curators can increase their cultural capital and that of their collections (and their status within the museum world) only by producing articles and exhibition catalogues about their holdings and propounding new theories about them to valorize their holdings as part of the larger continuum of art history.

Usually institutions have little or no money set aside for the purchase of artworks, so they rely on donations. This reliance establishes a dynamic three-way relationship involving the curator, the donor, and the dealers. The system starts with the dealer's selling the works to the collector, making a profit and gaining exposure for the gallery and its stable of artists. The collector displays the work and eventually donates it to the museum. The curator acquires works to build the collection; the donor gives works to the museum to increase his or her cultural standing and the overall value of the class of works themselves. This exercise is often accompanied by a modest tax deduction. Within this system, artworks flow in one direction: toward the public domain and a resting place within the museum.

Most museums operate under a conceptualization of art that prizes the perceived best—the masterpiece—by any given artist. "Museums are represented as disinterested accumulators of only the very 'best' quality, making their decisions objectively and not intuitively, as might the private collector."[3] Private collectors can regularly indulge personal taste, or even buy a middling work; public collectors (curators) need to ascertain what is the best of the field and secure it, all the while assessing their personal prejudices and collecting without showing them. This functional difference reflects an assumption that institutional collections are necessarily informed, intellectual statements that reflect a broad scope of knowledge. In reality, curatorial acquisitions are often ruled by hard practicality, institutional politics, and the vagaries of personality. It was these more pragmatic influences that proved to be fortunate for studio glass.

First-tier museums are the large, urban, universal-survey museums (termed *encyclopedic* within the field) and those smaller institutions that are recognized as undisputed leaders in the field. Therefore, the Metropolitan Museum of Art and the Museum of Modern Art in New York and the Los Angeles County Museum of Art are classified as first-tier museums, as are the Corning Museum of Glass and the Toledo Museum of Art.[4] Second-tier museums are often regional in the scope of their collecting, located outside urban centers, and have smaller collections and fewer staff members. It might appear that validation from first-tier museums would be the only recognition beneficial to the cause of studio glass, but this is not true; useful validation has come from the second-tier institutions as well.

The relative importance of these institutions and their contributions to the acceptance of glass is governed by the way in which each one functions within the overall art system. First-tier museums must contend with greater public scrutiny, as their actions and inactions are widely observed and commented upon. Given the essentially conservative nature of museums, such visibility can inhibit their selection of exhibitions and objects, as well as their willingness to open new areas of collecting. In a high-profile institution each curatorial selection is an opportunity for public comment and might even unduly affect the market. For example, if the Metropolitan Museum of Art were to announce that it intended to collect studio glass aggressively, the announcement would send a signal to the private collecting world and the dealer community that glass is a desirable art commodity. Thus the museum would be making judgments that affect dollar valuations before they had been established by the market. As a rule, museums that are not specifically dedicated to contemporary art wait until contemporaneous material has a track record of validation from dealers and collectors, and perhaps from other lesser institutions.

First-tier museums are not without their blind spots. In a candid lecture delivered at the annual conference of the Glass Art Society, held at Corning, New York, in 1991 R. Craig Miller, formerly the curator of decorative arts at the Metropolitan Museum in New York, commented on the glass holdings of universal art museums:

> For a number of reasons none of them simple, few of the really large, encyclopedic museums have been willing to make a long-term commitment [to glass]. First, the basic organizational structure of such large institutions works against it. Departments are most often divided by subject matter and media: painting and sculpture are in one department, decorative arts in another. When I was at the Metropolitan Museum, Picasso's ceramic plaques were catalogued in the design collection; they were two-dimensional surfaces just like a painting, but Picasso had not executed these particular heads on canvas. Likewise, sculptural pieces by Stanislav Libenský and Dale Chihuly were considered decorative arts since they were made of glass.[5]

Such considerations may seem quirky and illogical, but museums are not necessarily known for their seamless reasoning and such barriers to the understanding and appreciating of studio glass are found frequently.

Miller also commented that some curators did not naturally gravitate to glass and seemed put off by it. "The most serious obstacle, however, is the obvious one: compared to other craft media, many museum staffs simply did not understand this new work. They don't like it visually and they sure as hell aren't going to spend any money on it."[6] When a curator of sufficient power within a first-tier institution chooses to add glass to the collections, it is, therefore, an impor-

Teapot (Fabricated Weird Series #21), 1979. Richard Marquis (United States, b. 1945). Blown glass, cut, polished, and reassembled; 5 x 4 x 6 inches. Los Angeles County Museum of Art, gift of Anita and Julius L. Zelman through the 1987 Collectors Committee (M. 87.154)

right: *Amber Crested Form*, 1976. Harvey Littleton (United States b. 1922). Glass; 16 1/2 inches high. The Metropolitan Museum of Art, gift of William D. and Rose D. Barker, 1978 (1978.438)

Crystal Flow, 1983. Robert Willson (United States, 1912–2000). Glass, 14 inches high. Made with Alfredo Barbini, in Venice, Italy. Willson was, in the 1960s, the first of the American studio-glass artists to work in Italian glasshouses.

can sponsor, their ability to confer status on prospective donors, and their potential to attract large grants from funding agencies. For a so-called new medium such as studio glass, incomplete scholarship and the accessioning of inferior collections can be detrimental to the overall perception of the medium.[7]

Several key acquisitions of studio glass by first-tier museums occurred in the first years of the new movement and helped to create momentum. These acquisition were made in part because of an increased interest in what the high-art world then termed *new media* and in part because the curators were able to exercise their discretion.[8] The movement of studio glass into large, urban, encyclopedic museums began when the Metropolitan Museum of Art added examples to its permanent holdings during the mid- and late 1970s. Henry Geldzahler, then curator of twentieth-century art, saw a piece from the Dale Chihuly's Navajo Blanket Cylinders Series (1976) and promptly purchased it for the collection. The next year he accessioned *Amber Crested Form* (1977; see p. 143) by Harvey Littleton.

The significance of these acquisitions rests on three points: first, the works entered the museum early; second, they were brought in under the aegis of the contemporary art department, not that of the American decorative arts department, where glass by Louis Comfort Tiffany and Frank Lloyd Wright already formed part of the collection; third, they were purchased with scarce acquisition funds. Given the hierarchy of museum departments, the fact that the pieces were acquired by a department linked to painting and sculpture was a boon to studio glass, for although the department that accessioned the work is not mentioned on the label copy or any other public notice, it is known within the art and museum world.[9] Writing in 1990 Geldzahler justified his glass acquisitions by linking them to historical works already in the decorative arts collections: "I think that it is possible to compare what Dale Chihuly is doing with what Louis Comfort Tiffany did. . . . I believe his best glass rivals what Tiffany did a hundred years ago." Geldzahler also saw a similarity between the visual impact of studio glass and the "great traditions of watercolor and color field painting" in America.[10] By shifting the association of glass from decorative arts to painting, he provided a

tant statement, and often indicates a maverick interest in the medium. This interest is usually supported by the generosity of a glass collector. Because of this, the story of when and under whose aegis glass entered leading collections is, in reality, the story of curatorial discretion and personal taste coupled with the collectors' activism, rather than proof of a universal acceptance by institutions.

Second-tier museums have greater flexibility, as they operate with less public scrutiny and can be more adventurous in expanding into new areas. If a new medium were to join a second-tier collection, it may not garner worldwide acceptance, but it will get increased exposure, which may in turn broaden the audience. Indeed, exhibitions and acquisitions undertaken by regional or smaller museums often demonstrate the potential of glass and enable the staff of first-tier museums to see it afresh. Second-tier museums, however, have less clout and fewer economic resources, which can affect the level of scholarship they

more secure validation than the misplaced contemporaneous rage for new media would have.

In the early 1980s Penelope Hunter-Stiebel of the decorative arts department took over the championing of studio glass at the Metropolitan Museum of Art. Instead of finding the money to buy studio glass, she deployed a time-honored curatorial gambit in securing gifts of artworks from artists and donors.[11] She also actively exhibited glass. In 1979 she installed *New Glass: A Worldwide Survey,* a traveling exhibition from the Corning Museum of Glass that gave a significant measure of validation and exposure to the medium. The cachet of having the Metropolitan Museum as a venue for *New Glass* most likely influenced the decision of *ArtNews,* a periodical devoted to contemporary art, to publish an article on studio glass by Hunter-Stiebel in 1981. An early, cogent recounting of the development of American studio glass, her essay profiled several prominent studio glassmakers and was widely read.[12]

The Metropolitan Museum's interest in studio glass shifted once again when R. Craig Miller took over as curator of decorative arts between 1983 and 1990. His involvement in the early years was, he said, limited to "industrial and decorative design and only in the late 1980s were craft acquisitions allowed to resume."[13] Miller links the lack of interest in studio glass to a "modernist mandate" that had excluded the medium from consideration. He remembers that

the Metropolitan Museum . . . had been a major advocate for decorative design during the decades between the world wars, but by 1940 it largely abandoned the field for the next quarter century. The Modernist mandate became so pervasive, in fact, that it led to the myth at that time that only functional objects that were industrially made had any real aesthetic value. Both manufacturers and the public looked to architects and industrial designers—not craftsmen—for their best products. If craft was not a "dirty word," it was at least something not to be taken very seriously.[14]

As time passed and studio glass lost its association with craft, the Metropolitan Museum acquired works by Howard Ben Tré, William Carlson, Dale Chihuly,

Untitled 800808, 1980.
Steven Weinberg (United
States, b. 1954). Cast crystal;
8 3/16 x 8 3/16 x 8 3/16 inches.
Toledo Museum of Art, gift of
Dorothy and George Saxe
(1991.139)

Hanging Series #24, 1978.
Mary Shaffer (United States,
b. 1943). Plate glass, wire;
40 1/4 x 28 1/4 x 2 inches.
Toledo Museum of Art, gift of
Dorothy and George Saxe
(1991.136)

Plate Glass Vase #26, 1981. Sidney R. Hutter (United States, b. 1954). Plate glass; 11 3/4 x 7 1/16 inches. Toledo Museum of Art, gift of Dorothy and George Saxe (1991.120)

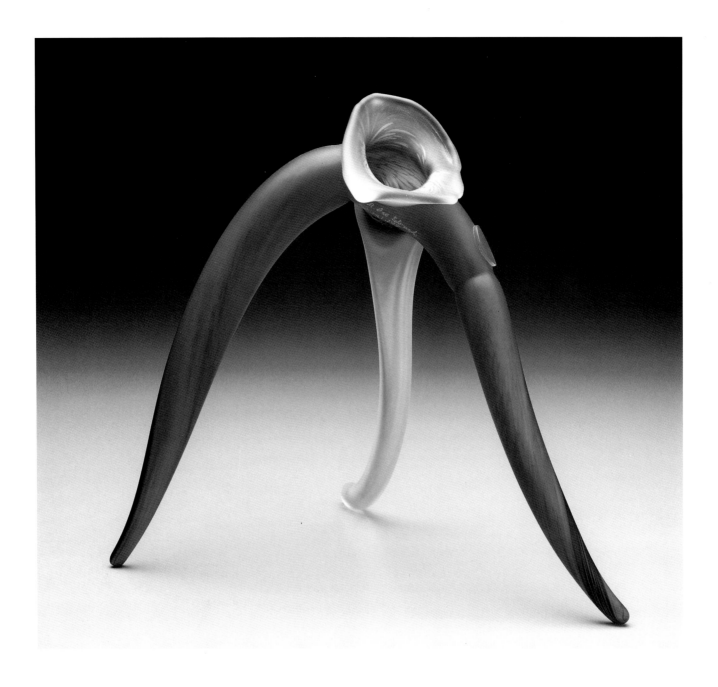

Tripod Sea Form, 1985. Stephen Dee Edwards (United States, b. 1954). Glass; 8 3/4 x 10 1/3 inches. Mint Museums, Charlotte, North Carolina; gift of Sonia and Isaac Luski (1986.28.4)

Dan Dailey, Michael Glancy, David Huchthausen, Joel Philip Myers, Narcissus Quagliata, and Steven Weinberg for its permanent collection.

The other leading New York institution to influence the acceptance of studio glass was the Museum of Modern Art. Favoring glass that was industrial in nature, rather than craft or art made from craft materials, the museum's interest was tepid during the period from 1975 to 1990. But it did mount two small shows drawn from its own collections: *Crafts from the Collection* (1986–1987), an exhibition of twenty-four

objects, and *Glass from the Collection* (1990), the presentation of work in a mixture of styles collected by the department of architecture and design since 1934. Despite this lack of interest in exhibiting glass, the museum did acquire during that time objects by the glass artists Sydney Cash, Dale Chihuly, Harvey Littleton, Tom Patti, and Toots Zynsky.

Both the Corning Museum of Glass and the Toledo Museum of Art took advantage of their ties to industrial glass to expand their support of contemporary glass through aggressive exhibition programs during the 1970s. The Toledo Museum of Art's activities tapered off during the 1980s, however, and would only be rekindled in the 1990s with the Saxe donation.

By contrast, support from the Corning Museum of Glass was sustained. In 1977 the museum began its series of annual exhibitions, *Contemporary Glass,* that recognized the importance of glass as an art medium and framed it in an international context. Originally the exhibitions offered a juried, international pictorial record of work in glass. In 1980 the format shifted to a printed volume with the name *New Glass Review,* which evolved into a valuable record of works donated to museums during the previous calendar year. Corning also actively collected studio glass, through donations from artists and collectors and through purchases. Its publication in 1989 of the seminal *Contemporary Glass: A World Survey from The Corning Museum of* *Glass* by Susanne K. Frantz provided scholarship and ready visual access to the collection. Corning's support was also expressed through the simple act of placing photographs of works by Dominick Labino and other notable studio glass artists in slide packs offered in the bookstore, which encouraged ready access to their contemporary glass.

Meanwhile, second-tier museums display their commitment to glass more consistently and without needing to resort to manipulating departmental classifications. Curators at these institutions—which had smaller audiences and were located away from urban centers—could exhibit works and artists not deemed acceptable in New York.[15] One regional institution that demonstrated a noteworthy commitment to glass was the Leigh Yawkey Woodson Art Museum in Wausau, Wisconsin.[16] In 1978, 1981, and 1984, the Woodson mounted a series of juried triennials entitled *Americans in Glass*, in which the museum sought to provide an overview of the work of studio glassmakers. Organized by David Huchthausen, these exhibitions traveled across the United States and to Europe. In the catalogue essay for *Americans in Glass* of 1981, David Huchthausen called for serious evaluation of glass art and criticized the artistic state of the medium: "One conclusion is inescapable: contemporary glass is not necessarily bad art as much as it is insignificant art"— comments that were prophetic and sharper than the collegial tone of most writing about glass at the time.[17] By 1984 Huchthausen's comments and those of the other jurors revealed further frustration and disappointment, as they questioned the validity of exhibitions based solely on the use of a common material.[18] The 1984 *Americans in Glass* exhibition would travel in Europe until 1986, but it was the last of the series. Huchthausen's writing and the Woodson's aggressive collecting strategy had placed this series of exhibitions in the vanguard.

The Huntington Museum of Art, Huntington, West Virginia, also contributed to the exposure of glass by sponsoring almost a dozen invitational exhibitions after 1976.[19] The first was a survey exhibition of 135 objects by 48 artists. In 1978, the focus was narrowed to the work of between two and four artists in depth. Notable exhibitions were *New American Glass: Focus West Virginia* in 1984 and *New American Glass: Focus 2 West Virginia* in 1986. The catalogue for the latter included color photographs, a brief history, and an emphasis on technique rather than critical assessment. As an afterthought an interleaved critique was added by Paul Hollister.[20] As further evidence of its commitment, the Huntington acquired a broad selection of studio glass for its permanent collection.

The American Craft Museum, now the Museum of Arts and Design, the preeminent craft museum in the country with its prominent location in New York City, would have seemed a natural champion for studio glass.[21] From its founding in 1956 until 1991, however, the museum mounted only three dozen exhibitions that included contemporary glass, and only sixteen devoted exclusively to the medium.[22] This stands in marked contrast to its record in clay and textiles. Indeed, as it was one of the first institutions to recognize the studio glass movement in the early 1960s and to see that American studio glass should appropriately be linked to the larger international glass movement, this record is surprising. A modest attempt was made in 1974 when the museum (then known as the Museum of Contemporary Crafts) showed works from six private collections in an exhibition entitled *The Collector*. Later, in 1977, the museum restructured its *Young Americans* show into three separate exhibitions organized by medium. Dale Chihuly was invited to serve as a juror for the reconstituted *Young Americans: Clay / Glass,* which opened in 1978 with the work of twenty-five glassmakers and sixty-seven clay artists. Sadly, as with other craft organizations then and now, the museum's catalogues usually consisted of general introductory essays, numerous photographs, obligatory biographies, and exhibition checklists, and only rarely included scholarly or critical essays.

Even with such activities, "the museum" as R. Craig Miller noted, "had begun in many ways to follow the movement rather than carefully examining and assessing it. Indeed, perhaps more than any American institution, the [American Craft Museum] has helped to perpetrate . . . [an] aesthetic and intellectual vacuum in the field."[23] Perhaps to avoid offending the artists who were once its core members, the museum produced survey exhibitions selected, not by its professional curatorial staff, but by living artists, who were charged with exercising curatorial discrimination. The museum did not attempt to place glass (or any other medium under its purview) within a larger historical or artistic context until the mid-1990s, when it attempted to write a history of craft.[24] As the final irony, the museum that first recognized the glass movement does not have a representative glass collection of its own. As of May 1991, after thirty years of familiarity with studio glass, the museum had only seventy-two glass objects in its holdings, and thirty-one of them were Christmas tree ornaments.[25]

Other second-tier museums sporadically honored studio glass and so influenced it acceptance. In 1983 the Tucson Museum of Art presented *Sculptural Glass*, an exhibition curated by Susanne K. Frantz. It was the first of several exhibitions of large-scale, site-specific glass sculptures, another being *Cast Glass Sculpture*, displayed at the Art Gallery, California State University, Fullerton, in 1986. The catalogue was notable for its essay by the art critic Donald Kuspit, who applied an outsider's eye and provided an intellectual framework from which to view the material. Moving away from references to the decorative arts and the table-sized scale of previous works, this exhibition heralded the arrival of glass as a serious sculptural medium.[26] A similar approach was taken by the Renwick Gallery's *Glassworks* exhibition in 1990, which presented constructions in the galleries and the public was invited in to watch the process.[27]

One hallmark of maturity for a movement is the retrospective exhibition of the work of a single artist. This style of exhibition assumes that an artist has produced a body of work of sufficient complexity and depth to warrant a sustained and considered examination. Here second-tier museums led the way. *Dale Chihuly: A Decade of Glass* was a ten-year retrospective organized in 1984 by the Bellevue Art Museum, Bellevue, Washington. In 1985 the High Museum of Art, Atlanta, originated *Harvey Littleton: A Retrospective Exhibition*, and in 1987 *Dan Dailey: Simple Complexities in Drawings and Glass, 1972–1987* was mounted by the Philadelphia Colleges of the Arts. In 1989 The Phillips Collection, Washington, D.C., circulated *Howard Ben Tré: Contemporary Sculpture.*

By the end of 1990 the collectors of studio glass had matured into a powerful force for the advancement of glass. Through their sophisticated and focused activities, glass became a modest presence at both first- and second-tier museums and was displayed alongside high art. One evidence of this growth was the acquisition by donation of approximately twenty pieces of studio glass by the top-tier Los Angeles County Museum of Art. These works were not assigned prime gallery space in the newly opened Anderson Building, but were exhibited in a small sunlit space adjacent to the collection of contemporary paintings and sculptures on the second floor. As the works were being installed with custom-designed cases and lighting, a senior curator remarked disparagingly that the only reason they were allowed into the gallery was because contemporary paintings were too large to fit into such a small space and that glass could more readily withstand the strong sunlight that flooded in. Museums may appear rational in their role as validating institutions, but the level of their actual participation often depends on such mundane realities as the scale of the artwork, the design of the building, and the light levels in the galleries.

NOTES

1. The donation of artwork was made attractive by tax regulations that permitted the increased value of the work to be deductible from taxable income. The federal tax code did not distinguish between those works that had already attained cultural status and those that were still striving. The change in this law did much damage to the growth of museum collections as the flow of artworks decreased markedly.

2. Curators are also technically responsible for the safe storage of the artworks under their care. More conceptual and managerial than actual, this responsibility involves their working in tandem with other museum staff who transport, install, and conserve the works.

3. A. Deirdre Robson, *Prestige, Profit, and Pleasure: The Market for Modern Art in New York in the 1940s and 1950s* (New York: Garland, 1995), 17.

4. In 1995 the Metropolitan Museum of Art (founded in 1870) had a staff of 1,654 full-time employees and a part-time staff of 791. It had a 250,000-volume library and its attendance was 4,400,000. The Museum of Modern Art was founded in 1929 and had a full-time staff of 500 and no paid part-time personnel. It had a 100,000-volume library and annual attendance of 1,300,000. The Los Angeles County Museum of Art was founded in 1910 and in 1995 had a curatorial staff of 40. The library boasted 117,000 volumes. Museum attendance in 1995 was over 1,000,000. The Corning Museum was founded in 1951, and in 1995 it had a full-time staff of 31 and a part-time staff of 4. The library had 50,000 volumes, and attendance in 1995 was 362,558. The Toledo Museum of Art was founded in 1901 and had a full-time staff of 90 and part-time staff of 140. The library had 50,000 volumes, and attendance was 275,779 in 1995. See R. R. Bowker, *The Official Museum Directory, 1995* (New Providence, N.J.: Reed Elsevier, 1995).

5. The term *universal art museum* is used in British literature and academic writing; the term *encyclopedic* is used

within the museum world. They both refer to museums that collect a broad range of materials over many cultures and time frames. R. Craig Miller, "Betwixt and Between: Contemporary Glass in American Art Museums," *Glass Art Society Journal* (1991): 29.

6. Ibid.

7. The literature about museums, their influence, and the nature of their constructed presentations is vast and is referred to here only as it directly relates to the display or acquisition of American studio glass. For further reading on the general topic, see Rosalind Krauss "The Cultural Logic of the Late Capitalistic Museum," *Art History* 54 (December 1980): 3–17; Carol Duncan, *Civilizing Rituals: Inside the Public Art Museums* (London: Routledge, 1995); Eilean Hooper-Greenhill, *Museums and the Shaping of Knowledge* (London: Routledge, 1993); Susan M. Peace, *Museums, Objects, and Collections: A Cultural Study* (Washington, D.C.: Smithsonian Institution Press, 1993); Didier Maleuvre, *Museum Memories: History, Technology, Art* (Stanford, Calif.: Stanford University Press, 1999); and Daniel J. Sherman and Irit Rogoff, eds., *Museum Culture: Histories, Discourse, Spectacles* (Minneapolis: University of Minnesota Press, 1994). For a history of American museums and their influence, see Steven Conn, *Museums and American Intellectual Life, 1876–1926* (Chicago: University of Chicago Press, 1998); Tamar Katriel, "No Two Alike: The Aesthetic of Collecting" (PhD diss., University of Haifa and Hebrew University of Jerusalem, 1987). For a discussion of the meaning of collections in terms of the completion of self, see Grant McCracken, *Culture and Consumption: New Approaches to the Symbolic Character of Consumer Goods and Activities* (Bloomington: Indiana University Press, 1988), esp., "The Evocative Power of Things: Consumer Goods and the Preservation of Hopes and Ideals," 104–17.

8. Glass hardly qualifies as a new medium, but that description illustrates how little the twentieth-century high- or fine-arts world, and perhaps some contemporary curators, knew about its history. This misconception led to anomalies such as the exhibition of glass by Harvey Littleton mounted by the first-tier Art Institute of Chicago in 1963. Sadly, the institution did not continue its support of the medium.

9. It is difficult for the casual observer to ascertain which department acquired a specific artwork. If a museum gallery is exclusively controlled by one department, a guess can be made. But even that can be misleading; for example, items brought into the Los Angeles County Museum of Art by the decorative arts department were often displayed in the Anderson Building, which was largely controlled by the twentieth-century department. The Museum of Modern Art design department acquired studio glass by Sydney Cash, Dale Chihuly, Harvey Littleton, Tom Patti, and Toots Zynsky in its design department. The Solomon R. Guggenheim Museum and the Whitney Museum of American Art in New York, as well as the Philadelphia Museum of Art, added a limited number of pieces to their collections through a variety of departments. Because of the concern about the suitability of glass as an art medium, curators have resorted to ruses to acquire controversial works. Items donated at year-end, with the deadline of December 31, tend to evade detailed scrutiny by both other curators and the board of directors. Also, items that are under a certain dollar amount can join collections with less review.

10. Henry Geldzahler, *Making it New: Essays, Interviews, and Talks* (San Diego: Harcourt Brace, 1994), 321.

11. Very little money is specifically designated for acquisitions in museums. One method of acquiring works of art for a collection is to locate donors who are willing to purchase the work and then donate it. In this system, selections are jointly made by the collector and the curator. This potentially places the donor on a par with the curator in the developing the collection and can lead to conflicts. To avoid this, curators who work with living artists can ask the artist directly for donations. But, this, too, is problematic as it places the curator and the museum in the business of potentially influencing the market and swaying collecting patterns. Museums are generally organized to acknowledge success already confirmed by the marketplace. The Corning Museum of Glass has received much of its twentieth-century glass as gifts from the artists. Museum policy on this point varies with each board of directors and institution. For a discussion of the relative influence of curators, see Michael Brenson, "The Curator's Moment," *Art Journal* 57, no. 4 (winter 1998): 16–27. Curators are perceived as being more powerful than they are. Indeed, their power is more evident outside their institutions than within, where they constrained by internal curatorial turf battles.

12. Penelope Hunter-Stiebel, "Contemporary Art Glass: An Old Medium Gets a New Look," *ArtNews* 80, no. 6 (June 1981): 130–35. Studio glass was not shown again until 1996 when Jane Aldin working with J. Stewart Johnson installed thirty-nine pieces of studio glass for an exhibition that ran from April 8 to October 6. This exhibition focused on conceptual works that were not vessel related. See the review, "Craftsman Hand: Multifaceted Glass: A Metropolitan Museum Exhibition Signals the Coming of Age of the Studio Glass Movement," *House Beautiful* (April 1996): 44 and passim.

13. Miller, "Betwixt and Between," 30.

14. Ibid., 28.

15. See Diane Crane, "Art Museums and the Reception of the Avant-Garde Styles," in *The Transformation of the Avant-Garde: The New York Art World, 1940–1985* (Chicago: University of Chicago, 1987), 119–36. Crane notes that, just as with studio glass, the acquisition patterns of high art in New York museums are markedly different from those in museums elsewhere.

16. Founded in 1973, the Leigh Yawkey Woodson Art Museum had an annual estimated attendance of forty-five thousand in 1995, with a staff of seven full-time and seven part-time employees. Its areas of collecting include paintings and sculpture depicting the natural world, glass, and porcelain. By the late 1970s and early 1980s, the collections of the Toledo Museum and the Corning Museum

were being emulated by a growing number of museums, among them the Chrysler Museum, Norfolk, Virginia; Cooper-Hewitt National Museum of Design, New York; the Detroit Institute of Art; High Museum of Art, Atlanta; Huntington Galleries, Huntington, West Virginia; Indianapolis Museum of Art, Indiana; Leigh Yawkey Woodson Art Museum, Wausau, Wisconsin; and the National Museum of American History and the Renwick Gallery of the National Museum of American Art, Smithsonian Institution, Washington, D.C.; Museum of Art, Rhode Island School of Design, Providence; and the Wheaton Museum of Glass, Millville, New Jersey. Most glass, like most studio crafts, is accessioned within the decorative arts or design departments, not the departments that deal with painting and sculpture.

17. See *Americans in Glass*, exh. cat. Leigh Yawkey Woodson Art Museum, Wausau, Wisc., 1981, 9.

18. Ibid.

19. The Huntington Museum of Art was founded in 1947 and in 1995 had an attendance of sixty thousand, a full-time staff of eighteen, a part-time staff of six, and a ten-thousand-volume library. It houses collections of nineteenth- and twentieth-century glass in addition to Georgian silver, nineteenth- and twentieth-century painting and sculpture, American and European graphics, pre-Columbian ceramics, and American decorative arts.

20. See Paul Hollister, *New American Glass: Focus 2 West Virginia*, Huntington Galleries, West Virginia, 1986, and *New American Glass: Focus West Virginia*, Huntington Galleries, Huntington, West Virginia, 1984.

21. Founded in 1956, the American Craft Museum has a fluctuating number of staff members. The library has thirty thousand volumes and its annual attendance is about one hundred thousand people.

22. In contrast, during the 1980s many small and large museums were mounting exhibitions that gave an overview of contemporary glass. In 1981 in *Glass Routes*, the DeCordova Museum and Sculpture Park, Lincoln, Massachusetts, offered a survey exhibition of glass created in New England. Anniversaries, especially of the Toledo workshops, provided opportunities for many exhibitions, including the twenty-year celebration *American Glass Art: Evolution and Revolution* at the Morris Museum, Morristown, New Jersey, in 1982. See Sharon K. Emanuelli, "Chronology: American Craft, 1851–1986," in *Craft*

Today: Poetry of the Physical (New York: American Craft Museum and Weidenfeld and Nicolson, 1986), 279–89.

23. Miller, "Betwixt and Between," 30.

24. In 1994 the American Craft Museum published a history of craft that cast its net so wide as to include industrial design and folk art. Perhaps driven by a rising interest in the work of post–World War II production designers and the increasing respectability of folk art, the museum strove to be inclusive and, as a result, obscured its craft roots. The authors—chosen from outside the craft field—evidenced little understanding of the history of traditional and contemporary crafts. The reception of these books (four were planned) was disappointing, and the fourth one was never produced. Janet Kardon, the director of the museum during this period and one-time curator of the ill-fated Robert Mapplethope photography exhibition, had unsuccessfully tried to reinvent high craft by removing its tainted craft associations. See Janet Kardon, *The History of Twentieth-Century American Craft: Centenary Project* (American Craft Museum, New York City, 1995–97).

25. Miller, "Betwixt and Between," 31.

26. Paul Hollister, "New American Glass: Focus West Virginia, June 15–November 9, 1986," *Glass Art Society Journal* (1986): 114–16. The glass artist Joel Philip Myers noted the same situation in a review ("New American Glass," *Craft Horizons* 36, no. 4 [August 1976]: 36–41). A photograph of the installation reveals a vessel-based formal vocabulary; only two of the pieces depicted presented a sculptural sensibility A connection between the factory and the artist was restored with the exhibition *New American Glass: Focus West Virginia* at the Huntington Galleries (later the Huntington Museum of Art), Huntington, West Virginia, in 1976. Half of the exhibition was devoted to studio glass, the work of fifty-one glassmakers from across the country, who had been invited to submit pieces. The other half consisted of earlier pieces produced in collaborations between six glass artists and six West Virginia glass factories.

27. The Renwick Gallery, as part of the Smithsonian Institution and under the jurisdiction of the National Museum of American Art, was little more than a *kunsthalle* (exhibiton space), although its location in the national capital positioned it to be a important venue. As of July 1990, its collection of studio glass included works by only fourteen artists.

Mi, 1984. Lynda Benglis (United States, b. 1941). Sand-cast glass with inclusions; 13 1/2 x 17 x 16 inches. Los Angeles County Museum of Art, gift of Daniel Greenberg and Susan Steinhauser (M.86.273.1)

Benglis was an artist-in-residence in 1984 and 1985 at Pilchuck Glass School, where she explored the possibilities of making knots from cast glass.

IT WOULD BE WRONG to think of the past fifty years of American studio glass as anything more than a small event when set against the previous five thousand years of glass history. Compared with the glass output of the Roman period, for example, the corpus of American studio glass is insignificant. During its brief span, however, it has made remarkable strides for itself and by extension for the other craft-based media, having successfully challenged what is accepted as art and what is relegated to the category of craft. This accomplishment is manifest in the flourishing, national marketplace and expanding collecting communities, private and public.

The challenges were many, with the first, and most enduring being the materiality of glass. John Perreault, an art critic and glassmaker, describes glass as "the most purely visual of all the art media, even more visual than painting, because in it light, color and material are one."[1] This visual appeal, while attractive for makers and collectors, made the medium suspect in the realm of high art that it sought to enter.

The second boundary that needed to be challenged related to the location where glass items were produced. To be considered high art, glass had to leave the factory and locate its production in a setting that paralleled that adopted by painters and sculptors. Mimicking high-art practice became an important adjustment on the road to acceptance. When glass moved successfully from the factory to the studio—a move accomplished by means of rediscovered technology and the invention of clever new technology by such leaders as Dominick Labino, among others—this telling and damning distinction was erased. Today artists working in glass have adopted high-art practices for their production and speak of themselves as artists.

The third boundary involved the educational system by which artists with ambitions in the high-art world were trained. After a brief period of identifying itself as a discrete field, studio glass found that it attracted enough practitioners to position itself within universities as a credible art medium, worthy of standing next to painting and sculpture. This was accomplished through the activities of the proto-studio glassmakers in the 1950s and 1960s and later by Harvey Littleton and his followers, who helped to move potters from clay to glass, and glass from vessel-oriented forms to sculptural ones. The last step was to place glass in the university art curriculum and extend education through seasonal and regional glass workshops.[2]

These accomplishments by the American studio glass community did not occur in a vacuum. There were social developments that drove the field. Anti-establishment sensibilities, the increased acceptance of art made in nontraditional mediums, the lure of a life outside the mainstream, and the powerful pull of group camaraderie all contributed to the formation of a community that was devoted to the making of art in glass. Soon collectors appeared, and a limited literature about the field emerged. Next, museums added their clout, mounting exhibitions that included glass artworks. Some of the most reputable museums began to

Black "Window" Bowl, 1992. Jane Bruce (United Kingdom, b. 1947; active in the United States and Australia). Blown, sandblasted, and electroplated glass, oil pastel; 9 inches high, 9 inches in diameter.

below: *Untitled* (from the Exotic Bird series), 1986. Mary Ann (Toots) Zynsky (United States, b. 1951). Fused threads of colored glass filaments; 7 x 10 x 9 inches. Indianapolis Museum of Art, gift from the collection of Marilyn and Eugene Glick (IMA 1991.228)

collect glass: the Metropolitan Museum of Art and the Los Angeles County Museum of Art, as did regional or medium-specific institutions such as the Indianapolis Museum of Art, the Toledo Museum of Art, and the Corning Museum of Glass. With high-art institutions joining their second-tier confreres, glass had successfully challenged established institutional boundaries.

These developments were supported by the growth of a private collecting community and the market apparatus to supply it. This occurred in the straight-line trajectory seen in other craft-based media with the distinction that in glass it occurred in a brief twenty-five-year period. The only aspect of this development that is still lacking is a sustained secondary market. There is till work to be done in establishing acceptance of American studio glass.

As with all sculptural endeavors, issues of content continue to play a role in the history and commodification of studio glass. The artist Michael Taylor defined two types of studio glass artists: those who work within the "modernist concepts of sculptural form as personal statement" and those "who love the material because of its raw beauty and enjoy making things with hot glass because it is challenging."[3] There still exist parallel universes: the one inhabited by content-driven makers, and the one inhabited by those who are engaged by the materiality of glass. The tension between those two universes remains a central concern and hamper the ambitions of the medium. With the dichotomy encapsulated on the one hand by the artists who declare that "technique is cheap" and on the other by those who recognize the need for craft in the successful creation of art, this issue continues to be replayed as individual artists work to gain technical proficiency in order to express the content of their work more effectively.

The acquiescence of artists working in glass in the imposition of high-art-world standards on glass raises the issues of the legitimacy of conforming to norms originally established for painting and sculpture. The issue of whether glass can be good sculpture—similar to objects made by those working in wood, metal, stone, or assembled materials—is incorrectly framed; the real issue is can glass function as an expressive art medium? The answer is yes—with varying levels of success, as is true for any art medium.

The consideration that still troubles studio glass is its place in the firmament relative to high art. Thomas Crow, an art historian, has noted that in Europe before the mid-seventeenth century, art was defined differently from the way we characterize it now. Painting, sculpture, furniture, glass, and so on, were made by artisans who belonged to guilds. In 1648 a dramatic transition began with the establishment of the Royal Academy of Painting and Sculpture by the French painter Charles Le Brun. The academy established a new category: the fine arts. The new fine artists rejected the association with guilds. Separate exhibitions were established, lectures about theory proliferated, classes with live models were instituted, and periodic exhibitions (salons) were mounted for the general public. These steps were taken deliberately so that artists could avoid the stigma of being considered "artisans who worked with their hands," rather than artists who dealt in concepts. The new "fine artists" became part of the literary and philosophical circles and removed themselves from the artisanal world by formulating an intellectual basis for their work.[4]

Many similar activities were attempted by American studio glassmakers both collectively and separately. Indeed each wrestles with formulating an intellectual basis for his or her own work. It is in this respect that studio glass has yet to achieve its goal of being regarded as high art, and this deficiency will continue to haunt it. Until an appropriate set of critical tools for assessing the validity of art made out of glass has been fashioned, American studio glass will be unable to cross the boundary permanently into the world of high art.

NOTES

1. John Perreault, "Conversation," *Glass* 64 (fall 1996): 13.

2. Paul Hollister, "American Studio Glass in the Next Decade: 1987–1997," *Neues Glas* 1 (1987): 6–13.

3. Michael Taylor, "Regional Glass Artists and Studios of Northwest New York State," *Glass Art Society Journal* (1991): 82.

4. Other guild artisans of the period followed this model. Architects established formal schools of architecture, which separated them from other designers. Public art museums accelerated the divisions within the art world. Galleries were, by definition, confined to painting and sculpture; museums were to collect the whole range of the arts. Even within the latter, though, separate departments were eventually created for the fine and applied arts. Even in museums devoted exclusively to the decorative arts, separate departments were established for different media, following the model of the Victoria and Albert Museum in London. Thomas E. Crow, *Painters and Public Life in Eighteenth-Century Paris* (New Haven, Conn.: Yale University Press, 1985).

Acknowledgments

TRADITIONAL ART HISTORY does not recognize crafts as a legitimate form of art-making, just as it once did not recognize the history of dress, or the artistic merit of photography. Perhaps this is because there have been few scholarly assessments of such work and no new field of intellectual inquiry can take its proper place in academe without first having a dispassionate history of the key moments and notable accomplishments in place. This book joins the few others extant as an attempt to establish some of that history. It is my hope that scholars with serious academic interest and credentials will take up similar subject areas and give the world of contemporary high craft its proper attention.

Many people helped me along the way with this project and I thank them all; among them are Dr. Trudie Abrams, Paul Anbinder, Doug Anderson, Gary Baker, Penny Beck, Dr. Gordon Berger, Mart Anne Biggs, Martin Chapman, Garth Clark, Shaula Coyl, Susanne Frantz, Dr. Barry Glassner, Audrey Handler, Dr. Selma Holo, David Huchthausen, Beth Hylen, Matthew Kangas, Lynne Kostman, Mark Leach, Marvin Lipofsky, Dr. Lynn Matteson, Dr. Richard Meyer, Tina Oldknow, Bruce Pepich, Dr. John Pollini, Nicole Revette, Ruth V. Roberts, Grant Rusk, Ruth Summers, Davira Taragin, Jill Thomas-Clark, William Warmus, and Mary White. Special thanks to Randall Perkins and Leslie van Breen of Hudson Hills Press, who took to the project with enthusiasm, to Frances Bowles, who added her skillful and intelligent editing, to Susan DeRenne Coerr, for the index, and to David Skolkin, who made it all beautiful. A section of this book was the basis for a presentation at the Ninetieth Conference of the College Art Association in 2002. Any errors, omissions, or misinterpretations are my own.

My final thank you goes to my father, Fred Drexler (1915–2003), who bore the up-front costs, and to my husband, Bob Danziger, who is my treat at the end of the day.

Glossary

Altered: Additional forming done after initial shaping, usually blowing (*see* **Blown Glass**).

Annealing: Applying heat to glass, followed by uniform cooling in order to prevent cracking or breaking.

Annealing oven: An oven used for cooling glass slowly after it has been formed. Without proper cooling the glass will experience stresses and often will shatter when cool.

Batch glass: A mixture of raw materials (typically silica, soda or potash, and lime) that is heated in a pot to form glass. Properly formulated batch is necessary for the longevity and workability of the **metal**.

Battulo: Literally, "beaten glass," a decorative device for which the surface of the glass is ground on a satin wheel, which produces irregular and adjacent markings that appear beaten; developed by Venini.

Blown glass: Molten glass gathered on the end of a hollow metal pipe which is blown into by the maker. The air causes the glass to expand and take on a variety of shapes.

Cage cup (*vasum diatretum*): An ovoid beaker with no foot and made up of two layers of glass, with the exterior layer carved away in filigree pattern but still attached to the supporting layer with struts; rare and of undetermined technique.

Cased glass: A thin layer of glass over a contrasting layer of glass; a relatively simply executed decorative device used in the early years of the studio glass movement.

Cast glass: Glass made either from **fusing** powdered glass in a mold or by pouring molten glass into a form made of sand, plaster, and other materials.

Cire perdue: *See* **Lost wax**

Cullet: Raw glass, often broken from a cooled melt, that is, remelted, with fresh ingredients, and used to form objects. Although it melts faster that fresh glass, cullet can be inferior. In periodicals published in the 1950s writers suggested that that remelted glass be used. Unfortunately this type of glass has impurities that can cause incorrect **annealing** and other flaws.

Cut glass: Glass that is decorated with facets, grooves, or depressions made by cutting onto the surface with a rotating wheel of iron or stone. This is a cold-working process. *See also* **Engraved glass**

Cut and assembled glass: Glass (often sheet glass) that is cut from larger pieces and assembled though **fusing** or gluing into different shapes.

Devitrified glass: A process in which glass is converted into a crystalline material.

Dichronic veiling: Glass coated to reflect colors not usually evident.

Engraved glass: A process of decorating glass by cutting the design into the surface of the glass with a diamond, metal needle, or other sharp implement or rotating wheel. *See also* **Cut glass**

Ferro: A piece of steel coated with clay and used as a plate under **murrines** when they are **fused**.

Filet de verre: A term invented by the American studio glass artist Toots Zynzky to denote her method of forming vessels out of fused filaments of glass.

Flameworking: *See* **Lampworking**

Float Glass: Flat sheets produced from glass that, in the manufacturing process, is flowed, while molten, over a bed of molten tin; the extreme heat burns out impurities.

Free blowing: *See* **Off-hand blowing**

Fusing, also **Kiln-forming**: A warm-glass process for shaping glass by heating it in a mold in the furnace, permitting it to melt enough to form a continuous whole.

Gaffer: The master craftsman in charge of the glass-making team, which usually consists of eight men. Traditionally the gaffer worked under the direction of the designer to fabricate items. In contemporary practice this has been modified—a gaffer now can lead a group and that group can be of any number.

Gather: A portion of molten glass picked up on the end of a blowpipe from the furnace.

Glass: An amorphous, artificial, noncrystalline substance, usually transparent but often opaque, made from fusing some form of silica (such as sand) and an alkali (such as potash or soda) sometimes with other additives. It is plastic when molten and can be formed into various shapes. It can be worked hot (as in **blown glass**), warm (as in **lampwork**), or cold (as in **cutting and assembling**).

Glasshouse: A building, often roofless and circular in shape, in which glass objects are made; usually equipped with a glass furnace that has several openings for working the hot glass.

Glory hole: An opening on the side of the glass furnace that is used for reheating the glass **gather** on a blowpipe. In the anti-establishment days of the late 1960s and early 1970s the double meaning was a great source of amusement to the male artists.

Inclusions: Pieces of extraneous material that either intentionally or unintentionally become incorporated into the finished work.

Kiln-forming: A warm-glass technique for shaping

glass by heating it in a mold in the furnace; **slumping**, *pâte de verre*, and **fusing** are three kiln-forming techniques. **Proto-studio glass artists** worked with kiln-forming because they could use equipment that was already set up for forming clay.

Laminated glass: Glass that is built up in layers to provide greater strength or variations in coloring.

Lampworking (flameworking): Preformed glass tubes or rods of fusible glass are heated section by section over a small flame. The heat softens the glass and allows it to be shaped or attached to other glass tubes. Originally the work was done over a fire flame, later Bunsen burners were employed. Probably invented in the Roman era, the technique became popular in the seventeenth century for making small figures and glass beads. In the twentieth century it devolved into a carnival staple. Only in its use with paperweights did lampworking keep its connection to art. Many lampwork pieces are small in scale as the tubes are small; larger works are made by contemporary artists, such as Ginny Ruffner.

Latticino: Glass originally made in Venice and on Murano with a clear body in which white threads (*latticino*) are embedded. Dale Chihuly and other studio makers have taken up the traditional technique.

Lost wax (cire perdue): A method of glass forming adopted from metal forming. The object to be formed is modeled in wax and then cast in plaster. Hot molten glass is poured into the form and the wax melts and drains out through vents, leaving the glass to conform to the plaster mold. The work is **annealed** and then released, ready for hand finishing.

Malfin: Glass **batch** with impurities.

Marver: A flat, smooth metal, forming surface on which warm glass, usually while still on the blowpipe, is rolled to form it.

Metal: Formulated but unformed glass.

Mold-blown glass: Glass that is blown on a blowpipe into a mold that imparts a shape to the finished object.

Murrina; murrine: A type of modern mosaic glassware. Mosaic glass is made from molten glass in different colors that are heated together and then pulled to form thin canes. These are then cut into disks, and placed side by side and **fused**. The resultant sheet is then formed into the desired object by various methods including **slumping** and **blowing**. Murrina is the singular; murrine the plural.

Off-hand blowing: Working molten glass on the end of the blowpipe through the introduction of air.

Off pipe: Working hot glass after it has been separated from the blowpipe.

Pastorale: Italian for shepherd's crook; in glassmaking it refers to the surface that the **ferro** is placed on to be transferred to the furnace.

Pâte de verre: French for glass paste; a material produced from grinding glass into a powder and adding a binder and flux, usually with colorants. This mixture is then placed in a mold to fuse the material. Released from the mold, the work produced is usually hand finished. Popular during the nineteenth century, this technology was lost until late-twentieth-century studio glassmakers rediscovered it.

Proto-studio glass artists: Artists who worked to make glass artifacts in their studios before the Toledo workshops in 1962.

Pulled glass: Glass that is formed by being elongated (pulled) while molten. Often used for applied handles for vessels.

Sheet glass or **plate glass:** Glass produced commercially in large flat sheets by a variety of processes that have changed over time. Since 1959 it has been made by the **float glass** process. The point for studio glass is that the material is the result of an industrial process and it is then mediated by the artists. In this, it is unlike the early blown glass that was controlled in all aspects of the forming by the artists.

Slump: To heat glass until it is soft but not liquid, and will sag under its own weight to create a form.

Soda lime glass: A very malleable type of glass produced when small quantities of sodium carbonate (soda) and calcined limestone (lime) are added to the to the **batch glass**.

Style: A visual representation specific to a particular time and/or place that conveys information about the identity of the makers and the context of use; usually refers to decorative or surface embellishment but may also refer to technological traits.

Triple-hinge door: Door for the glass melting furnace that permits the opening to be accessed in thirds, so that the work area is not obstructed and heat from the furnace is not lost; invented by Dominick Labino.

Top-burning furnace: A furnace in which the heating element is located at the top.

Vasum diaretrum: See **Cage cup**

Veiling: A decorative effect created by trapping air bubbles in hot glass; often seen in factory-made Scandinavian glass.

Verre églomisé: An unfired, engraved decoration usually made of gold leaf (sometimes silver) applied to the reverse side of a glass form. It is frequently covered by another layer of glass or lacquer.

Byrd, Joan Falconer. *Harvey K. Littleton: A Retrospective Exhibition*. Exh. cat. High Museum, Atlanta, 1984.

Corn, Wanda. "Coming of Age: Historical Scholarship in American Art." *Arts Bulletin* 70, no. 2 (June 1988): 188–207.

Crane, Diana. *The Transformation of the Avant-Garde: The New York Art World, 1940–1985*. Chicago: University of Chicago Press, 1987.

Csikszentmihalyi, Mihaly, and Eugene Rochberg-Halton, *The Meaning of Things: Domestic Symbols and the Self*. Cambridge: Cambridge University Press, 1981.

Crimp, Douglas. *On the Museum's Ruins*. Cambridge, Mass., MIT Press, 1993.

Doss, Erika. *Benton, Pollock, and the Politics of Modernism from Regionalism to Abstract Expressionism*. Chicago: University of Chicago Press, 1991.

Duncan, Carol. *Civilizing Rituals: Inside the Public Art Museums*. London: Routledge, 1995.

Forty, Adrian. *Objects of Desire: Design and Society, 1750–1908*. London: Thames and Hudson, 1986.

Frantz, Susanne K. *Contemporary Glass: A World Survey from the Corning Museum of Glass*. New York: Abrams, 1989.

Glass 1959: A Special Exhibition of International Contemporary Glass. Exh. cat. Corning Museum of Glass, Corning, N.Y., 1959.

Hooper-Greenhill, Eilean. *Museums and the Shaping of Knowledge*. London: Routledge, 1993.

Lynn, Martha Drexler. *Masters of Contemporary Glass: Selections from the Glick Collection*. Exh. cat. Indiana Museum of Art. Bloomington: Indiana University Press, 1997.

McCracken, Grant. *Culture and Consumption: New Approaches to the Symbolic Character of Consumer Goods and Services*. Bloomington: Indiana University Press, 1988.

Manhart, Marcia, ed. *The Eloquent Object: The Evolution of American Art and Craft Media since 1945*. Seattle: University of Washington Press, 1987.

Muensterberger, Werner. *Collecting: An Unruly Passion*. Princeton, N.J.: Princeton University Press, 1994.

Mukerji, Chandra. "Artwork: Collecting and Contemporary Culture." *American Journal of Sociology* 84, no. 2 (1978): 348–65.

Nordness, Lee. *Objects: USA*. New York: Viking Press, 1969.

Oldknow, Tina. *Pilchuck: A Glass School*. Seattle: Pilchuck Glass School in association with the University of Washington Press, 1996.

Taragin, Davira, ed. *Contemporary Crafts and the Saxe Collection*. Exh. cat. Toledo Museum of Art, Toledo, Ohio. New York: Hudson Hills Press, 1993.

Index

Abramson, Anne and Ronald, 120n18
abstraction, avant-garde, 31nn1, 32n15, 89n18, 144
acid etched glass, 29
Alderson, Ben, 54
Alsop, Joseph, 11
America House, 32n15, 70, 71, 72, 89n11
American Artist periodical, 90n22
American Craft Council, 70
American Craft magazine, 71, 74–76, 89n20
    see also Craft Horizons
American Craft Museum, 32n15, 71, 121n34, 131, 136, 150, 153n21, 153n24
American Craftsmen's Council (ACC):
    conferences, 40, 42, 46n8, 51, 52–53, 70
    exhibitions, 32n29, 89n7
American Glass Now exhibition, 78
American studio glass, equation, 7, 9, 11–12
Americans in Glass exhibitions, 4, 110, 150
Anderson, Dale and Doug, 113, 128
annealing, 55, 160
annealing oven, 30, 52, 160
announcements, gallery, 94, 97
anonymous makers, 16n8
antiquity, glass in, 4n1, 33n35, 74, 138n9
applied art, definitions of, 5, 157, 158n4
apprenticeship system, 6
Argy-Rousseau, Gabriel, 28
Arneson, Robert, 46, 47n22, 90n33, 111
Arnheim, Rudolph, 66n16
Art Alliance for Contemporary Glass, 2, 116, 121n32, 128, 137, 138n9, 139nn23;37
art and craft:
    distinctions between, 7, 9, 11–12, 23, 157
    no distinction between, 4n1, 132
art dealers, 93, 94, 103n6, 124–125, 157
    see also dealers, studio glass
Art Dealers Association, 93
art disciplines, 11, 157, 158n4
    and new media, 71, 89n14, 104n20, 124, 126, 133, 152n8
    separation of the, 4n1, 131, 145, 157, 158n4
    status of the, 4n1, 16n6, 23, 31n6, 82, 84–85, 119, 124, 128–129, 131, 132, 144–145, 157, 158n4
"art for art's sake," 31nn4;11
art glass versus glass art, 5, 16n2
art history, 18n40, 25–26, 104n14, 157
Art Institute of Chicago, 43, 82, 152n8
art market, 94–96, 103n2, 104nn13;19, 114, 124–125, 131
    and museums, 141–142, 144–145, 152nn7;11;15
    see also dealers; galleries
Artforum, 117
artist craftsmen:
    designer, 14–15, 19n42, 27, 39, 40, 76, 157
    pioneers, 33n32, 35, 36, 39
artists, 16n6, 96–97, 104n20, 139n22, 157
    and artisans, 4n1, 157
    attire of, 46n1, 65, 67n47, 72
    as collectors, 79, 129, 139n22
    craftsmen versus, 14, 18n34, 75, 91n47
    figurative, 22–23, 31n11
    generational links between, 60, 62, 79
    high-art, working in glass, 17n22, 67n30, 117, 121n34
    instructors and teachers, 26, 59–60, 62, 65, 71
    studio, 6, 18n37, 30
artists, glass:
    attrition among, 76
    books by, 76–77
    definitions of, 15, 19n44, 30, 32n28, 157
    gifts to museums, 152n11

artists, glass: (cont.)
    intention and location of production, 14
    names of, 120n14
    number of, 60, 67n39, 69, 89n9
    in residence, 57
artists, studio glass, 15, 30
    ambition and techniques of, 50–54, 85, 87–88, 157
    galleries and, 94, 96, 104n18
ArtNews, 145
Arts and Crafts movement, 21, 22, 31nn3;9;10
Asilomar conference 1957, 40, 40, 42, 46nn8;11, 70, 72
Atkinson, Tracy, 52
auctions, art, 104n13, 112–114, 114, 121nn28;29;30
Australia, studio glass in, 67n41

Bailey, Clayton, 55, 66n24
Barbini, Alfredo, 47n17, 57, 144
beauty, 138n5, 139n20, 155
    as collecting motive, 126
    the expression of ugliness or, 6, 17n19
    handcrafted, 18n31
Becker, Howard, 12, 14, 17nn12,19
Bell, Larry, 9, 17n22, 117
    Untitled (Terminal Series of Boxes), 7, 8
Benglis, Linda, *Mi*, 117, 154
Bernstein, William, 71
    Teddy Bear on Bird Throne, 60, 72
Billeci, Andre, 59, 78
Black Mountain School, 17n13
Blenko Glass Factory, 18n37, 26, 89n12
blown glass, 9, 14, 29–30, 50, 160
    as true studio glass, 55, 59, 62, 77, 99
    as vessels, 9, 43, 46, 87, 89n18
body-referent artworks, 11, 18n29
Boone, Thomas J., 71
Boone, Thomas J. and Linda, 71, 96, 105n23
Boris, Eileen, 23
Bourdieu, Pierre, 138nn6;12
The Brooklyn Museum of Art, 89n9
Bruce, Jane, *Black Window Bowl*, 11, 156
Brychtová, Jaroslava, 47n17, 101, 121n30
Buechner, Thomas S., 43, 52
Burlyez, Million K., *Encyclopedia of Working with Glass*, 76
Burton, John, 19n47, 44, 79

cage cups (*diatreta* vessels), 28, 160
California Ceramics and Glass Competitive Exhibition, 1974, 88n6
canes, glass, 15, 134
Carder, Frederick, 28, 33n34, 54
    Diatretum Vase, 20, 28
Carlson, Nils, 55
Carlson, Robert, *Apis Arcana*, 106
Carlson, William, 99, 145
Carpenter, Jamie, 11, 119
cartoon, Dings & Fractures, 2
Cash, Sydney, 148
    Untitled, 109
cast glass, 38, 39, 160
Cast Glass Sculpture exhibition, 139
Castelli, Leo, 103n3, 117
catalogues, 114
    of donated works, 131, 132–133
    gallery, 95
    museum, 120n16, 141
    see also exhibitions
Cellini, Benvenuto, 4n1
Center for Craft Creativity and Design (North Carolina), 17n13
ceramic kilns, 46n3, 52, 161
ceramists, 41, 66n24, 121n25
    as glass artists, 87
Chambers, Karen S., 35
Charles Cowles Gallery, 18n37, 101, 117, 119, 121n37

Chase, Bette, 81
Cheek, Leslie, 43
Chihuly, Dale:
    collaborative works by, 11
    exhibition titles of, 15, 19n45, 139, 151
    fame of, 2, 96, 117, 119
    influence of, 60, 65, 90n34, 150
    museums collecting, 144, 145, 152n9
    Sea Forms, 9, 10, 11
    techniques of, 9, 142, 161
    Wedge Weave, 61
Chochinov, Allan, 2
Christie's auctions, 113–114, 114, 135
cire perdue. *See* lost wax (cire perdue)
Clark, Garth, 16n6
Clark, Jon, 72
class, social:
    and craft work, 23, 25, 138n7
    of dealers and collectors, 91n37, 124, 125, 138n7
clay, 41, 90n33, 129
    glass versus, 55, 67n33, 88n3, 89n10
    high-art recognition of, 31n6, 32n15, 51, 65n1, 67n44
    pricing of, 88n3, 89n9
    technique of, for glass, 40, 46n3, 87
Cleveland Museum of Art, 70
Clifford, James, 94
cold-worked glass, 14, 15, 22
collectable commodities: alienable or inalienable, 137n2
collecting:
    literature on, 137n4, 139n32
    private, 129, 131–133, 141–142
collections of glass, 132–133
    as accumulations, 79, 139n23
    corporate, 113, 133, 135–136, 139n34
    historical material, 115, 133, 138n9
    see also museums
The Collector exhibition, 78–79
collectors, 32n28, 70–71
    ceramics, 81, 88n2
    display and symbolic language of, 125–126, 138n15
    early glass exhibitions and, 77–79, 82, 150
    social class of, 91n37, 124, 125, 138n7
collectors, glass, 78–79, 81, 123–126
    activism of, 128–129
    artists as, 79, 129, 139n22
    blue-chip (first-tier), 129, 131–133
    books for, 100
    characteristics of, 124–126, 139n23
    connoisseurship of, 129, 131, 138n11
    corporate, 113, 133, 135–136, 139n34
    and museums, 82, 129, 131–133, 150
    organizations of, 2, 82, 116, 121n32, 126, 137
    and patronage, 123–137
    private, 129, 131–133, 139n23, 141–142
    see also community, the American studio glass; *names of specific collectors*
commissions, artwork: 4n1, 37, 39, 120n18
community, the American studio glass, 60, 79
    camaraderie in, 57, 59, 62, 65, 67n35, 70, 104n15, 124, 126, 132, 137
    early exhibitions and collectors, 77–79, 82
    local and regional groups, 137
    size of, 26, 60, 126, 129
    social cohesion and camaraderie of, 139n36
conferences and events, 40, 42, 46nn8;11, 51, 52–53, 66n23, 67n47, 71, 74, 75, 117, 137
    see also specific conference names
contemporary art:
    collectors of, 124, 126, 133
    versus traditional crafts, 40, 42, 44, 46n8, 124
Contemporary Art Glass Gallery, 93
Contemporary Art Glass Group, 71, 100–101
Contemporary Art Glass (Ray and Lee Grover), 76

Contemporary Crafts and the Saxe Collection, 132
content, artistic:
  beyond the vessel, 78, 82, 87, 99, 153n26
  expression of, 6, 11, 17n19, 46, 126, 157
  and form, 66n16, 78
Corn Dolly, 3
Corn, Wanda, 104n14
Corning Glass Works, 50, 52
  see also Steuben Glass Works
Corning Museum of Glass, 121n33, 139n35, 142, 151n4
  collections of the, 111, 141, 152n11, 157
  Contemporary Glass: A World Survey from The Corning Museum of Glass, 149
  exhibitions, 47n16, 53, 78, 108, 110, 129, 148, 149
  and the *Glass 1959* exhibition, 42–45, 47n16, 78, 108
  international slide collection, 90n31
  New Glass Review, 90n31, 149
Cowles, Charles, 93, 101, 107–108, 117, 119
craft and contemporary, 7, 9, 11–12
Craft and Folk Art Museum, 17n12, 80, *81*
Craft Horizons magazine, 14, 15, 40, 45, 53, 71, 74–75
  founding of, 25
craft scholarship, 111, 131, 132, 145
  lack of, 2, 116, 138n6, 144, 150
craft shops, 69, 71
crafts, 5, 23, *70*, *71*
  characteristics of, 7, 9, 11–12
  functionality of, 11–12, 32n15, 46
  history of American, 78, 153n24
  internationalization of, 89n20, 150
  meanings of, 7, 67n45, 90n22
  separation of art from, 11, 31n4, 66n16, 145
  survival of, 21–22
  see also traditional craft
Crane, Diana, 94, 120nn5;17, 152n15
Creative Glass Center of America, 137
Cribbs, Kéké, *Sailing to Byzantium*, *125*
Crimp, Douglas, 16n5
  critical perspective as missing, 4, 95, 124, 138n6, 150
Cros, Henry, 28
crossovers. *See* high art
Crow, Thomas, 157
crucible, 52
cullet, 22, 30, 160
culture, issues of:
  collectors' motivations, 124
  and cultural capital, 124, 125, 132, 138nn5;12
  lack of discussion of, 18n28
curators:
  acquisitions and discretion of, 144, 152nn9;11
  gallery relationships with, 103
  roles of, 128–129, 132, 141–142, 151n2, 152n11
  see also museums
curriculum. *See* education and training
cut and assembled glass, 14, 160
Czechoslovakia, glass artists in, 15, 42, 44, 49n17, 101, 105n29, 121n30

Dahle, Richard, 7
Dailey, Dan, 60, 72, 97, 99, 120n18, 121n37, 148, 151
  Café, 7, *8*
  Ocean-Linear Beach-Grass, *118*
dealer's collection (dealer's shop), 103n6, 131
dealers, studio glass, 104nn11;13;17;18
  backroom sales, 112
  dedicated galleries and, 93–96
  functions of, 125
  primary and secondary, 112, 157
  social class of, 138n7
  see also galleries

Dearborn Glass Company, 39, 44
decorative arts, 5–6, 16n6, 17n20
  definitions of, 5, 7, 157, 158n4
  departments in museums, 144–145, 152n16, 158n4
Décorchemont, François-Emile, 28
  Pâte de verre, 24
Depression, the, 23, 25, 88n4
design, home furnishings, 32n24
  and display practices, 72, 125–126, 138n15
  of glass, 36, 39
designer-craftsmen, 14–15, 19n42, 27, 39, 76, 157
  see also proto-studio glass artists
designers, 12, 16n4, 32nn24;27
  European, 28, 33nn36;37, 40, 157
Detroit Institute of Art, 82, 137
devitrified glass, 30, 90n27, 160
dichronic veiling, *135*, 160, 162
display. *See* status or display functions
domestic spaces:
  of collectors, 125–126
  and contemporary art, 16n5, 70–71, 72, 89n15, 138n15
donations. *See* museums
Dormer, Peter, 123
Dowler, David, 33n37
Dreisbach, Fritz, 57, 59, 72
  flyers drawn by, 74, 75
  Super Star-Studded Charlotte 500 Winner, 56
Drutt, Helen, 108

Eames, Ray and Charles, 26, 32nn24;27
Eckhardt, Edris, 36, 39–40, 42, 44, 70, 74, 78, 79
  Archangel, 39, 40
  Uriel, 38
Edgewood Orchard Gallery, 137
education and training:
  art world, 89n11
  craft schools, 17n13, 57, 65, 72, 74, 112, 117, 136
  curriculum issues, 62, 67n33
  GI Bill, 25–26, 32n23, 51
  of proto-studio pioneers, 36, 39
  of studio glass artists, 50–51
  university-level, 50, 57, 59–60, 62, 155
  workshops, 35, 54–55, 57, 59, 62, 72, 75, 111, 117, 155
Edwards, Stephen Dee, *Tripod Sea Form*, *148*
Egg and Eye gallery, *80*, *81*
Eisch, Erwin, 45, 75, 113
  Buddha, *114*
The Eloquent Object exhibition, 111
Emergence in Glass catalogue, 99–100
Emmerich, André, 103n3, 119
enamel techniques, 36, 46n4
Europe:
  designers in, 28, 33nn36;37, 40, 157
  factory art and production in, 28–30, 33nn36;39, 52, 57, 144
  glasshouses in, 15, 40, 46n9, 52, 57, 67n35, 144
  guilds and fine art in, 4n1, 157, 158n4
  names of glass artists in, 15, 44, 47n17, 67n41, 75, 101, 113, 131, 139n30
  recognition of American artists, 90n28
  studio glass in, 29–30, 35, 115
exhibitions:
  collectors and, 77–79, 82, 101, 124, 129, 133
  gallery, 94, 100–101
  international, 40, 42–45, 43–44, 149, 150
  invitational, 71, 78, 99, 100, 105n23, 150
  juried, 43–44, 52, 70, 108, 149, 150
  naming strategies for, 15, 119
  openings of, 95, 98, 107
  regional, 79, 137, 150–151
  retrospective, 139
  survey, 79, 108, 110, 111, 150, 153n22
  see also specific exhibition names

fabrication separate from creative process, 12
factory:
  glassmaking outside the, 18n41, 28–30
  relationship of glass to the, 21–22, 26–28
factory glass, 7, 26–27, 32n31, 33n32, 39, 40
  craft glass versus, 21–30, 55
  production (design), 5, 12, 108
  studio glass versus, 12, 14–16, 153n26, 155
fairs, regional and craft, 69–70, *70*, *81*, 89n9
Florian, Robert, 79
folk art and traditional crafts, 3, 6, 16n7, 17n11, 89n9
forming methodologies. *See* glass-forming methodologies; *names of specific techniques*
Fragile Art competition, 115
France, 104nn12;13;19, 157
  influences from, 15, 28–30, 33nn36;39
Franklin, Edith, 54, 55, 66n24
Frantz, Susanne K., 16nn3;6, 35, 44, 111, 149, 151
Frey, Viola, 139n24
Fritz, Robert, 79, 89n17, 99
Fugita, Kyoto, 98
functional theory of art, 14, 18n34
functional versus decorative art, 16n3, 82, 145
fundraising, charity, 112–113
furnaces, 27, 30, 33n32, 162
fused glass, 8, 161

gaffers, 15, 59, 126, 161
Gagan, Larry, 55
Gallé, Emile, 28, 33n37, 105n29
galleries, 88nn1;3, 104n22
  craft arts, 69, 71, *81*
  New York, 71, 103n3, 107
  number of, 71–72, 103n3
  painting and sculpture, 71, 104nn13;19, 158n4
  see also museums
galleries, studio glass, 71–72, 79, 82, 88n3
  and artist, 94, 96, 104n18
  cards and flyers, 94, 97
  and dealers, 93–103, 103n3, 131
  differentiation among, 95–96, 104n17, 119
  installations, 94, 97, 99, 103
  names (lists), 104n22, 105n29
  three exemplars of, 96–103, 97–99, 103n3, 104n22, 131, 132
  urban single media (dedicated), 88n1, 89n13, 93–96, 93, 99–101, 107, 131
Geldzahler, Henry, 119, 144
GI Bill (Public Law 346), 25–26
Gilbert, John, *Torso Series*, 115
Glancy, Michael, 148
  Pierced Celestial Ambit, 3
glass:
  ancient and historical, 9, 25–26, 30, 66n20, 115, 124, 133, 138n9
  beauty and visual appeal of, 17n22, 79, 126, 129, 131, 139n20, 144, 155
  dangerousness of, 11, 82
  definition of, 161
  fragility of, 82, 138n13
  handling, 124
  materiality of, 7, 126, 155
  melting point of, 66n4
  remelting, 45–46, 47nn20;21
  spirituality associated with, 18n31, 25, 30
  tactility and texture, 11
  transparency of, 7, 8, 92
Glass 1959: A Special Exhibition of International Contemporary Glass, 40, 42–45, 47n16
Glass Art Magazine, 60, 114
Glass Art Society (GAS), 2, 66n23, 72, 116, 137, 139n36, 142
  flyers, 74, 75
  members' photograph, 72
Glass Art Society Journal, 2, 107, 116–117

glass artists. *See* artists, glass
Glass Focus (newsletter), 2, 116
glass-forming methodologies, 15
  historical, 9, 17n25, 28–29
  status hierarchy of, 14, 15, 18n41
Glass Gallery, 88n17
Glass (*Glass Arts Magazine*), 93, 114–115
"Glass Lovers Weekend," 128–129, 137
Glass magazine, 93
glass-only galleries. *See* galleries, studio glass
Glass State of the Art (books), 100
Glass Studio magazine, 115
Glass Workshop Report (Toledo), 55, 57, 76
glassblowing, 57, 59, 161
  experiments, 28, 54
  as happenings, 90n32
  Littleton's book on, 17n26, 76, 77, 90n27
  off-hand blowing, 14, 17n25, 162
  skill of, 15, 22, 53
  solo, 42
  teamwork, 27, 62
  see also blown glass
glasshouses, 15, 27, 67n35, 144, 161
  names of American, 22, 26, 28, 33nn34;37,
    47n17, 54, 89n12
  small family, 47n20
  see also factory
Glassner, Barry, 133n13
Glassweekend, 121n32, 138n8
Glick, Marilyn and Eugene, 105n25, 113, 114,
  135
government policies:
  encouraging crafts, 25–26, 108, 111
  and glass collections, 136, 139n34
Greenberg, Clement, 7, 31n11
Grotell, Majlis (Maija), 51, 66n9
Grover, Ray and Lee, 76
Gruenig, David, 42, 46n3
guild artisans, 4n1, 157, 158n4
Gunther, Charles, 54
Guthrie, Derek, 111
Guzman, Kathleen, 113, 121n28

Habatat Gallery, 71, 96–100, 105nn23;24,
  121n28, 131, 132
  books, 99–100
Halem, Henry, 62, 72, 72, 88, 91n47
  Square Penetration, 63
Hampson, Ferdinand, 71, 96, 105n23, 107,
  110
hand arts, 4n1, 14, 157, 158n4
  as virtuous, 25
Handel Glass Company, 32n31
Handler, Audrey, 72
  An American Breakfast, 65
handmade, 129
  values attached to, 7, 16n5, 21–22, 26, 31n5
Hansen, Sally, 89n17
Hauberg, John H. and Anne, 65, 79, 90n14,
  112
Haystack Mountain School of Crafts, 57
Heaton, Maurice, 35–37, 44, 46n4
  Africa, 36, 37
Heller, Douglas and Michael, 93, 100–101,
  108, 110
Heller Gallery, 71, 93, 100–101, 103n3, 112,
  131, 132
Herman, Samuel J., 45
  Vase, 44
Higgins, Frances Stewart, 44, 70, 89n6
  Vessel, 34
Higgins, Michael, 42, 52, 70
  Sawed Box, 8, 39
Higgins, Michael and Frances, 36, 39, 44
  *Country Gardens, Arabesque Apple, Butter-
    cup,* and *Sunburst*, 36
  Plate, 36
high art:
  crossovers from glass to, 30, 117, 119,
    121n37, 157

high art: (cont.)
  the evolution of, 104n14, 157
  functions of, 12
  masterpiece category, 5–6, 142
high-art world, 2, 16n1, 138n6
  artists, 111, 117
  attitudes toward craft-based work, 82, 85,
    87, 108, 115, 128, 144–145
  critical and commercial acceptance in, 88n5,
    100–101, 114, 119, 128, 129
  critics and reviews, 110–111, 115–116, 119
  of New York, 31n11, 71, 100–101, 103n3,
    104n22, 107, 144–145, 148, 152n15
  power structures, 4, 104n19, 141–142,
    144–145, 152nn11;15
  the urban, 6, 31n11, 89n13, 107
  see also museums
Hilton, Eric, 33n37, 78
hobbyists, 25, 32n28, 54, 69, 75, 76, 90n22
Hollister, Paul, 150
hot-glass techniques. *See* glassblowing
Houghton, Arthur Amory, 33n34
Huchthausen, David, 4, 7, 9, 113, 148, 150
  Alpine Landscape #67, 83
  Leitungs Scherbe LS 282, 127
Hunter-Stiebel, Penelope, 108, 132, 145
Huntington Museum of Art, 150, 153n19
Hutter, Sidney R., *Plate Glass Vase #26*, 147

inclusions, glass, 8, 161
industrial design, 36, 145
*Insight: A Collector's Guide to Contemporary
  American Glass*, 100
installation works, large-scale, 11, 151
installations, glass art gallery, 94, 97, 99
Italian glass:
  artists, 44, 47n17, 113
  factories, 52, 57, 144
Ivor Kurland Gallery, 97, 98, 103

Jervis, Margie, and Susie Krasnican, *Spotlit
  Bowl*, 130
Johns-Manville Fiber Glass Corporation,
  53–54, 59
Johnson Collection of Contemporary Crafts,
  78, 90n30, 136
Johnson, J. Stewart, 111, 152n12
Jolley, Richard, *Female Bust with Leaves*, 110

Kallenberger, Kreg, 139n20
Kamm, Gloria and Sonny, 103
Kaufmann, Edgar, Jr., 43, 52
Kaziun, Charles, 19n47, 33n32
Kehlmann, Robert, *Composition #55*, 64
Kester, Bernard, 17n12
Kilby, Ruth Maria, 78
kiln-forming techniques, 52, 161
Kinney, Kay, *Glass Craft: Designing, Forming,
  Decorating*, 76
Kirkpatrick, Joey. *See* Mace, Flora
kitsch, craft as, 7, 111, 120n15
Klein, Dan, 15, 113, 114, 120n16, 121n25
Kubler, George, 6
Kurland, John, 98, 103
  Kurland/Summers Gallery, 94, 98, 103, 131,
    132
  installations, 97, 99
Kuspit, Donald, 151

Labino, Dominick, 49
  career of, 53–54, 54–55, 59
  exhibitions, 78, 79, 90n28, 105n23
  inventions by, 54, 66n19, 88, 155, 162
  and Littleton, 53–54, 66n13, 87–88, 99
  photograph of, 50
  Visual Art in Glass (book), 17n26, 76–77
  —, works by, 149
  Emergence Four-Stage, 92
  Untitled, (1968), *viii, 1*
  Untitled (Emergence series), *135*

Labino, Dominick, works of, (cont.)
  Vessel, 53
  Vessel (1966), 43
Lalique, René, 28, 33n37
laminated glass, 40, 161
lampworking (flameworking), 15, 19n47,
  33n32, 59, 161
Le Brun, Charles, 157
Leafgreen, Harvey, 55
Leigh Yawkey Woodson Museum, 110–111,
  150, 152n16
Leighton, John, *Miranda VI*, 149
LeQuier, K. William, *Sentinel III*, 130
Levin, Robert, *Vessel with Prunts*, 76
Lewis, Albert, 115
Lewis, John, *Moon Bottle*, 56
Libbey Glass factory, 54
Libenský, Stanislav, 142
Liebman, Jon C., 139n23
lifestyles, alternative, 62, 65, 67nn44;45;47
lighting, gallery, 94, 97, 99, 103, 151
Lipofsky, Marvin, 60, 67nn35;45, 79, 99,
  105n25
  California Loop Series, 58
  Glass Form, 56
  Pair of Vessels, 58
  photographs of, 45, 57, 72, 98
  poster, 81
  Series Crystalex-Hantich #11, 116
literature:
  about museums, 152n7
  art history, 18n40, 25–26, 104n14, 157
  art periodicals, 90n22, 115, 117, 119, 145
  on collecting, 137n4
  high-art world, 111, 145
  technical treatises, 4
literature, American studio glass, 74–77
  by artists, 17n26
  books, 2, 4, 26, 76–77, 100, 111
  catalogues, 4, 95, 99–100, 110, 114, 120n16,
    132–133, 141, 148–151
  chronological surveys, 100
  gallery ephemera and, 94–95, 97
  periodicals, 2, 53, 74–77, 114–117, 119,
    138n6, 145
Littleton, Bess, 81
Littleton, Harvey K., 31n8, 91n47, 113, 132
  career of, 51–53, 112
  ceramic work by, 51, 66n10
  collecting by, 79, 129
  education and training of, 50–51
  in Europe, 15, 30
  exhibitions, 82, 151, 152n8
  glass workshops, 35, 54–55, 57
  Glassblowing: A Search for Form (book),
    17n26, 76, 77, 90n27
  influence of, 14, 35, 46n1, 49–50, 59–60, 62,
    155
  and Jean Sala, 30, 33n36, 42
  and Labino, 53–54, 66n13, 87–88, 99
  and MOMA, 82, 84–85
  photographs of, 49, 50
  on pricing, 69, 88n3, 89n4
  "technique is cheap," 87, 157
Littleton, Jesse, 50, 66n4
  —, works by, 81, 89n17, 148, 152n9
  300° Rotated Ellipsoid, 84
  Amber Crested Form, 143, 144
  Blue Lined Loops #14, 30
  Ceramic Vessel, 41, 51
  Green Loop, 77
  signature in glass, 9
  Three bottles, 12, 13
  Three-Part Vessel, 9, 9(detail)
  Torso, 48, 51
  Vase, 43
  Vessel, 12
location of production and art making, 14,
  18n37

Los Angeles County Museum of Art, 103,
  120n18, 142, 151, 151n4, 152n9, 157
lost wax (cire perdue), 20, 38, 39, 161
Lotton, Charles, 99
Luebtow, John Gilbert, *Glass Sculpture*, 116
Lukens, Glen, 46n3, 71–72, 88n3, 89n10
  Plate, 24
Lynes, Russell, 43, 43, 108

MacDonald, Dwight, 66n16
Mace, Flora, and Joey Kirkpatrick, *First Doll,*
  Portrait/The Chinaman, 81
machines: the role of, 12
Macleod, Dianne Sachko, 124, 126
mainstream art. *See* high-art world
malfin, 30, 45–46, 161
Maloof, Sam, 89n7
Manhart, Tom and Marcia, 111
marbles, #475 fiberglass, 54–55, 59, 91n44
Marer, Fred, 88n2
Marinot, Maurice, 29–30, 33n39
  Vessel, 29
marketing:
  of crafts, 6, 31n3
  secondary, 112–114, 157
  of studio glass, 93–96, 119
  urban high-art, 6, 89n13, 107
Marquis, Richard, 57, 60, 99
  Teapot (Fabricated Weird Series #21), 143
  Witch's Ball, 45
  Wizard Teapot and *Murrine Teapot*, 134
marver, 40, 161
materiality of craft-based art, 7, 17n20, 155
McCutchen, Earl, 44, 45, 74, 79
McGlauchlin, Tom, 59–60, 66n24, 105n23
  NS38 (1982), 60
Meitner, Richard, *Untitled* (1984), 68
Mensch, Martin and Jean, 114, 135
methodologies. *See* glass-forming methodologies
Metropolitan Museum of Art, 43, 108, 119,
  142, 151n4, 152n12
  glass acquisitions, 144–145, 148, 157
Miller, R. Craig, 82, 84, 108, 142, 145, 150
Milles, Carl, 50
Mingei-kai movement, 18n31, 31n10
Mint Museum of Craft + Design, 17n13
Moje, Klaus, 67n41
mold-blown glass, 14, 161
Moore, Guy and Rodessa, 81
Morris, William, 21
movement, defined, 15–16
  see also studio glass movement
Moyano de Muñiz, Lucrecia, 44, 45
Murray, William Straite, 88n4
murrina (murrine), 134, 161–162
Museum of Arts and Design, 71, 150
Museum of Contemporary Crafts, 71, 78, 82,
  150
Museum of Modern Art (New York), 26, 142,
  151n4
  and studio glass, 82, 84–85, 148, 152n9
museum shops, 70, 80, 89n9, 149
museums:
  categorizing glass within, 18n29, 144–145
  and collectors, 82, 131–132, 141–142, 144
  departmental classifications within, 82, 142,
    144–145, 149, 152n9, 152n16, 158n4
  display practices of, 132, 151, 152n9
  donations to or purchases by, 82, 91n41,
    131–132, 141, 144, 151, 151n1, 152n11
  exhibitions at, 78–79, 108, 110, 131–133
  first-tier urban encyclopedic, 142, 144–145,
    148–149, 151nn4;5, 152nn9;15;16,
    158n4
  glass acquisitions by, 82, 84–85, 91n41,
    141–151, 152nn9;11
  literature about, 152n7
  permanent glass collections of, 78, 111,
    120n16, 141, 144–145, 148–150,
    152nn9;11

museums: (cont.)
  second-tier, 142, 144, 149–151, 152n16
  statistics and staffing, 151n4, 152n16,
    153nn19;21
  see also curators; *names of specific museums*
Musler, Jay:
  Cityscape, 134
  Rock Around the Clock, 133
Myers, Joel Phillip, 71, 79, 148, 153n26
  CFTBLUECLEARKSG 1984, 100
  "D" Black Form, 64
  Dr. Zarkhov's Tower, 26, 121n29, 135
  Hand Forms, 136

Nagle, Ron, 18n29
Nakashima, George, 43
National Council on Education in the Ceramic
  Arts (NECA), 72
National Glass Invitational exhibition, 96
Natzler, Gertrud and Otto, 41, 70–71
Navarre, Henri, 33n39
Nelson, Jim, 55
networks, 70
  marketing and collecting, 65n3, 137
  studio group, 89n20
  of traveling glassmakers, 57, 59, 67n35
Neues Glas, 115–116
New Glass: A Worldwide Survey exhibition,
  108, 110, 129, 145
new media. *See* art disciplines
New Work magazine, 115, 119
New York State University at Alfred, 59
Newcomb Pottery, 31n4
Nordness, Lee, 71, 78, 80
North Carolina Glass, 79
Nygren, John, *Bottle with Internal Form*, 85

Oakland Museum of California, 88n5, 131
Objects: USA exhibition, 78, 79, 80, 90n30,
  136
Oldknow, Tina, 1

Pacific Northwest Arts Center, 65
painting styles, 22–23, 119
Palusky, Robert, *Globe Form*, 86
Parkman, Paul and Elmerina, 79
pâte de verre, 17n25, 18n30, 24, 30, 145, 162
  technique, 28–29
patronage, 123–126, 128–129
  see also museums
patrons. *See* collectors, glass
Patti, Thomas, 71, 121n37, 148, 152n9
  Convexed Green with Gray, 109
Peiser, Mark, 57, 62, 69, 71, 72, 88n3, 105n23
  Lilies of the Valley PWV 034, *ii*, *v*, 117
  Paperweight Vase series, *ii*, *v*, 105n25
Penland School of Crafts, 17n13, 57, 72, 74
Perkins, Flo, *September Cactus*, 127
Perreault, John, 23, 111, 155
Perrot, Paul, 42, 45, 51–52, 52, 53
Philadelphia College of Art, 59
Philbrook Museum of Art, 111
Pilchuk Glass Center, 79, 90n32
Pilchuk Glass School, 65, 112, 117, 136
plate glass, 147, 162
Plexiglas and glass, 7, 8, 17n22
Polak, Ada, *Modern Glass*, 76
Ponti, Gio, 43, 44
Portnoy, Sy and Theo, 78–79
posters and flyers, 74, 75, 81
powdered glass techniques, 36, 160
pricing:
  and art status, 7, 88n3, 104n20, 126, 131
  courtesy discount, 107–108, 126
  of crafts, 26, 88n3, 89n9
  escalation in, 10n5, 107–119, 121n30
  of glass art, 11, 69–70, 71, 88n4, 96, 99,
    103, 119, 131, 136
  and museum collecting, 131, 142
  resale, 112

procedural theory of art, 14, 18n34
proto-studio glass artists, 14, 29, 44, 70, 79,
  111
  definitions of, 33n38, 162
  kiln-forming by, 161
  pioneers, 35–46, 100, 155
Pulos, Arthur J., 22

Quagliata, Narcissus, 98

Racine Art Museum, 136
Reeves, Ruth, 36
Renwick Gallery, 151, 153n27
Reynteins, Patrick, 112
Richmond Art Center (California), 81, 96, 99
Ricke, Helmut, 115
Risatti, Howard, 31n4
Ritter, Richard, 82, 105n23
  YC-39-1982, 128
Robson, A. Deirdre, 123–124
Rosenberg, Harold, 66n16
Rosenblatt, Joshua, 71, 100
Rothenberg, Polly, *Complete Book of Creative*
  Glass, 76
Rothko, Mark, 88n5
Ruffner, Ginny, 161
  Beauty's Alter Ego as a Tornado, 140
rural arts, 6, 16n8, 107
Ruskin, John, 21, 31n4

Sala, Jean:
  Footed Bowl, 30
  and Littleton, 30, 33n36, 42
sales notation system, 95
Saxe, George and Dorothy, 110, 131–132
scale and size of glass art works, 11, 18n29,
  151
Scanga, Italo, 117, 119
Schmidt, Jack, *Soda Steins*, 62
Scholes, Samuel R., *Handbook of the Glass*
  Industry, 52, 76
Schuler, Frederic, 42, 74
Schulman, Norman, 54, 60, 79
scientists, glass, 42, 50, 66n4, 66n19, 74
sculptors, 15, 29–30, 40, 67n30, 119
Sculptural Objects and Functional Arts
  (SOFA), 137
sculpture, glass, 14, 15, 28, 78, 99, 119, 142,
  151, 157
  non-utilitarian, 82, 87, 153n26
Seattle Art Museum, 119
Seattle conference, 42, 53
self-expression, autonomous, 12
self-sufficiency, craftsman, 23, 25
Shaffer, Mary, 99
  Hanging Series #24, 146
Sheets, Millard, 22
  Sun, Sea and Rocks of Sonoma, 23
Shifman, Barry, 114
signed glass works, 9, 16n8
Silberman, Robert, 4, 110–111, 119
Sim, Patterson, 107
Slivka, Rose, 25, 26, 31n5, 40, 111
slumped glass, 22, 24, 95, 162
Smith, Dido, 74, 75
Smith, Paul J., 78, 108
Smithsonian Institution, 17n11
Smyers, Steve, 98
socialism and crafts, 66n16
Sosin, Hilbert and Jean, 79, 82, 91n37
Southern California Designer Craftsmen, 76
stained glass, 19n46, 36, 37, 99
Stankard, Paul, 121n37
  Cloistered Block with Cactus and Spirits, 109
Statom, Therman, 60
  Chair on Base, 120n18, 122, 123
status or display functions, 18n28, 72, 138n15
  and conspicuous consumption, 124, 125–126
  of decorative arts, 6, 16nn5;6, 124, 138n12
  and utility, 11–12